THE JAMES SPRUNT STUDIES IN HISTORY AND POLITICAL SCIENCE

*Published under the Direction of
the Departments of History and Political Science
of the University of North Carolina*

VOLUME 46

———————— * ————————

Editors

FLETCHER M. GREEN, CHAIRMAN
WILLIAM WHATLEY PIERSON
KEENER C. FRAZER
J. CARLYLE SITTERSON
GEORGE V. TAYLOR

WALLACE EVERETT CALDWELL

LAUDATORES TEMPORIS ACTI

Studies in Memory of Wallace Everett Caldwell Professor of History at the University of North Carolina by His Friends and Students

By

Mary Francis Gyles and Eugene Wood Davis

CHAPEL HILL
———— * ————
THE UNIVERSITY OF NORTH CAROLINA PRESS
1964

COPYRIGHT © 1964 BY
THE UNIVERSITY OF NORTH CAROLINA PRESS
Library of Congress Catalog Card Number: 64-64799

PREFACE

It is appropriate to adapt a phrase from Horace (*Ars. Poet.* 173—ignoring the gentle sneer) as a title for these studies in memory of Professor Wallace Everett Caldwell. Professor Caldwell was fond of Horace, he was a "praiser of times past," and he encouraged his friends and students in the same art. His interest in ancient history and the classics was boundless, and his care and affection for friends and students were limitless. It is appropriate that we offer praises of times past in his honor, and in memory of his life-long achievement.

Every person acquainted with our effort has helped to make it a success. People who could not contribute essays have given generously of money, suggestions, time or encouragement. Among them are: the James Sprunt Fund, Mr. Selby C. Parker, Professor Lillian Parker Wallace, Professor James M. Grimes, Professor Elizabeth Rogers, Dr. Helen Lanneau Moore, Dr. Laura Bland Clayton, Dr. Evelyn Lee Way, Mrs. J. M. Bergman, Mrs. Herbert L. Bodman, Jr. and many other friends. The Caldwell family is particularly to be thanked for making available all necessary information. We are grateful, too, to the University of North Carolina itself, to the library of the University for important materials, and to Leon Godown of the Oxford Orphanage Press for the excellent portrait used as our frontispiece. All of us together are *laudatores temporis acti*.

Mary Francis Gyles
Brooklyn College

Eugene Wood Davis
Trinity College

March, 1964

ABOUT THE AUTHORS

The contributors of the essays in this volume were colleagues, friends and students of Professor Wallace E. Caldwell. Those colleagues on the faculty of the University of North Carolina are: Professors Henry R. Immerwahr, B. L. Ullman (Kenan Professor Emeritus), and Robert J. Getty of the Department of Classics; and Professors Henry C. Boren and Loren C. MacKinney (Kenan Professor Emeritus) of the Department of History.* Completing the list of colleagues is Professor Robert Samuel Rogers of the Department of History at Duke University.

The rest of us have had the pleasure and profit of studying under Professor Caldwell. We are: Professor Barnaby C. Keeney, President of Brown University—who writes our Foreword; Professor Francis R. Bliss, Department of Classics at Western Reserve University in Cleveland, Ohio; Professor Paul A. Clement, Department of Classics at the University of California at Los Angeles; Professor Eugene W. Davis (co-editor), Department of History at Trinity College in Hartford, Conn.; Professor Ronald E. White, Department of Classics at McMaster University in Hamilton, Ontario; Professor Robert E. Wolverton, Department of Classics at Florida State University at Tallahassee, Fla.; Professor Mary Francis Gyles (co-editor), Department of History at Brooklyn College of the City University of New York; Dr. John M. Riddle, Department of History at Wisconsin State College, Eau Claire, Wis.; Mr. Thomas Herndon (joint author with Professor MacKinney) who is a candidate for the Ph.D. in History at the University of North Carolina; and Professor Herbert L. Bodman, Department of History at the University of North Carolina.

The essays have been arranged in historical order—which is to say chronologically—so that in spite of the variety of topics, the reader may catch something of the grand sweep and drama of the history of the ancient world.

* Professors Getty and MacKinney died in the Fall of 1963, not long before the publication of this volume. We are glad that their papers were completed and could be included.

FOREWORD

Wallace Everett Caldwell was one of the most remarkable teachers I have known in three universities. Some of the fruit of his success as a graduate teacher is shown by the work of his students in this volume.

I write of him as an undergraduate teacher, though, in fact, much of the work I did with him at Chapel Hill was in graduate seminars. The first course I took with him as a sophomore so delighted me that I was in his classes almost every quarter thereafter. He procured his material with erudition of a breadth and depth that rarely occur in the same man, organized it with extraordinary clarity, and presented it with wit and verve. He treated his students with the understanding and consideration that are the essential qualities of a really great teacher. It was well known to the students in my day that persons of modest intellectual endowment were not unlikely to pass his elementary courses; but it was also known that they could not do so without profiting from the courses, for, whether they wished to or not, they were drawn into a study of things they could never forget. It was known just as well that to achieve distinction in his courses required great effort and careful thought. Thus students at all levels were able to benefit from his instruction.

The breadth of his repertoire was extraordinary: of course, he taught general ancient history, but he taught more advanced courses on Greece, Rome, Mesopotamia, and Egypt and he gave seminars in all these subjects. He knew more history, I think, than almost any man I have ever known, and at whatever level he was teaching—or indeed letting his students teach one another and themselves—he kept these remote times constantly relevant to the present and to what was then the future of his students. I remember very well his discussion of the Oriental mystery cults in the Hellenistic period and his explanation of why people chose these enchanting but illogical religions in preference to the logical and precise philosophy of the Greeks. He told us that the world had grown too big for ordinary men; with the destruction of the city as the unit, there was no longer anything for an ordinary man to hold to or with which to identify himself; thus, men turned to the mystery cults which provided a warmth unavailable elsewhere. The same need was evident throughout the world in the 30's, and may well have been the reason that Professor Caldwell became so deeply interested in Masonry. The same need exists today; it is better understood if compared with the classical precedent.

Professor Caldwell liked to play tricks upon his students. In the middle of a serious discussion of some historical development, without change of tone or expression, he would embark upon some bit of nonsensical fiction, very well disguised as fact; watch his students write it down carefully in their notebooks; and then remind them that in order to learn it is necessary to think.

He knew his students well, in the classroom and out, (sometimes too well for their own comfort) and he took great interest in their academic and non-academic activities. He was rarely absent from an athletic contest in the sports that he enjoyed. He knew when his students were troubled, and when they were sick, and he helped take care of them. When they called at his home, as they frequently did, he and Mrs. Caldwell combined to an extraordinary degree in their entertainment the charm of society and the erudition of the faculty, an example which should be before every undergraduate—and seldom is—throughout his years.

On the morning of my graduation, he drove me to the exercises in his ancient car, partly out of kindness, but partly because by then it was necessary for a heavy person to sit in back and hold down the transmission. In the process I was shaken up considerably and the burning ash of my cigar set fire to my academic robe. One might have expected that I would have left his life then in a blaze of glory, but this was not so, for we corresponded and visited each other throughout the years; sometimes we fished together, sometimes we talked together, occasionally we just sat.

The privilege of his friendship has meant much to many who were fortunate enough to know him well. Let us hope that his students will carry on not only his scholarship, but his humanity.

BARNABY C. KEENEY

CONTENTS

Preface	v
About the Authors	vi
Foreword	vii
by Barnaby C. Keeney	
Ἡδυ εν Σικελιαι: Democracy and Pleasure	3
by Francis R. Bliss	
Some Inscriptions on Attic Pottery	15
by Henry R. Immerwahr	
The Beginning of Coinage by Olynthian Chalcidians	28
by Paul A. Clement	
The Persian Battle Plan at the Granicus	34
by Eugene Wood Davis	
Cicero and His Hoped-for Triumph	45
by B. L. Ullman	
Cicero's Concordia in Historical Perspective	51
by Henry C. Boren	
The Unity of Propertius 2. 34 and 3. 20	63
by Ronald E. White	
Lucan and Caesar's Crossing of the Rubicon	73
by Robert J. Getty	
Speculum Caesaris	82
by Robert E. Wolverton	
Freedom of Speech in the Empire: Nero	91
by Robert Samuel Rogers	
Effects of Roman Capital Investment in Britain Under Nero	99
by Mary Francis Gyles	
Amber: An Historical-Etymological Problem	110
by John M. Riddle	
Tradition Against Independent Investigation in Pre-modern Craniology	121
By Loren C. MacKinney and Thomas Herndon	
The *Sator*-Formula: An Evaluation	131
by Herbert L. Bodman, Jr.	
List of Publications by Wallace E. Caldwell	142
Index	145

LAUDATORES TEMPORIS ACTI
Studies in Memory of Wallace Everett Caldwell
Professor of History at the University of North Carolina
by His Friends and Students

ΗΔΥ ΕΝ ΣΙΚΕΛΙΑΙ—DEMOCRACY AND PLEASURE

FRANCIS R. BLISS

Although the evidences lie all around us that there is a close and vital connection between the economic growth and the spiritual advancement of a people, the weight of opinion supports the argument that riches corrupt. In the ancient world almost no voice is heard for the opposing side: Circe and her pigs have the final word. To debate this question in detail would be matter for more than a single paper. Here I shall confine myself primarily to the evidence of Thuc. 2.38 and Ps.-Xen. *Resp. Ath.* 2.7-10, in an attempt to show that, though perhaps never fully explicit, there was in the fifth century a theory that Athens' spiritual and political growth sprang from her open system, her free market for products and ideas.[1]

The common view of Greek philosophers, and indeed of Greek writers in general, was that human society goes from bad to worse as it becomes richer and freer, and that justice is to be found in returning to a more ascetic and even primitive virtue. To some extent these notions are conventional and commonplace, but we cannot look on them as meaningless, for they are in harmony with the deep-seated pessimism of Greek thought of all periods; the greatest thinker of the Greeks reechoes them in only more ideal form. Most recently Professor Havelock has suggested that the Pre-Socratics, and especially those whom he designates 'Greek anthropologists,' mounted a counter-argument to Plato's view. These liberals, he suggests, looked at the world and its history as progress rather than regress, were materialists, made use of a calculus of pleasure similar to that later employed by Epicurus, and in general took a more 'dynamic' (if I may use a word of modern cant) and optimistic view of the human condition. But in fact, as Professor Welles has remarked, Havelock's "liberals fell back on a natural right as dogmatic as Plato's ideas." To put it another way, materialist as well as idealist in antiquity presents us with a limited view of man's

---

[1] I should like to avoid the use of such a 'dernier cri' term as 'open society' in a paper like this in which there is little room for abstract discussion. This well-known phrase comes from K. F. Popper, *The Open Society and its Enemies* (revised edition, Princeton, 1950), who says in a footnote to the Introduction that he traces its use back to Bergson's *Two Sources of Morality and Religion*. The most thorough-going refutation of Popper's position is in R. B. Levinson, *In Defense of Plato* (1953). The most recent approach to the question is that of Eric Havelock, *The Liberal Temper in Greek Politics* (New Haven, 1957); a good view of questionable points in these works may be found in the numerous reviews of Havelock's book. By 'open system' I refer to Athens' readiness to accept innovations and novelty, especially in terms of material goods, without restricting their introduction in accordance with any abstract principle.

capacity for growth; perhaps the clearest evidence for this is to be seen in the ascetic form in which Epicurus' hedonism is phrased.²

The plain facts of Greek life, however, tell a different story. Freedom, when it was not a dirty word (ἐλευθέρα Κόρκυρα, χέζ' ὅπου θέλεις, Strabo 7. frg. 8), was a warcry. And the ancient world did not come to an end in 404 B.C. or 338 either. The city-state form was replaced more than once by different and progressively larger political combinations before the force of the great intellectual effort which begins with Homer spent itself. Ancient man, in fact, was not politically static. Furthermore, what we today recognize as an absolute requirement for a progressive society, namely an open and expanding economy, was precisely what the Greeks worked towards and the Romans for a time achieved. As an old writer on their technological life remarks, "Weder die graue Theorie der Denker noch der blasierte Hochmut des Adels ... konnte dem Griechentum den Ruhm rauben, ein fleissiges, betriebsames, erfinderisches Volk ... zu sein ..."³ Practical men, traders, orators, inventors, explorers, founders of cities, from the Seven Wise Men to Archimedes and Polybius, are no small part of the glory of Greek history. In directing our view solely at the critical and metaphysical sides of Plato's system we miss one of its most important features. Plato did not write without practical intent; he was not uninventive, and his purpose, if ever any man's, was social change. We speak here of Greeks in general, but the rest of our paper will confine itself to Athens. The reason lies not merely in the texts to be studied but in the striking fact that the Athenians early won a kind of prescriptive right to these aspects of Greekness: the inventive, inquiring, restless mind. From the fifth century on these terms make up the common picture of Athens.⁴ One thinks at once of St. Paul at Athens, where "all the Athenians and strangers which were there spent their time in nothing else, but either to tell, or to hear some new thing (*Acts* 17.21)."

The earliest formal account of Greek political theory we possess is

---

² B. Welles, review of Havelock (above, note 1), *AHR* 63 (57/8) 641-2. N. W. DeWitt, *Epicurus and his Philosophy* (Minneapolis, 1954) in a chapter entitled "The New Hedonism" (216-248), does not seem to me to free Epicurus fully of this charge.

³ Max C. P. Schmidt, *Realistische Chrestomathie aus der Litteratur des Klassischen Altertums*, vol. 3 (Leipzig, 1901) 5.

⁴ Plato and Isocrates in criticising Athens clearly reflect this already stereotyped view of the Athenians. Even Paul's speech, which follows directly on the passage quoted above, has one or two terms which fit the conventional picture. The best example to be found is a work, a fragment of a *Description of Greece* now attributed to one Herakleides Periegetes (formerly referred to as Ps.-Dicaearchus) and recently reedited by R. Pfister in *Sitzber. der Akad. der Wissenschaften zu Wien* 227.2 (Wien, 1951). Pfister has in his lengthy commentary missed, I believe, several important points, and in fact emended one of the nicer ones out of existence. I hope in a later paper to study the evidence of this work and to make clear how much light it throws not only on the standard account of Athenian character but on the ways of Greek sociological thinking.

that in Herodotus. There, in a group of set speeches (3.80-82) we learn of the three great political types: Democracy, Aristocracy, Monarchy. Otanes, who speaks for Demos, assails Tyranny, while Megabyzus attacks the masses in his plea for the rule of the Best. Each of the views presented is a static, one might say an 'administrative' one. The polities presented are good in proportion as they provide pleasure or fulfilment to their citizens. So Otanes starts his remarks by saying that to be ruled by a monarch would be neither pleasurable nor good. Herodotus may be said to assume an ideal and invariable state of pleasure for the individual. Humanity has reached the end of the line. Government is simply a matter of balancing the more or less equal claims of pleasure and utility; it seeks not to improve men, but to preserve the status quo.[5]

In Thucydides we have, attributed directly to Pericles in the Funeral Oration and seen from different points of view in a number of other passages, an account of the nature of democracy in general and of democracy as practiced at Athens in particular. The most striking feature of Pericles' account is that he attributes the εὐτραπελία which enemies may consider a vice of instability, etc., but which he holds to be the primary virtue, of the Athenian character to the training of the Athenian democracy and way of life. Here clearly is a "growth concept." The aim of Athens is to produce not "good" men, nor "free" men, but "adaptable" men. The world is a changeable place, and changeable though not fickle men are needed.[6]

Let us start with a brief outline of Pericles' argument in the Funeral Oration. 1. (2.36) Athens got where it is, he says, by gift of the ancestors in the past, but we moderns have done much to improve her. This improvement has come from our ἐπιτήδευσις, πολιτεία, τρόποι (The latter two are the embodiments of the former, which is not separately

[5] J. A. O. Larsen in *Essays in Political Theory presented to George H. Sabine* (Ithaca, 1948), 1-16, presents in the essay entitled "Cleisthenes and the Development of the Theory of Democracy of Athens" the suggestion "that *isonomia* is an earlier name for what was later called democracy..." (p. 6), and makes some point of the fact that in 3.82.1 Herodotus refers to *demos* rather than to democracy. The evidence seems to me to suggest equally well that 'democracy' was already a fighting word, and something to be avoided in reasonable debate.

[6] These ideas are not set forth as simply as all this in the text, in part because of Thucydides' well-known idealizing style of presentation, in part, I believe, because Pericles himself, a master politician as well as statesman, knew that he must step cautiously in leading people along paths that ran contrary to fundamental beliefs. Larsen (above, note 5) 13, notes correctly that in 2.37.1 in characterizing Athens' constitution as a democracy "the speaker appears to be on the defensive." The standard commentaries (Gomme, Poppo, Classen-Steup) do not point out that *eutrapelos* (2.41.1) involves a bold perversion of the pejorative view of change expressed by the word *ektrapelos* (cf. Theognis 290). This is the normal view: cf. *Inferno* 33.151, "Ahi Genovesi, uomini diversi,/d'ogni costume..." with its clear Vergilian reference; and let us not forget that our own founding father came from Genoa.

discussed.) 2. (2.37) The *politeia* used is a democracy, which means, here at least in Athens, that talent is used by the city regardless of the social level from which it springs (e.g., equal rights under law in private suits; freedom of individual ἐπιτήδευμα from censure; general favorable reaction to unwritten law). 3. (2.38) For mind and body as well, both in public and in private, material and intellectual pleasures are largely available to our citizenry. 4. (2.39) The evident result of this policy is our success against the enemy abroad and our happy life at home, for our people join as readily in military as in peaceful activities. 5. (2.40) Free-thinking and material riches have not weakened us; we do not boast of wealth unless it *does* something, nor shun the poor—unless he be merely lazy. We all take part in all aspects of civic life, and this eventuates in a wise and calculated courage. Abroad, on the other hand, we win friends by free giving, for our aid is not self-interested: our aim is to spread liberty. 6. (2.41) Taking all in all, Athens is the school of Greece and Athens puts out the best human product, most variable, most free, and most ready to turn his hand to aid the state. The proof is in the present pudding: our power as a whole and the virtue of these men here fallen.

The point of Pericles' speech is character, of course. But the paths to it are only allusively expressed. These are: primarily, freedom of intercourse within the state, secondarily a larger standard of living both intellectual and material.[7] The great summary statement "we are lovers of beauty with *euteleia* and lovers of wisdom without softness" is not intended, as often thought, to point up the frugality of the Athenian way, or to contrast their bare esthetic with Oriental lavishness.[8] Rather this phrase rebuts the charge usually directed at a materialist civilization, that its love of beauty is based on principles of conspicuous waste, and that its philosophy is destined to go the way of all hedonism.

Now this is a bold argument. One may recall that even Herodotus does not stress this *apolaustic* aspect of democracy (3.80) in the speech of Otanes. Pericles in fact blurs the sharper outlines, placing main stress on the recognized results rather than on the material details, which might have been too distressing for many conservative members

[7] It has not usually been noticed how clearly Thucydides separates the *politeia* from the *tropoi*. In Pericles' view the causations of Athenian democracy are two: the social-political (discussed in par. 37) and the social-economic (discussed in par. 38). For reasons that it would be idle to dwell upon, the academic mind has been at one in disregarding the materialistic side, though it has been common practice to notice his failure to mention the new temples and public buildings.

[8] So Gomme in part, *ad hoc*. Other references simply to *Gomme* in the text are to this great work, A. W. Gomme, *A Historical Commentary on Thucydides*, vols. 1 and 2 (Oxford, 1944, 1956). Gomme himself pretty well throws up his hands at the attempt to explain *euteles* suitably for this passage.

of his audience.⁹ This smoothing out of the argument is best seen in par. 38, where he refers to the well-known richness of life both public and private at Athens. As the city herself supplied more festivals, more food both for body and mind, so the port brought in goods from all over the Mediterranean world; the result was of course greater strength of body and mind, greater variability of taste and understanding, but Pericles does not say so until par. 41. Instead he mentions the contests and perennial sacrifices as the reward of the Athenians' labors and a relaxation from their ennui. Furthermore, by tying all these ideas together under the heading γνώμη, leaving out the σῶμα which logically should introduce the second half of the paragraph, he manages to stress the richness of the intellectual diet and obscure the crasser aspects of the argument.

The modern reader tends to forget that there is a perfectly good reason for mentioning the sacrifices in such a connection. The ancient festivals had a dual function apart from the purely religious observance involved. First, they supplied a rest period—so the Hebrew sabbath, which was one of man's first steps out of the sunless caves of savagery. Second, the city festivals were closely connected with their food supply. When we find a particular state increasing the number of its festivals we can be assured that its population was growing, probably also that the status of urban labor was rising, to say nothing of the general well-being. The meat did not all go up in smoke: ancient society, one may say, was Kosher society. This at least was part of what the Athenians meant when they boasted of the great number of their festivals.¹⁰

Another aspect of ancient society well known to all is its parochial character, and this of course is the point of the final observation of par. 38: when Pericles says "the result is that we harvest our own goods with no more native enjoyment than we do those of other men" he means that Athens' maritime situation made her citizens less parochial. It all seems obviously a good thing to us, but the ancients were not so sure. What they saw as results of foreign importations were change and in-

⁹ One should notice also that this stressing of the results, Athens' current power and success, assists Thucydides in making one of the most dramatic points in the whole history, for the funeral is followed directly by the account of the plague.
¹⁰ See Stengel, *Die Griechischen Kultusaltertümer*, 2nd ed. (Munich, 1898), vol. 5, part 3 of Müller's *Handbook.*, 95. The new festivals, the ἐπὶ Θέτοι ἑορταί, were added to satisfy the growing population, while older ones, established to meet a smaller social need, were often disregarded. This is the meaning of Isocrates' criticism (*Areop.* 29): "... celebrated magnificently supplementary festivals which involved any banqueting, while fobbing off the holiest rites on some cheapjack public contractor." These same facts underlie the biting comment (*Clouds* 984) that the Just Argument's words recall the Dipolia, a festival not only archaic in ritual but poorly provided with barbecue. For newer work on this interesting subject see F. Sokolowski, "Partnership in the Lease of Cults in Greek Antiquity," *HTheolR* 50 (1953) 133-143, as well as more recent studies by the same writer.

stability. Cicero puts it wittily in a discussion of the same topic at the beginning of the second book of the Republic (2.9): *quid dicam insulas Graeciae? quae fluctibus cinctae natant paene ipsae simul cum civitatum institutis et moribus.* In addition this view does violence to the traditional wisdom that sees how quickly pleasure leads to decadence of taste and manner: hence Pericles' quibble, which seems to say that the products enjoyed may be *foreign*, but the taste that enjoys them is *native*.

How widespread was this view of the Athenian character and of the factors that brought it about may be seen in the curious similarity between several phrases in the speech of the Corinthian ambassadors in book one and this same paragraph of the Funeral Oration. Athenians' favorite idea of a holiday, say they, is a day on which they get a chance to do their neighbor in the eye. (1.70.8). (So much, that is, for talk about their being so taken up with the soft life of *festivals* and sacrifices that they can't fight a war). They are congenitally incapable of keeping the peace themselves or of letting anyone else do so either (1.70.9), for they consider ineffective peace as great a misfortune as unceasing labor (1.70.8). As for body and mind, they spend their bodies in the service of the state as though they were *foreigners*, while they are in the fullest *native* possession of their wits when using them for her (1.70.6). This famous phrase contains, in the words σώμασι ἀλλοτριωτάτοις and γνώμη οἰκειοτάτη, a clear echo of the σῶμα-γνώμη antithesis Pericles makes use of in describing Athens' festal richness (2.38), which paragraph concludes, one recalls, with the difficult remark that the Athenians enjoy their own products with no οἰκειοτέρᾳ ἀπολαύσει than they do those of others. Perhaps an even clearer parallel to this phrase about enjoyment occurs a few lines later, where we hear that as for enjoyment, they get less than anyone out of what they've got because they're always so busy acquiring more (1.70.8). Festivals, relaxations, peace and quiet or busy activity, mind and body, pleasure or *apolausis*, the 'other' (foreign) and the 'own' (native)—these are the topics which recur when one talks of democratic theory and practice.

Only one other well known passage from ancient literature speaks of wealth in this way, and that also is an Athenian text, possibly even written prior to Pericles' presentation of the Funeral Oration. This is the Pseudo-Xenophontian *Constitution* of Athens, often referred to as 'The Old Oligarch.''[11]

[11] In dating this text so early I agree with H. Frisch, *The Constitution of the Athenians* (Copenhagen 1942), but the question is a complex one and no general agreement on it has yet been reached. The late Professor Gomme preferred a date around 425 B.C. see "The Old Oligarch," in *Athenian Studies Presented to William Scott Ferguson (Harvard Studies in Classical Philology,* Supplementary volume I), Cambridge, 1940, 211-245. I shall refer throughout the rest of this paper to the Ps.-Xen. as the 'Old Oligarch.'

In this brilliant early example of Athenian prose—actually the earliest complete Attic prose work we possess—a full-scale justification of democracy is presented in the form of an anti-democratic tract. The writer purports to be an oligarch in tastes (his language, as well as his use of the first person, betoken him an Athenian) lecturing to exiled and foreign oligarchs on the character and weaknesses of the Athenian constitution.[12] The central section of the work is a lengthy discussion of the advantages and disadvantages of empire (in total bulk one half of the account of the constitution, two fifths of the work as a whole). Towards the end of his account of the advantages the Old Oligarch turns in a brief digression to mention some minor cultural advantages.[13] These are as follows: 1. Produce from every port is readily available at the Piraeus; 2. as a result of this constant foreign contact the Athenians have a newer and richer mixed vocabulary—in fact, where other Greeks are parochial in φωνῇ, διαίτῃ, σχήματι, the Athenians are the reverse: 3. they have a much greater number of θυσίαι, ἱερά, ἑορταί, τεμένη; 4. there are available a great number of public facilities similar to the aristocratic gymnasia, baths, dressing-rooms. The list is much the same as that of Thucydides 2.38 except that it seems to be in reverse order. Thucydides speaks, that is, of Public Festivals and Private Establishments, then of Resources coming from Every Land, last of the Effect of these on the Public Taste. That is: Festivals—Private Establishments—Imports—Taste. In the Old Oligarch the items fall in the order; Imports—Taste—Festivals—Private and Public Establishments. It is striking that both passages end with a statement about ἀπόλαυσις and a kind of equation of pleasure. In the Old Oligarch the *demos* is said to get as much *enjoyment* from its public facilities as do the rich from their private ones; in Thucydides the *demos* gets as much *enjoyment* from imported goods as do the original producers of those goods themselves.

[12] I have never been able to persuade myself that this was in fact an anti-democratic work. G. Murray (*Hist. of Ancient Greek Literature*, New York 1897, 168-9) long ago expressed interesting doubts about the writer's tendency, and a laughable list of various scholarly conclusions is given on the first page of Gomme's article referred to in the preceding footnote. It should be noticed that Oligarch's net conclusion is a warning to Athens' enemies not to expect her to fall as a result of internal dissensions, nor to expect much help from the exiles. If someone were to disseminate such an argument today with reference to the new government in Cuba we would not be deceived, but would surely call it 'Communist propaganda.'

[13] His account presents us with an almost classic example of so-called 'ring composition,' the main theme of which is the antithesis πένητες / χρηστοί, which is followed by further comments on social relations, first internal, then with allied populaces. Quite logically the very center of this 'ring' is an account of the material goods which allow the Athenian πένητες to become χρηστοί. The exposition of H. Haffter, "Die Komposition der pseudoxenophontischen Schrift vom Staat der Athener" in *Navicula Ciloniensis, studia philologica F. Jacoby...oblata* (Leiden, 1956) 79-87, differs considerably from my own views on the structure of this work, which I hope to present in another paper.

There can be no question that both these passages apply to the characterization of Athens a consideration of the actual physical conditions under which she lived. Secondly, in their interpretation of character and character growth there seems to have been present a theory of pleasure as an economic and cultural good which is reflected in their somewhat obscure use of the words ἀπολαύει (Old Olig.), ἀπολαύσει (Thuc.). Thirdly, in the order of presentation of the particular examples we may see some similarity, though in fact the relation of A-B, C-D to C-D, A-B, where B and D can be shown to have an inherent relationship to A and C respectively, is not compelling.[14] In three striking ways, then, these two passages show a structural similarity. But perhaps even more important are the omissions. These are essentially two: first, Thucydides' passage is far briefer; second, the clearly stated materialistic point of view of the Old Oligarch is avoided by Pericles, and specifically there is no mention of φωνή, δίαιτη, σχῆμα nor of the various luxury installations of the aristocracy and of the public.

Furthermore, Pericles is extremely vague. The transition from the word πόνων to the word γνώμη is confusing; editors seem in doubt whether he meant recreations of mind or of body. But if only intellectual recreations are meant as Gomme austerely writes, then what are the ἀγῶνες and θυσίαι διετήσιοι doing here? Surely these words cannot be confined to an allusion to tragic drama. Nor does anyone really know what is meant by the ἰδίαι κατασκευαί. Then in the second part of the paragraph, where the values derived from the harbor are to be pointed out, though he says "everything from every land," a plain reference to importing activities, he says that these goods accrue to them through the greatness of the city and not, as the Old Oligarch does, through their maritime empire.

Now if these ideas are as simple as they appear to be, and if their order is reasonably logical, why will Thucydides have presented them in so obscure and confused a fashion? The answer, I believe, is not hard to seek. The various counter-arguments: that physical well-being leads (especially for those who formerly were poor and knew their place) to civic and moral breakdown; that the port city was the place where you couldn't tell the difference between slave and free (so Old Oligarch himself, 1.10-11); that extensive public works, and private too, fall into the class of extravagant and god-tempting acts of tyrannical Hybris; all these arguments were well-known to the audience, a large number of whom were frugal propertied middle-class folk. They were, for example, the parents of these young soldiers who had died and therefore

---

[14] The order in which these items are brought forward in the Old Oligarch is influenced by his argument as a whole; he has been talking about the advantages of empire and therefore naturally mentions the goods in the harbor first. If there is a more logical or a more conventional order I should say it was that in which they are found in Thucydides.

must have been in the hoplite class.[15] Their reactions can readily be imagined by recalling that they were also the audience for whom Aristophanes wrote his scathing attacks on sophism, warm baths and luxury. To have spoken so baldly of material goods as the sources of Athenian greatness would have damned the speaker's reputation.

Stress should be laid at this point on the neatness with which the Old Oligarch has epitomized the nature of cultural change. With the method so typical of the idealizing habit of Greek art he selects and isolates the particular concrete items which will best typify the total process; he does not deal in abstractions; he has no ambiguous word for 'culture.' Instead he tells us of vocabulary, diet, dress and manners, for both words translate *schema*. These are terms for surface changes, but Aristophanes will show us how seriously they concern the inmost man. When his Unjust Argument (1073) offers the enticements of "Boys, women, gambling, meat, drink, and merriment (κιχλισμῶν)" the only thing he seems to have omitted was drag-racing in chariots, to which Pheidippides was already accustomed. But perhaps even more than diet and *schema* the problem of vocabulary is central to the *Clouds*. Zeus is out, Dinos is king; cock must have his 'cockress.' Yet these are only simple examples: Socrates' redefinitions destroy conventional meaning; society is made up largely of εὐρύπρωκτοι. In Thucydides (3.82.83), in Plato (*Rep.* 560d), in Isocrates (*Areop.* 20) we see that this idea of the breakdown of the terms for moral values had become regularly associated in people's minds with freedom. But the Old Oligarch seems to be even more concrete; he says that by hearing all languages the Athenians adopt one thing from one language, one from another.[16] Thus he is referring not only to changes in value, new words for old things, but to new products (and concepts) arriving to break up the old standarized way of life. So in our own language are great numbers of the newer words, and especially those which come from languages which otherwise have contributed relatively little to our own tongue: julep, tobacco, gin, sari, mumu, dungarees, hashish, cocaine, goulash. And what do the old fogeys of Paris, London, Rome, and Zagreb think of their children guzzling that insidious tonic Coca-Cola? Yet of course they all want the best of the West. "Ὅ τι ἐν Σικελίᾳ ἡδὺ ἢ ἐν Ἰταλίᾳ ἢ ἐν Κύπρῳ . . .

It is striking that we ourselves in America have an attitude toward material luxuries so similarly compounded of opposites. From the richest to the poorest we tend to base our criticism of Europeans (to say nothing of the rest of the world) on their lack of modern plumbing;

---

[15] For a recent very sober view of the social make-up of the Athenian people in this period see A. H. M. Jones, *Athenian Democracy* (New York, 1958) 81. See also above, note 6.

[16] On the difficult question of the meaning of φωνή see Frisch's Commentary (above, note 11) 253, also Gomme (above, note 11) 212.

it is standard that we judge a people's culture by the frequency of their bathing habits. Yet at the same time there is a whole raft of apocalyptic voices in our public press making a fat living on amplifications of the cronippian theme, all filled with cicadas and smelling of must and garlic, that we are corrupt with too much good living, softer than those pioneers our own *Marathonomachoi*. (Not that there is not a good deal of soundness in both views.) This latter attitude, which is that of the *laudator temporis acti*, was well known to the Greeks of fifth century Athens; the line of argument so frequently followed by Aristophanes, especially in the *Clouds*, would be incomprehensible had it not been so. But it is a wisdom of much greater antiquity. It stands behind Hesiod's myth of Pandora. It is present all through Theognis: what else is the meaning of οὐ χρὴ κιγκλίζειν ἀγαθόν βίον (303) if not that the old and stable life is better than the new and changeable? One may note how similar it is to the fascinating word κιχλίζειν, which seems to mean 'to live it up.'[17] It connotes the idea of sophisticated humor and 'modern attitudes' (as in Catullus's *cachinnare*, which sometimes translates it), while at the same time it means 'to live luxuriously' (presumably on quail). The word is several times repeated during the *Agon* in the *Clouds*. But the Greeks had no corner on this market. One recalls the "fleshpots of Egypt" (*Exod*. 16.3): Moses was worried from the beginning that the children of Israel would be enslaved by Egyptian bounteous living more than by any violence of Pharaoh (see *Exod*. 15.12: "Is not this the word that we did tell thee in Egypt ....").

Yet the other view is equally ready to the Greek mind, and we should not be so led astray by simplistic moralizing as to swallow whole the Golden Age commonplace. The fulminations of prophets both major and minor on which our grandfathers were suckled, and Christian asceticism in its more disgusting forms are really neither enlightening nor humane. The truly great figures of both the Judaic and the Greek traditions (Socrates and Christ, for example) have strong currents of hedonism and utilitarianism running through their teaching, nor would Western democracy be what it is without their sound good sense.

Homer himself gives us our preliminary sketch of the uses of pleasure in his account of matters on the island of Phaeacia, where

---

[17] How violently people can react to this association of material goods with cultural greatness is a little surprising. Even the normally judicious Professor Gomme rises in his wrath at the thought: "This is the oligarch's account of Athenian political ideas, ἰσονομία and ἐλευθερία, of the festivals, of tragedy and comedy and dithyramb, of the great temples ... nothing but ... greed ..." (above, note 11) 221. Great indignation; but in fact Thucydides didn't mention these things either. One may wonder whether κιγκλίζειν and κιχλίζειν are not in fact the same word. Our only use of it in this sense seems to be this line in Theognis and an entry in Hesychius defining it as equal to κινεῖν or πειράζειν; both words are derived from the names of birds, though the 'dabchick,' whatever that may be, was traditionally as poor as a church mouse.

> Ever to us is banquet beloved and
> cithara and dance,
> And changes of clothing and warm
> baths and bed (*Od.* 8.248-9[18])

Solon's beautiful lines on the happy life present us with a picture of pleasure both physical and social:

> Happy is he who has boys to love
> and firm-footed horses
> And dogs for the hunt, and a guest
> from a foreign land. (frg. 13D)

Much else too of the great trader and patriot shows how aware he was of the difference between pleasure and wealth, between the rich man and him:

> whose riches all were this:
> with belly and side and foot to live
> daintily and of boy and woman, when
> the time for this too comes, the blossom...
> this is mortal riches—the rest is
> vanity... (frg. 14 D 3-7)

(One wonders whether it has been noticed how closely these terms are repeated in the wonderful old song from *Gammer Gurton's Needle,* "Back and side go bare, go bare,/ Both foot and hand grow cold;/ But belly, God send thee good ale enough,/ Whether it be new or old.") Perhaps Mimnermus is not a good example: he seems too conscious of the waste and fret of Time. But by and large, all through the archaic period, we hear the ring of a hearty pleasure not at all dissociated from notions of wealth, virtue, and sound politics. To archaic man, goods were still good.

As we have already mentioned, pleasure was an integral part of Herodotus's theory of government. Plainly he considered Pleasure and 'Goodness' the primary criteria for the excellence of an institution. Now whether Herodotus's ἀγαθόν means Utility or some other standard of excellence may be not at once clear, but as to ἡδύ there can be no doubt. The difficulty here is that Pleasure for him was an invariable human emotion. Our comparison of the Old Oligarch and the Thucydides passages testifies to something much more striking, a real defence of pleasures (intellectual and material goods) as productive of change and growth and therefore providing a dynamic rather than a static view of

---

[18] In fact, however, if one adds up the whole evidence of books eight and nine it is clear that the poet of the *Odyssey* was aware of the problem more or less in the form in which we have put it, and that with great restraint he takes a somewhat ambiguous position towards the pleasure-principle. The ancients were not at all unaware of this, see for example the *Certamen Homeri et Hesiodi* 6.

human destiny and development. Yet in one way pleasure is not static for Herodotus: for him, as for other men of his time, it did move things, only the direction was usually downward. The moralizing picture of what happens when the pleasure-principle is let loose was fully available to men of the early fifth century in the form of the fables of Sybaris and of Polycrates. The story of how Cyrus and Croesus changed the character of the Lydians by causing them to wear feminine dress and to teach their sons singing and dancing and huckstering (Herod. 1.156) is only comprehensible in terms of a generally accepted theory that ἁβροδιαιτεῖν produces slack people incapable of defending themselves and preserving their own liberties.

For the opposite view we have but one supporting text, a fragment from Heraclides Ponticus's lost dialogue *On Pleasure* where he is quite explicit that "to have pleasure and to live luxuriously are properties of free men: for they relax the soul and augment it."[19] This fascinatingly liberal view, which comes near to saying what people have been suggesting in recent years about social development and modern Western democracy, was then no strange idea to the fourth century. The aim of the present paper has been to show that this idea was part of the pro-democratic argument in fifth century Athens, that it found its clearest expression in the tract of the Old Oligarch, and that Pericles makes direct but covert reference to it in the Funeral Oration.

Western Reserve University
Cleveland

[19] Hercleides Ponticus (Ath. 12.512a) frg. 55.6-7 Wehrli (*Schule des Aristoteles, Texte und Kommentar*, vol. 7, Basel 1953) is right in pointing out that these ideas are probably not those of Heracleides himself but of one of the interlocutors in his dialogue. But this is not an argument invented ad hoc, for traces of it can be found as early as the *Gorgias* (so Wehrli *ad hoc*); I myself feel quite sure we can demonstrate tradition from Homer right on down, and echoes can even be seen in Hericleides Periegetes (above, note 4).

SOME INSCRIPTIONS ON ATTIC POTTERY

Henry R. Immerwahr

Several thousand scratched and painted inscriptions on pottery were published in the first edition of the Berlin Corpus of Greek inscriptions (*CIG*) well over a hundred years ago. Since then, their study has not kept pace with the general progress of Greek epigraphy. Only recently have scholars (in particular Sir John Beazley and currently Miss L. H. Jeffery) begun to pay sufficient attention to these important testimonia for Greek, and especially Athenian, social and cultural history. No longer do monumental stone inscriptions suffice to give us an adequate picture of the history of Greek writing and of ancient language and customs. As a by-product of a complete collection of published Attic vase inscriptions undertaken by the author, some new readings and interpretations of such inscriptions are here offered as a small tribute to the memory of Professor Wallace E. Caldwell.[1]

1. A Potter's Dedication

A black-figured plate by the painter Lydos and dating to about 550 B. C., said to have been found in Attica, formerly belonged to the collection of D. M. Robinson but is now at Harvard.[2] The subject is probably the sons of Boreas. On the front of the plate (which is not completely preserved) is the beginning, and on the rear the end, of an incised inscription interpreted by Robinson as ''Εριν ἐς ἔργον or ''Εριδες ἔργον, with an understood reference to the figures of the plate, which he thought wrongly to be female.[3] However, the figures are male, and the goddess Eris has no connection with the subject. Since the lower part of the plate is broken away, there must also be a gap in the middle of the inscription, for as Robinson rightly saw, the letters are likely to belong to a single inscription written on front and back of the plate, although

---

[1] The majority of the readings in this paper go back to 1946-47. I received much help from Miss Edith Marshall and the late Professor G. H. Chase at the Boston Museum of Fine Arts; from Professor Martin Robertson in the British Museum; and from Sir John Beazley who gave me access to his collection of photographs. For bibliography on Attic vase inscriptions, see G. M. A. Richter, *Attic Red-figured Vases: A Survey*,[2] 1958, pp. 14 ff.; J. D. Beazley, "Some Inscriptions on Vases I-VIII," *AJA* 31, 1927, pp. 345 ff. and later; L. H. Jeffery, *The Local Scripts of Archaic Greece*, 1961, *passim*. Figs. 1 and 2 are museum photographs sent me through the kindness of Dr. Cornelius Vermeule and published by courtesy of the Boston Museum of Fine Arts.

[2] Published by D. M. Robinson, *AJA* 34, 1930, pp. 353-59; cf. *CVA*, Baltimore fasc. 1, pl. 19,1. Beazley, *ABV* 112 no. 54. Cf. Beazley, *The Development of Attic Black-figure*, 1951, p. 47.

[3] Robinson, *op. cit.*, p. 356 and *CVA* text to pl. 19,1. Cf. Beazley, *JHS* 54, 1934, p. 89.

the letters on the reverse are smaller than those on the front. When examining the plate in Baltimore in 1947, I thought that the letters had been redrawn, but that enough remained of the ancient strokes to allow for certain readings. Thus the obverse reads ΕϷΙΑ . . . (the *alpha* about two thirds preserved) and the reverse . . . ΕϟΕΡΛΟΝ, the *gamma* being redrawn, but certain. Thus the inscription ends in ἔργον or ἔργων, which suggests a dedication by an artisan, since in early dedications the "work" referred to seems to be always that of the dedicator himself.[4]

It seems likely, then, that the inscription was meant to be read as a continuous text on both sides of the plate when it was hung up from the branch of a tree or the like, for which purpose it has two suspension holes. When the plate was in this position, the inscription would have started near the center of the obverse and have run down to the right in the direction of 4 o'clock on a dial; it would then have curved to the left and at one point have turned to the reverse (no doubt running along the rim for a while), where it would arrive near the center pointing toward 2 o'clock. This conjectural course of the inscription would involve a change of direction to retrograde writing at some point. The amount of text lost is difficult to determine, because the letters are of uneven size and the following restoration is given merely *exempli gratia*:

Ἐριά[νϑες? ἀνέϑεκεν or divinity, or possibly both τε͂ς? τέχν]ες ἔργον.[5]

Since this is presumably an artisan's dedication, the possibility must be admitted that we have here the name of the Attic potter of the plate, for it cannot be the painter's name, since that is known to us from other vases.

2. A Hermes Dedication from a Cairn?

A triangular piece broken off from a tile and containing the unusual scratched inscription ΗΕΡΜΕΙ | ΜΑΛΑL | ΜΑ was published in 1939 by Eugene Vanderpool. It was found in a well-marked stratum of a well, situated just south of the Athenian Agora, and the pottery associated with it dates the sherd in the third quarter of the sixth century.[6] The inscription was written on the piece after it had been broken off and rather neatly fills the available space. Vanderpool gives the reading by E. Schweigert: Ἑρμ' εἰμ' ἄγαλμα, "I am Hermes' statue," but does not speculate about the exact nature or purpose of the text. Miss Jeffery prefers a different reading; hερμε͂ι μ' ἄγαλμα . . . , and suggests that the inscription "may be an imperfect draft . . . for a sculptor who was mak-

[4] See the author, *AJP* 81, 1960, pp. 273-74, and note 33.
[5] Not [σοφί]ες ἔργον, which would have to be poetic, but does not scan. [περικαλλ]ὲς ἔργον is possible, but I know of no parallel. For τέχνες ἔργον cf. Raubitschek, *Dedications from the Athenian Acropolis*, 1949, no. 244, as restored.
[6] E. Vanderpool, *Hesperia* 8, 1939, pp. 258-59, no. 9 and fig. 15. Jeffery, *Local Scripts*, p. 78 no. 33 and pl. 4.

ing a Hermes statue for some client."⁷ Neither reading, nor Miss Jeffery's explanation, seems entirely satisfactory.

Schweigert's reading, if I understand it correctly, presupposes the elision of the genitive ending, which is unlikely, since the vowel is long. It would be preferable to assume that the writer omitted the dative ending of Hermes' name by haplography: hερμ<εῖ> εἴμ' ἄγαλμα, which gives an Ithyphallic. Miss Jeffery's text is admittedly incomplete (the word ἀνέθεκεν and the dedicator's name are missing) and one would perhaps have to assume that the other part of the inscription was written on a second sherd. At any rate the inscription hardly looks like a model for a stone inscription, which would rather have been written in its entirety on a single sherd. Furthermore, a third version for the reading of the text may be suggested: hέρμ(α) εἰμ(ὶ) ἄγαλμα, i.e. "I am a *herma* (intended for) an offering." The word *herma* is often translated "stone heap," but it is better taken as a "stone," or the individual item in such a heap.⁸ The grammatical construction of this dedicatory text would be similar to a well-known inscription from Miletus: "I am Chares . . . , Apollo's offering."⁹ The two elisions suggest that the text is metrical; it has the form of a *colon Reizianum*. If complete, the inscription has two peculiarities, in that both the dedicator's name and the name of the divinity are absent.

A decision between the three suggested readings is difficult, although the last seems to me most probable. For the purpose of the sherd two interpretations suggest themselves. It may either have accompanied some other object as a label, or it may itself be the object dedicated. The labels cited by Miss Jeffery are mostly of bronze, although some are of pottery, among them a curious dedication at the Ptoum.¹⁰ But against the theory of a label is the incompleteness of the information given on the sherd. Hence it is most likely that the sherd itself was the dedication: an *agalma* is not necessarily a statue, but may be any dedication pleasing to a god.¹¹ In that case we have here a most unusual piece, which is so far as I know unique. I would suggest that an unknown person in the sixth century B.C. tossed the sherd onto a stone heap sacred no doubt to Hermes. The dedicator's name is missing because he was just a passer-by; and the god's name is omitted, because the association of Hermes with stone heaps was obvious.

This is not the place to discuss in detail the association of Hermes

---

[7] Jeffery, *op. cit.*, p. 74 and note 2.
[8] H. Frisk, *Griechisches Etymologisches Wörterbuch*, s.vv. ἕρμα, Ἑρμῆς.
[9] Jeffery, *op. cit.* p. 343, no. 29 (cf. p. 414).
[10] Bronze labels: Jeffery, *op cit.*, p. 168, no. 2; p. 199, no. 19; p. 220, no. 14; p. 234, no. 10. Pottery labels: p. 76, no. 9c, cf. p. 70; p. 95, no. 10, cf. p. 92, note 4 (the suggestion that this, the Ptoum dedication, was a label is mine, not Miss Jeffery's. I believe the object was neither a tile nor a plaque, but was finished all around and thus meant to be hung up.)
[11] C. Karouzos, "Περικαλλὲς Ἄγαλμα," *Epitymbion Tsounta, passim.*

with stone cairns. Whether or not there exists an actual etymological connection between *herma* and Hermes (by which the god would be "he of the stone heap"), such a connection is attested as a popular etymology, albeit in a later time.[12] It also does not matter here whether or not we accept the theory that cairns in early antiquity were always funerary, or the less likely theory that they were originally *Fluchmale* or curse markers.[13] Their use as road markers was certainly also widespread.[14] It is futile to speculate what kind of stone heap our piece comes from. It was found in a fill consisting of "dark grey mud and stones;" the well into which it was finally thrown was rather far from the image of Hermes by the Areopagus mentioned by Pausanias; but the well was situated near several ancient roads leading up to the Acropolis from the area of the market place.[15]

While I know of no exact parallel, there exist various similar monuments. On a farm near Sparta, a longish rough stone was found many years ago, inscribed in sixth-century letters: hερμᾶνος; the inscription is on the upper part of the stone, showing that it was meant to be stuck in the ground or in a base. Nilsson follows the original report in assigning funerary significance to the stone, but it has also been considered a boundary marker—at present it is impossible to be sure.[16] Boundary markers and boundary cairns are at any rate well known in the Peloponnesus, especially from Arcadia.[17] The main evidence for cairns surrounding herms is a fifth-century vase painting showing the hero Cephalus sitting near an ithyphallic herm, probably of Priapus, placed in a cairn.[18] In a famous passage, the Odyssey mentions a Ἑρμαῖος

---

[12] See in general M. P. Nilsson, *Geschichte der griechischen Religion*, vol. 1 2nd ed., 1955, pp. 503 ff. Also Nilsson, *Griechische Feste*, 1906, pp. 388 ff. *RE* s.v. Steinkult (Latte, 1929), col. 2300. L. Curtius, *Die Antike Herme*, Diss. Munich, 1903, pp. 9 ff. R. Lullies, *Typen der griechischen Herme*, 1931, pp. 35 ff. M. W. de Visser, *Die nicht menschengestaltigen Götter der Griechen*, 1903, pp. 102-107. H. Goldman, *AJA* 46, 1942, p. 58. J. Chittenden, *Hesp.* 16, 1947, p. 94.

[13] Funerary: Nilsson, *Gesch. der Griech. Rel.* I², p. 504, following Curtius, *op. cit.* (above, note 12), pp. 12-13. Curse markers: B. Schmidt, *Neue Jahrbücher für klass. Philol.* 147, 1893, pp. 369 ff.

[14] See Pfuhl, *JdI* 20, 1905, p. 80. Passages in de Visser, *loc. cit.* RE s.v. Steinkult, col. 2300.

[15] E. Vanderpool, *Hesp.* 8, 1939, p. 256. Altar of Hermes: Paus. 1.28,6 and D. Burr (Thompson), *Hesp.* 2, 1933, p. 638. Ancient roads: see Vanderpool, *op. cit.*, p. 255. *Hesp.* 25, 1956, pp. 47 ff. (South Road). The well lies west of the modern Areopagus Road and south of the ancient South Road (= modern Asteroskopeiou).

[16] *IG* V 1, no. 371; cf. *AM* 2, 1877, p. 434, no. 4 and Nilsson, *Gesch. der griech. Rel.* I², p. 504, note 3. *IG, loc. cit.* Schwyzer, *Delectus*, no. 8, and others consider the stone a boundary marker. Cautiously, Curtius, *op. cit.* (above, note 12), p. 23.

[17] Paus, 8.34,6, etc. (the passages are collected in *IG* V 2, *passim*, under the several Arcadian localities). K. A. Rhomaios, Οἱ μεθόριοι Λακωνικοὶ Ἑρμαῖ, *Athena* 1908, pp. 401 ff. is not available to me. Another *terminus: IG* V 2, no. 558; cf. XII 5, no. 1076, lines 30-31; XII 3, no. 345, line 14.

[18] Nilsson, *Gesch. der griech. Rel.* I², pl. 33,1. Lullies, *Typen der griech. Herme*, pp. 72, no. 7, and 75; pl. 8,2. Watzinger, *Griechische Vasen in Tübingen*, pl. 41. The vase is Boeotian.

λόφος, which the scholiast defines as a cairn. Similar terms, e.g. Ἕρμαιον, Ἅρμακα, and Ἑρμαϊκόν (a common name for mines at Laurium) occur in literary texts and inscriptions, but it is usually not possible to tell whether they refer to temples, monuments or simple cairns used as markers.[19] Finally, one might cite an archaic inscription on a longish uncut stone from Corcyra, Μῦς με hίσατο, although as Six has pointed out, this object was probably not a herm, but an aniconic representation of Apollo Agyieus. This inscription agrees with ours in the omission of the name of the divinity.[20] The parallels cited are of course insufficient to prove the proposed interpretation, but they help to render it more probable.

3. "Hail thee and buy me."

The majority of Attic vases are found in Etruria where they were brought no doubt by wholesale dealers who bought them from the Athenian potters and from private owners in bulk. However, Athenian potters also sold their wares directly to individual customers, and this aspect of their trade was in fact foremost in their minds as we can see from many indications, including occasional references in inscriptions to the selling of vases.[21]

Thus a curious variation of the common drinking inscription on Little-Master cups (χαῖρε καὶ πίει εὖ) appears on a band cup in Copenhagen, Chr. VIII 961, and on an early lip cup in the Spencer Churchill Collection at Northwick Park, namely χαιρην καὶ πριομην. These two inscriptions have been explained with reference to the more intelligible inscription χαῖρε καὶ πρίο με on a band cup in the Louvre; the last recurs on fragments in Florence and Adria.[22] Blinkenberg interpreted πρίο με as πρίω με, and read the last inscriptions as "Hail thee and buy me." Against this Pottier raised the objection that the inscription should refer to the banquet rather than the market; he interpreted πρίο με as

[19] Od. 16. 471; cf. J. F. Crome, *AM* 60/61, 1935-36, pp. 309 ff. *Hermaion*: Thuc. 7.29. Paus. 8.34,6. Schwyzer, *Delectus*, nos. 709, line 9 (Ephesus) and 720, line 27 (Priene). Nilsson, *Gesch. der Griech. Rel.* I², p. 205, note 12. It is often not possible to decide whether the term refers to a temple or a cairn. *Hermax*: *SEG* 6, no. 673, line 4 ("Αρμακα). *Hermaikon*: see M. Crosby, *Hesp.* 19, 1950, p. 307 (index).

[20] *IG* IX 1, no. 704. Cf. Six, *AM* 19, 1894, pp. 340-45.

[21] "Two obols and you got me," on a sixth-century black-figured amphora, according to a probable interpretation: see Amyx, *Univ. of Cal. Publications in Class. Archaeol.* vol. I, pp. 179 ff.; but cf. Beazley, *ABV* 136 no. 50, and see further Amyx, *Hesp.* 27, 1958, pp. 300 ff. "Buy me and you will make a good bargain," on a black-figured lekythos soon after 500 B.C.: Beazley, *AJA* 54, 1950, p. 315, no. 8. "Lakon bought this...," graffito on a (non-Attic?) bowl from Olympia: *JdI* 56, 1941, Olympia Bericht 3, p. 39 and fig. 25.

[22] *CVA*, Denmark fasc. 3, pl. 117,5a-b and text (Blinkenberg). Beazley, *JHS* 52, 1932, p. 182 (Northwick Park cup and Florence fragment). E. Pottier, *BCH* 55, 1931, pp. 432 ff. and fig 1 (Louvre). Beazley, *AJA* 39, 1935, p. 476, no. 2 (Adria). For the χαῖρε καὶ πίει εὖ formula, see G. M. A. Richter, *CVA*, USA fasc. 11, p. 5.

πρίου μή, and read "Hail thee and do not worry." Sir John Beazley rightly preferred Blinkenberg's interpretation.

A plain lip cup in the British Museum (B 414) definitely settles the matter in favor of Blinkenberg's interpretation.[23] The cup is restored and had been made to read, on A, χαῖρε καὶ ριο ἐμέ, which in the British Museum Catalogue was reproduced as ΧΑΙΡΕΚΑΙΓΙΟΕΜΕ. However, the seventh and eighth letters, and part of the ninth, were modern, and were too widely spaced. After a cleaning, the inscription appears as:

+ΑΙΡΕΚ'..ΡΙΟΕΜΕ   Χαῖρε κα[ὶ π]ρίο ἐμέ.

The form ἐμέ shows clearly that this is the personal pronoun rather than the negative μή.

On B, there is a nonsense inscription:

ΧΑΙ⊳ΕΤΕΝΕΓΓϟΤϟΤ

4. A Kalos-name.

A black-figured hydria in the Boston Museum (28.46), attributed by Beazley to the Lysippides Painter, bears a *kalos*-name which has been listed as Philon.[24] The final *nu* is missing, as are the first two letters of καλός. The *omikron* of the name, near the break, was a smudge. A cleaning with alcohol revealed the lower part of an upright stroke, *iota* or (less likely) *tau*. It seemed to me that five letters would just fill the break, but it is possible that the inscription curved up and around the missing head of one of the figures, giving a longer name. Nevertheless, Philippos is a probable restoration:

ΦΙΛΙ[ΓΟϟΚΑ]ΛΟϟ   Φίλι[π<π>ος κα]λός.

This name does not seem to occur as a *kalos*-name elsewhere.

Under the foot of the vase is a graffito with *alpha* and *pi* in ligature (cf. Hackl, *Münchener Archäologische Studien,* 1909, no. 52c), perhaps retrograde. On the right, a vertical stroke. There seems to be also a very faint figure-eight sign, painted in dilute glaze (?); this last is not listed in Hackl.

5. A Casual Encounter

Greeting scenes are common on vases and often have inscriptions added. The obverse of a red-figured skyphos in Boston (01.8076), by the Euaichme Painter,[25] shows Heracles (ΗΕΡΑΚΛΕϟ) confronting a bearded man leaning on a stick, from whose mouth issues the greet-

[23] *CIG* 4, no. 8103 and pl. VI (incorrect). H. B. Walters, *Cat. of the Greek and Etr. Vases in the Brit. Mus.* 2, 1892, p. 221. Smith and Pryce, *CVA*, British Museum fasc. 2, IIIHe, pl. 12,5 (erroneous readings).
[24] Beazley, *ABV*, 261, no. 38, and p. 672. On Philon, cf. also Caskey-Beazley, *Attic Vase Paintings*, 2, p. 5 (our vase is not mentioned there).
[25] Beazley, *ARV* 524, no. 1. See figs. 1-2.

ing +AIRE.²⁶ If this figure is Zeus (despite his very human look) then we have here Heracles' entry into Olympus and the greeting is ceremonial. More interesting, however, is the reverse, on which a youth confronts a bearded man holding a purse. From the man's mouth (which is shown open) issue the letters EΦEVSO, complete. This too ought to be a greeting, and I would suggest ἤ, φεῦ σου, "Hey, what a boy." Both ἤ and φεῦ are known individually from Aristophanes, although I have not found them in combination; the first is a rather low-brow form of address, the second an expression of admiration.²⁷

Erotic conversations between men and boys are commonplace on vases. Sometimes, as here, the man holds a bag, and the question arises whether this purse contains stones for a game, or money. However that may be, the inscriptions range from high-class to what is definitely the lowest.²⁸ Our text is thus not as bad as it might seem. The two sides of the vase draw a nice contrast between the heroic and the realistically human.

6. Preliminary Sketch.

A single fragment of a red-figured skyphos in Boston (10.224), showing parts of a youth in a sleeved costume, of a woman attacking, and the hand of a second woman, has been interpreted by Sir John Beazley as the Death of Orpheus and attributed to the Pantoxena Painter.²⁹ Above and between the two preserved heads appears an inscription, painted on the glaze in applied red in four lines, which is rendered in *ARV* as follows:

ΓΑΝΤΟΞΕΝΑ ΚΟΡΙΝΘΟΙ ΗΟṢΙΑ ΚΑLΑΙS.

Between the lines of this inscription, and under the glaze, is another inscription in three lines, written in thick paint or glaze in such a way that the letters stand out in slight relief:

ΓΑΝΤΟΞΕΝΑ | ΚΟΡΙΝΘΟΙ | ΚΑLΗ.

²⁶ For the identification of the man, cf. J. D. Beazley, *Apollo*, Boll. dei Musei del Salernitano, 1, 1961, p. 25. For the greeting, see Eur., *Medea*, lines 663 ff. Other greeting scenes with χαῖρε: Rome, Villa Guilia, bf. neck amphora *ABV* 693 bottom, cf. Greifenhagen, *JdI* 72, 1957, *AA* pp. 13-14; London E 41, rf. cup *ARV* 37, no. 40 (Theseus and maiden); Vatican, rf. amphora *ARV* 120, no. 2 (Herakles and Athena); Munich 2409, rf. stamnos *ARV* 196, no. 7 (two men); Boston 98.880, head vase *ARV* 200, no. 4 (symposium). I owe these references to Mr. Mario Pellicciaro. Cf. also Beazley, *AJA* 33, 1929, p. 363, no. 6, and above, note 22.

²⁷ ἤ Ξανθία, Arist. *Frogs*, line 271, cf. *Clouds*, line 105. φεῦ τοῦ κάλλους, Arist. *Birds*, line 1724 (lyr.).

²⁸ London E 398, rf. pelike: a man greets a woman on the other side of the vase, saying εἶ σφόδρα - χαλή (on the other side also); cf. C. Smith, *Cat. ... Brit. Mus.* 2, pp. 252-53. Vulgar: Beazley, *AJA* 54, 1950, p. 316, no. 10.

²⁹ Beazley, *ARV* 694, no. 2. Beazley, *Attic Red-figured Vases in American Museums*, 1918, p. 175. Furtwängler-Reichhold, *Griechische Vasenmalerei*, 3, p. 358, fig. 169 (drawing by Beazley without the inscriptions); cf. p. 357, note 10. I want to thank Miss G. M. A. Richter and Dr. Dietrich von Bothmer for additional information on this vase and for sending me an infra-red photograph.

This three-line inscription was not written with the relief-line instrument, but no doubt with a brush. Its relation to the four-line inscription can be seen in the sketch made by Miss Suzanne Chapman of the Boston Museum (see Fig. 3). The three-line inscription was written before the vase was glazed, the four-line inscription after glazing; it is reasonable to assume that the first inscription served as a model for the second.

The three-line inscription is written partly in Attic letters and the lines slant upwards. The dot of the *theta* seems to be missing; the second and third *omikrons* are open at the top; *alpha* appears as A and A. The four-line inscription is *stoichedon* except for the last three letters and somewhat more careful in appearance, except that the vertical spacing of the lines is uneven; the second and third lines are close together, while the third and fourth are rather widely separated. The third letter of the third line, given by Beazley as a doubtful *sigma*, is nearly illegible, but I thought that I saw, both on the original and in a photograph, the top of what might be a *rho*, but could not be a *sigma*. Hence I read: HOPIA.[80] The lettering of the two inscriptions is similar (especially ΘO of KOPINΘOI), but one cannot state that they were written by one man; this is for other reasons unlikely.

It would seem most natural to consider the first inscription a preliminary sketch to be copied after the vase was glazed. In any case, it was so used, for the second inscription was clearly copied from the first, and with a good many errors. In particular, the painter seems to have copied the second line twice; his second attempt was worse than his first, and he was perhaps looking for a new word then. His H is similar to the badly written K of the first inscription, and although the N of the first inscription is clear, this is a letter easily misread for Λ or A. In line four, the painter seems to have been confused by the ὁ παῖς καλός formula so common on vases. Thus we have here an unusual case showing us how vase inscriptions were copied at times from models, and indicating at least one common source of errors. Surely, the writer of the four-line inscription was not the same man as the writer of the three-line inscription, and despite his attempt at *stoichedon* (which is not uncommon on vases of this period) he was hardly literate, although he knew how to make letters and could probably read some words.

The first (or three-line) inscription has the merit of being intelligible: Παντοξένα Κορίνϑοι καλή means "Pantoxena (seems) fair to Korinthos" (δοκεῖ is to be supplied). The same inscription appears, with a slight variation, on another skyphos by the Pantoxena Painter, in the Bibliothèque Nationale.[81] It too is in three lines and *stoichedon*, with the

---

[80] Dr. von Bothmer and Miss Richter considered the third letter illegible (*ca.* 1947).

[81] Cab. Med. 846; Beazley, *ARV* 694 no. 1. A third vase by this painter has a fragmentary three-line inscription also (*ibid.*, no. 3).

Fig. 1: No. 5 (Boston 01.8076, A).

Fig. 2: No. 5 (Boston 01.8076, B).

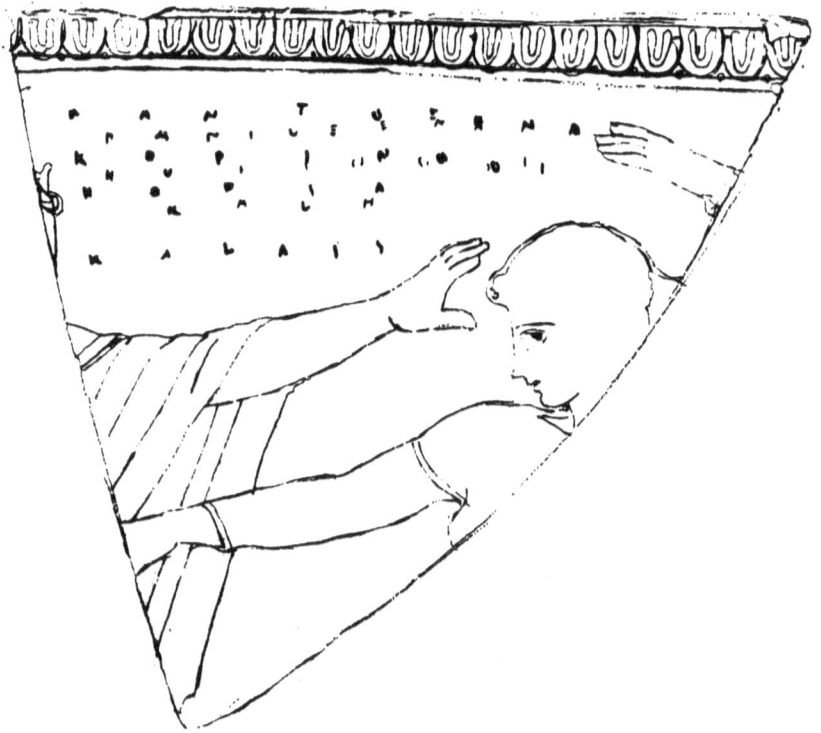

Fig. 3: No. 6 (Boston 10.224).

second word centered on the first: Παντοξένα καλὰ Κορίνθοι. Here not only the ending of the name Pantoxena, but also the adjective, show Doric forms.

A red-figured cup by Oltos in Berlin exhibits the same method of making a preliminary sketch for a painted inscription, and a small fragment of an undetermined black-glazed pottery object from the Agora (P 9,978) has the dedicatory inscription lightly incised under the glaze with the instrument used for preliminary sketches and then repeated over the glaze in applied white. In Furtwängler-Reichhold, the latter scholar remarks on two Meidian vases which have terrain lines drawn in relief before glazing and then incised after glazing, but (as Miss G. M. A. Richter has pointed out to me) in this case the relief lines as well as the incisions were meant to be seen. On a cup in the British Museum (D 4), both white-ground and red-figured, by the Tarquinia Painter, the inscriptions on the white-ground Interior were first incised into the white ground and then painted over. This last procedure is not very similar to our case, but reminds one rather of a remark of Plato's, in the *Protagoras,* that teachers would draw outlines of letters for their pupils to follow.[32] The method followed on our vase seems to be uncommon, although models of inscriptions for the use of vase painters were probably quite frequent.

I have not found the name Pantoxena elsewhere; the ending is not Attic, although καλή has the regular form, unlike the καλά of the vase in the Bibliothèque Nationale. Pantoxenos, with the first letter missing, but surely to be supplied, occurs on a red-figured amphora in the manner of Euphronios in the Louvre.[33] It is there doubtless a love name, with καλός omitted. Korinthos is also an odd name, for a personal name it must surely be. It occurs, in Attica and elsewhere, only in late inscriptions; my earliest example is a fourth century inscription from Argos.[34] Heroic names are said not to occur in Attica for free citizens until the end of the fifth century.[35]

Usually inscriptions of this sort refer to a (real or hypothetical) user of the vase praising another person who is mentioned at a drinking

[32] Cup by Oltos: Furtwängler, *Beschreibung der Vasensammlung in Antiquarium* 2, 1885, no. 2264. The Agora fragment is unpublished. Meidian vases: Furtwängler-Reichhold, *op. cit.,* 1, p. 299. London D 4; *ARV* 570 no. 33. Plato, *Prot.* 326d.
[33] Louvre G 106, cf. *ARV* 18 no. 3. D. von Bothmer, *Amazons in Greek Art,* 1957, p. 150, no. 37. Love name: Hartwig, *Meisterschalen,* pp. 152-53; D. M. Robinson and E. J. Fluck, *A Study of Greek Love Names,* 1937, p. 85, no. 31. The name Pantaxenos occurs in a later period: see Preisigke, *Namenbuch,* s.v.; Collitz-Bechtel, no. 4782 a 2 (Pantaxenos).
[34] *IG* IV, no. 516.1 (Argos). See also Fick and Bechtel, *Die Griechischen Personennamen,* 1894, p. 349, cf. 351.
[35] E. Fränkel in *RE,* s.v. Namenwesen, cols. 1642 f. Fick and Bechtel, *op. cit.,* pp. 304 ff. and 315 f. Bechtel, *Historische Personennamen des Griechischen,* pp. 571 ff.

party, but in our case the non-Attic name of Korinthos, the dialect forms, and the fact that the vases are by the same hand, make one suspect that Korinthos may possibly be the name of the painter himself (the potter is less likely). I do not know if this possibility (it is no more than that) has been suggested.

7. Diokles of Halae.

In 1931, the late Professor D. M. Robinson published a red-figured bell krater then in his possession, dating to about 430 B.C. and depicting, on A, the hero Bouzyges with the first plough, and on B three youths.[86] The vase was said to have been found in a cemetery near Vari. On the reverse and on the left side of the obverse is a graffito in large letters, given by Robinson as: ΔΙΟΚΛΕ[Σ] ΗΑΛ[ΑΙΕ]Υ[Σ] ΚΕΚΡΟΠΙΑΣ. However, the vase is much restored, and the ancient strokes have been gone over with an instrument in modern times. A photograph in the possession of Sir John Beazley shows part of the vase before the modern additions were made and gives the letters ΚΡΟΓΙΔΟΣ for the end of the inscription. Using only those traces which I thought were genuine, plus the photograph, one may read:

ΔΙΟΚΛΕ[Σ] ΗΑΛ[ΑΙ]ΕΥ[Σ] | [Κ]ΕΚΡΟΓΙΔΟΣ.

There is no doubt that the restorer reproduced the deme correctly, guided perhaps by more traces than can now be seen. The alphabet is evidently mixed.

The inscription was written in such a way that it more or less avoids cutting into the figures, which necessitated wide spacing. Since Κεκροπίδος is written on the left of the obverse, it is no doubt, as Robinson saw, the continuation of the inscription on the reverse. The combination: *name—deme—tribe in genitive* is unusual, but Professor B. D. Meritt has pointed out to me that the name of the tribe may have been added to distinguish the deme Halae Aixonides from Halae Araphenides (which belonged to Aegeis).[37] Otherwise the combination of these three items of information is known to me only from the monument for the heroes of Phyle,[38] and from later ephebic inscriptions.

A *Diokles Halaieus Kekropidos* is listed by Kirchner as belonging to the early fourth century B.C.[39] He is known only as the father of a

[86] Robinson, *AJA* 35, 1931, pp. 152-60. Cf. *CVA*, Baltimore fasc. 2, pl. 48,2. The vase is now at Harvard. By the Hephaistos Painter: Beazley, *ARV* 391, no. 19. Cf. A. B. Cook, *Zeus*, 3, pp. 606 ff. and pl. 45. Arvanitopoulos, *Polemon* 3, 1947, pp. 53-55. Mentioned by M. Jameson, *TAPA* 82, 1951, p. 59, note 26. On the mistaken identification of the figure as Athena, see Beazley, *JHS* 58, 1938, p. 268.

[37] Cf. *RE* s.v. Halai, nos. 1-2 (Kolbe). C. W. J. Eliot, *Coastal Demes of Attika* (Phoenix suppl. 5), Toronto, 1962, pp. 25 ff.

[38] A. E. Raubitschek, *Hesperia* 10, 1941, pp. 284 ff. Ephebes: e.g. *IG* II/III² 478, 665, 766, etc.

[39] J. Kirchner, *Prosopographia Attica*, no. 4014.

[Phil]agros of about 360-50 B.C.⁴⁰ Our Diokles is likely to be a member of the same family, but hardly the same man, especially if Robinson was right in thinking the vase funerary, since some bones were said to have been found in it. This last point, however, is doubtful, since a bell krater is not very suitable for a burial and Robinson does not mention a cover of any kind. Another possibility would be that the vase was a prize vase, perhaps for some local festival. At any rate, our Diokles is apparently about forty years earlier than the father of Philagros.

8. Syllabic Heta.

The famous pair of red-figured cups by Aristophanes and Erginus in Boston (00.344 and 00.345) was published long ago in Furtwängler and Reichhold, but so far as the inscriptions are concerned, the drawings are not up to their usual standards of accuracy since they were made from photographs. E. Robinson, both in the *Annual Report* and in notes contributed to Furtwängler-Reichhold, had better readings, but I took somewhat more accurate readings in 1947.⁴¹ In the following list, I give the inscriptions mechanically from left to right. C. stands for Centaur. It will be recalled that the vases are nearly exact duplicates showing, on the Interior, Heracles and Nessus, and outside, both on A and B, the battle of Lapiths and Centaurs.

00.344:

Interior: 1. ΗΡΑΚΛΕΣ
2. ΝΕΣΣΟΣ   C.
3. ΔΕΙΑΝΕΙΡΑ

In Exergue: Ἐργῖνος:ἐπο[ίε]σεν. | Ἀριστοφά[νε]ς:ἔγραφε.

Exterior, A: 1. ΣΚΙΡ[.]ΟΣ   C., Σκίρ[τ]ος
2. ΑΙΟΛΟΣ
3. ΓΕΡΙΘΟΣ = Περίθους
4. VⱯΙΓVΛΟΣ   C.
5. ΘΗΣΕVΣ
6. ṄVΚΤΕVΣ   C.

B: 1. ΕΓΡΕΤΟΣ   C., Ἔγρετος
2. ΑΣΜΕΤΟΣ = Ἄδμητος
3. ΑΝΤΙΒΑΤΕΣ   C.
4. ΕVΡVΓVΛΟΣ
5. ΜΑΙΝΕVΕΣ   C., Μαινεύ{ε}ς
6. ΑΝΤΙΟΗ... = Ἀντίθης[ος]

---

⁴⁰ *P.A.* no. 9110, with stemma. *IG* II² 2820, line 24; cf. W. K. Pritchett, *Hesperia* 15, 1946, pp. 162-63.
⁴¹ Furtwängler-Reichhold, *op. cit.*, pls. 128-29 and text. E. Robinson, *Annual Report of the Museum of Fine Arts, Boston*, for 1900, pp. 49 ff., nos. 17 and 18. Beazley, *ARV* 842, nos. 2 and 3.

00.345:

Interior: 1. ΗΡΑΚΛΕΣ
2. ΝΕΣΣΟΣ   C.
3. ΔΕΙΑ̣ΝΕΙΡΑ

Exergue blank.

Exterior, A: 1. ΕΥΡVΒΟΤΟΣ   C.
2. ΚṘΕΘΕVΣ = Κρε̄θεύς
3. ΓΕΡΙΘ[.]Σ
4. Ν[.]ΚΤΕVΣ   C., Ν̣[υ]κτεύς
5. ΘΗΣΕV[.]
6. ΝΕΩΝ   C.

B: 1. ΑΝΤΙΝΟΜΟΣ   C.
2. ΑΣΜΕΤΟΣ
3. ΑΙΘΩΝ   C.
4. ΓΟΛVΑΙΝΟΣ
5. ΤΕΛΕΣ̇   C.
6. ΝΕΣΕVΣ =Νεσεύς

Only a few readings of 00.344 are new, since it is the better preserved. For exact details, see Robinson in the *Annual Report* and Hauser in Furtwängler-Reichhold. Important is B,6: as Robinson states, the fifth letter is a certain *theta*, not a *phi;* this is followed by a certain *eta* (only the top of the right vertical hasta is missing). Surely, this is a miswriting ('Αντίθηος) for 'Ατίθεος, as Hauser saw. In 00.345, A,1, a centaur's name, has been read as Εὐρύβατος, but the sixth letter is an *omikron* made in two halves, with the right half prolonged toward the bottom; the same shape occurs for the first *omikron* of B,1.[42] A,2: the *theta* is uncertain, with *omikron* and *phi* the other possibilities. *Kappa* is certain. A,4 had not been read before and is extremely faint. B,4: the *alpha* is faint, but certain. B,5: cursive *lambda* (λ).

From the epigraphical point of view, the most interesting feature of the writing is the misspelling 'Αντίθη[ος]. Both vases use an alphabet

[42] Eurybotos occurs as the name of an Athenian Olympic victor of 672 B.C. (Paus. 2.24,7; Dion. Hal., *Ant.* 3.1,3 has Εὐρυβάτης); cf. also *IG* I², no. 943, line 22. For Σκίρτος cf. Athens, Agora P 21,860 Σκ[ί]ρτων, surely a proper name (*Hesp.* 22, 1953, p. 66, no. 9). "Εγρετος: the name of the hero of an Attic ἱερὸν το[ῦ] 'Εγρέτου, *IG* II/III², 2499 (306/5 B.C.) is usually rendered 'Εγρέτης, but it may equally have been "Εγρετος. See C. D. Lord, *AJA* 3, 1899, p. 47, and E. Ziebarth, *Rhein. Mus.* 55, 1900, p. 501; cf. also Dittenberger, *Syll.*² 937, note 1, and Syll.³ 1097 (name 'Εγρετίων). Egertius was an Ionian founder of Chios (*RE.*, s.v.), and Nonnus has the name 'Εγρέτιος (*Dionys.* 30, 309, etc.). Thus "Εγρετος is fairly certain as a mythical proper name. Μαινευες: probably confusion between -ευς and -ης endings, cf. P. Kretschmer, *Die griechischen Vaseninschriften*, 1894, pp. 191-92.

that is mainly Ionic, including *omega,* but they do not use the Ionic *eta* as can be seen from the spellings of 00.344, Int. 1; B,2; B,3; B,5; and 00.345, Int. 1; A,2; B,2; B,5; B,6. I assume that Deianeira, on both vases, has the first vowel shortened to *epsilon.*[43] In 00.344, A,4, we note the absence of H = *h*. The letter H then stands for syllabic *heta* (i.e. for *he*—) in the first syllable of Herakles (on both vases); in 00.344, A,5 and 00.345, A,5 (Theseus); and in 00.344, B,6 (Antitheos). The vase painter seems to have used syllabic *heta* both for *hē* and for *hĕ* not only in the name of Heracles, but also improperly after *theta* (i.e. th+e = th+he). He neglected to do this only in 00.345, A,2 (Kretheus), possibly because the diphthong *eu* was too familiar to him.

The same improper use of *heta* after *theta* occurs on a pair of Panathenaic amphorae in Hildesheim which Peters has attributed to Aristophanes.[44] The inscriptions are identical, except that one vase omits the last *theta:*

ΤΩΝΑΘΗΝΕΘΗΝΑΘΛΩΝ

These vases use *omega* and Ionic *lambda,* but *epsilon* for *eta* and H for *hē* and *hĕ* after *theta.*

These four vases are of the very end of the fifth century and it seems strange that they should still use a feature seemingly so archaic as the syllabic use of *heta.*[45] However, we know from stone inscriptions that there is a good deal of confusion in the alphabet in the last decades of the fifth century, at the time when the Ionic alphabet was finally officially adopted.[46] It seems likely that this use of *heta* has nothing to do with an old "inherited" syllabic *heta,* but is due merely to a confusion between the Attic and Ionic alphabets. We find here the following combination of factors: (1) a dialect which pronounces *h*; (2) an alphabet—the Attic—which writes it; (3) another alphabet—the Ionic—which gives to what had been *h* the new value of *eta* and thus makes it impossible to write *h*. It would go beyond the scope of this paper to investigate to what extent this explanation is applicable to earlier occurrences of syllabic *heta.*

University of North Carolina
Chapel Hill

[43] ει for ηι is common from the early fourth century on: see Meisterhans, *Grammatik der attischen Inschriften,*⁸ 1900, pp. 36 ff.
[44] Hildesheim 1253 and 1254: K. Peters, *JdI* 57, 1942, pp. 143 ff.; the attribution is not accepted by Beazley, cf. *ABV* 412, nos. 2 and 1. The readings are taken from Beazley, *AJA* 47, 1943, p. 455, nos. 2 and 1, and (for the missing *theta* on 1253) from my note on a photograph in Beazley's possession. H. K. Süsserott, *Griechische Plastik des 4. Jahrh.*, p. 69 has dated the vases, from the shield device, to 403/2 B.C. Peters, *op. cit.*, p. 143, assumes a simple confusion between *eta* and *epsilon,* but the above explanation seems more likely.
[45] See most recently Jeffery, *Local Scripts*, p. 28.
[46] See e.g. *IG* I², 108; 304; 372-74. Cf. W. Larfeld, *Griechische Epigraphik,*² 1914, pp. 260-61.

THE BEGINNING OF COINAGE
BY OLYNTHIAN CHALCIDIANS

PAUL A. CLEMENT

In his note on Thucydides, I, 57, 5, A. W. Gomme declined to accept the dates for the Chalcidic coinage proposed in Olynthus IX because he thought it very doubtful that literary and inscriptional evidence indicated with certainty that the Chalcidic state did not exist before 432 B.C. and supposed that the chronology of the coinage had depended for its *terminus post quem* entirely on the truth of the proposition that literary and inscriptional evidence did indeed bear certain witness to the formation of the state in that year.[1] A specific year for the *terminus post quem* of the coinage does of course depend on literary and inscriptional evidence. But what Gomme's doubt ignored was the significance of the newly developed body of numismatic evidence in *Olynthus* IX. This indicated without regard to literary and inscriptional evidence for the formation of the Chalcidic state, that the *terminus post quem* of the state's coinage (Apollo/Cithara ΧΑΛΚΙΔΕΩΝ) was to be sought around the middle years of the reign of Perdikkas II, king of Macedon from *ca.* 454 B.C. to *ca.* 413 B.C.—or so it seems to me, and I very much regret that I can not now submit the elements of the problem to the judgment of the scholar whose interpretations of Greek and Roman history gave me at Chapel Hill great pleasure and much profit.

Briefly, the numismatic evidence was, and is, this. In fabric, tetrobols of Chalcidic Groups A-D are like tetrobols of Perdikkas II, and tetrobols of Chalcidic Group E like those of Archelaos (*ca.* 413-*ca.* 399), and the tetradrachms of Chalcidic Groups E-K like staters of the kings from Archelaos through Amyntas III (from *ca.* 413 to some time in the period *ca.* 392-370). In style there is a very close likeness between the male heads on Chalcidic Group F tetradrachms and those on staters of Archelaos, Aeropos, Amyntas II (?), and Pausanias (*ca.* 413-*ca.* 392). In the hoards found at Olynthus the attrition shown by coins of Perdikkas II corresponds to that shown by the hoard-coins of Chalcidic Groups A-G; this is indication of like periods of circulation, therefore, roughly, indication of contemporaneity; and, since Chalcidic Groups A-G contain about a third of the die-combinations known for the unit denomination in the whole coinage, it can be expected that they occupy in the uninterrupted series of the coinage, *ceteris paribus,* approximately a third of the time occupied by the whole.[2] This evidence of course yields interpretations

[1] *Historical Commentary on Thucydides,* I, p. 206, note 2.
[2] The detail of the evidence is given *Olynthus,* IX, pp. 125-128.

which are approximations. Its value in arguing the *terminus post quem* depends upon the fact that the numismatic history of this particular mint is now so well known that it is possible to estimate closely variables and imponderables such as ratio of preservation (high),[3] changing intensities of mint-production (locatable),[4] periods of no mint-activity (none of practical significance).[5] In the circumstance which in fact prevails the indications of the numismatic evidence alone, however approximate, are yet sufficiently definite to place the beginning of the coinage in the reign of Perdikkas II and neither too close to its beginning nor too close to its end.[6]

The evidence and the interpretations of evidence which caused Gomme to suspect that the Chalcidic state (and consequently the Chalcidic coinage) may have existed before 432 are not new[7] (though I believe no one has suggested before that it is possible that the Apollo/Cithara coinage of the Chalcidians could have started earlier than 432). Herodotos, VIII, 127: Ἀρτάβαζος . . . ὑποπτεύσας . . . τοὺς Ὀγυνθίους ἀπίστασθαι ἀπὸ βασιλέος, καὶ ταύτην ἐπολιόρκεε· εἶχον δὲ αὐτὴν Βοττιαῖοι . . . . ἐπεὶ δέ σφεας εἷλε πολιορκέων, κατέσφαξε ἐξαγαγὼν ἐς λίμνην, τὴν δὲ πόλιν παραδιδοῖ Κριτοβούλῳ Τορωναίῳ ἐπιτροπεύειν καὶ τῷ Χαλκιδικῷ γένεϊ, καὶ οὕτω Ὄλυνθον Χαλκιδέες ἔσχον. Gomme argued: " 'Ὄλυνθον Χαλκιδέες ἔσχον agrees excellently with the evidence of Thucydides. . . . Χαλκιδεῖς was the official name of the state. . . . Athens, in the fifth century, refused to recognize the official name; and, since Herodotos uses Χαλκιδεῖς in the same way as Thucydides, . . . this refusal belongs to the period before 432 (the tribute-lists) as well as after (the Treaty of Nikias) . . . . we seem to have the relics of an old union in the grouping of Olynthos, Skable, and Assera and of Mekyberna and Stolos on the tribute-lists of 454-453; the disappearance of these groups may well be the last step in ἀπόταξις of what had been one state; and Thucydides, I, 58, 2 would then describe what was politically a reversion to an older condition." But surely it is far from clear that Χαλκιδεῖς in Herodotos is used with the meaning it has in Thucydides. What substantiates the

[3] *Op. cit.*, pp. 129-131.
[4] Complexity in the combinations of interlinked dies provides the index. The varying intensity of production of coinage is noted at appropriate parts of the section "Correlation Between Coinage and the Political and Commercial Activity of the Chalcidians," *op. cit.*, pp. 142-161, and it can be checked in the summary of evidence for the relative chronology of the coinage, *op. cit.*, pp. 87-112, as well as in the detail of the catalogue of dies and their combinations, *op. cit.*, pp. 1-86.
[5] *Op. cit.*, pp. 1-112, particularly pp. 87-112.
[6] See now the arrangement of the coinage of Perdikkas II by Doris Raymond, *Num. Notes and Mon.*, 126 (1953), pp. 136-166. The coinage of the king accommodates itself nicely to the arrangement of the Chalcidic coinage proposed in 1938.
[7] Gomme's interpretation derives in part from Hampl, *Hermes*, LXX, 1935, pp. 177-196, and in part from Kahrstedt, *A.J.P.*, LVII, 1936, pp. 416-444, though the latter destroyed most of the former's argument (cf. *Olynthus*, IX, pp. 120-121).

interpretation of Χαλκιδεῖς in Thucydides is the use of the name for the state in official (non-Athenian) documents including the state's own coinage; evidence of like clarity in connection with the events of 479 does not exist. The histories of Skable, Assera, Stolos (and Polichnitai-by-Stolos) are unclear, except that two are recorded with Olynthos and two with Mekyberna in the quotas granted Athena from the amounts paid in to Athens by the allies in 454/3, and thereafter all are recorded separately.[8] Why the quotas are so grouped in the first list, we do not know. And if in fact the grouping of the quotas reflects joint payments, the cause may well be no more than convenience, implying nothing about the political status of the towns listed—to claim that they constitute the remnant of a Chalcidic state is to pile guess on top of conjecture. The literary and inscriptional evidence which might indicate the possible existence of the Chalcidic state before 432 seems to me to amount to little or nothing.

"The evidence of the coins" Gomme held to be "confusing." About the time of the events of Thucydides I, 58, 2, "there was a change in many mints of the Chalcidic peninsula including that of Olynthos, from the Attic standard to the 'Phoenician' . . . and many . . . have connected this change with the revolts from Athens between 432 and 422. Now there is an old coin of the Olynthos mint with the legend ΧΑΛΚ, another with ΟΛΥΝ, both of the Attic standard; these can be easily explained —the former corresponds to Herodotos' evidence, the latter will belong to the period of Athenian pressure, when Olynthos was isolated; but there are also coins of the Phoenician standard with ΟΛΥΝΘΙ. These Gaebler puts in the period 431-420 . . . ." The fact is the attribution of the "old coin . . . with the legend ΧΑΛΚ" (two tetrobols were known in 1938, both from the same pair of dies) to a "Chalcidian" mint at Olynthus is so completely uncertain that the coins are worthless evidence to establish a point of history.[9] A second fact: there is not in existence

---

[8] Meritt, Wade-Gery, McGregor, *Athenian Tribute Lists*, I, chapter VII, The Register, under the names of the several communities.

[9] The coins: Obv. Horse galloping r. Rev. Eagle flying r., grasping with beak and claws a serpent; incuse square. The argument for attribution, whether to Euboean Chalkis or to Thraceward Chalcidians, is reviewed in *Olynthus*, IX, pp. 292-293. Subsequently D. W. Bradeen, arguing the Euboean origin of Thraceward Chalcidians, claimed an Olynthian mint for the coin without adducing either new evidence or new argument (*A.J.P.*, LXXIII, 1952, pp. 363-364, 374; so too E. S. G. Robinson in his discussion of the effect of the Athenian Currency Decree, *Hesperia*, S VIII, 1949, p. 335). Miss Raymond also argued the coin to a mint at Olynthos and to connection with the events of 479, relying (she as others before her) on comparisons with Macedonian horses (*Studies Presented to D. M. Robinson*, II, pp. 197-200 and pl. 60). Specifically, she notes that pose and type of horse are paralleled on coins of the so-called Tyntenoi (*ibid.*, pl. 60, 7 = Gaebler, *Ant. Münz. Nord-Gr.*, III², pl. XXIV, 40, and p. 211, 42, "Berlin, unter den Fälschungen"), of Ichnai (*ibid.*, pl. 60, 8-9, the latter = Gaebler, *op. cit.*, pl. XIV, 12, and p. 65, 10: beginning of 5th cent. B.C.), of the Orreskioi

any coin with the legend ΟΛΥΝ struck on the Attic standard.[10] And a third fact: there are no "coins of the Phoenician standard with ΟΛΥΝΘΙ" dated by Gaebler in the period 431-420.[11] Finally, if Gomme, when he wrote (p. 206) "I am inclined myself to put . . . the 'Olynthian' coins of the 'Phoenician' standard . . . to the 10 or 15 years before the revolt [of 432]," had in mind the tetrobols Horse/Eagle ΟΛΥΝ, in fact the only ". . . 'Olynthian' coins of the 'Phoenician' standard . . ." known, then it seems clear that in his text he accepted the very chronology proposed in *Olynthus* IX (pp. 296-298 and 112-142) which in the footnote to his text (p. 206, note 2) he wrote that he could not accept. And if he had in mind the coins with ΟΛΥΝΘΙ from Chalcidic tetrobol anvil-die A32, he was indeed plagued by a momentary confusion. This same footnote 2 is unhappy in another respect. "It is . . . possible, though hardly . . . likely, that Olynthos was the official name of the state for [a] short period after 421." Such is the view Gomme attributed to *Olynthus,* IX, pp. 148-152, which "would place the 'Olynthian' coins in this period, and explain the use of 'Ολύνθιοι by Thucydides and in the Peace of Nikias accordingly." But in the pages of *Olynthus* IX cited there is certainly no talk of placing "Olynthian" coins in the period of the Peace of Nikias; there is indeed no talk of Olynthian coins at all, but rather of Group D of the Chalcidic series and, in particular, the significance of the subsidiary inscription ΟΛΥΝΘΙ on tetrobol anvil-die A32 (all punch-dies of Group D have, of course, the usual principal legend ΧΑΛΚΙΔΕΩΝ), and the suggestion is there made that the subsidiary inscription on this one die may reflect the brief existence of a separatist, pro-Olynthian, anti-Chalcidic element within the Chalcidic state which nevertheless during this period, as earlier and later, con-

---

(*ibid.,* pl. 60, 10 = Gaebler, *op. cit.,* pl. XVIII, 12, and p. 91, 15: *ca.* 500-480 B.C.), of Sermylia (*ibid.,* pl. 60, 11 = Gaebler, *op. cit.,* pl. XXI, 4, p. 107, 2; and pl. 60, 12 = Gaebler, *op. cit.,* pl. II, 6 p. 107, 4: *ca.* 500 B.C.), and of Alexander I (*ibid.,* pl. 60, 13 = *Num. Notes and Mon.,* 126, pl. IX, 105 a, and p. 107: *ca.* 475-460 B.C.). But it seems to me that type and style of horse vary through the series of animals compared. And so, I think, does the pose: the horse on the tetrobol inscribed ΧΑΛΚ appears to have the off hind-foot, as well as both front feet, raised from the ground and therefore may be presumed to be galloping (see the illustrations *Olynthus,* IX, pl. XXXIV, a-b); it was perhaps the intention of the engraver of Alexander's tetrobol anvil-die A32 to render his horse in like fashion, but certainly the other animals compared have both hind feet on the ground and presumably, with forelegs raised, the intention was to represent the horses prancing (except of course the Sermylian coin illustrated on Miss Raymond's pl. 60, 11, which is rightly not compared for pose). That no single specimen of the series Horse/Eagle ΧΑΛΚ was found in the course of the extensive excavations at Olynthus will perhaps weigh with field archaeologists, but doubtless with no one else.

[10] For the list of die-combinations of the coinage of the Olynthian mint (Horse/Eagle ΟΛΥΝ) known in 1938 see *Olynthus,* IX, pp. 294-298.

[11] For the inscription occurs only on tetrobol anvil-die A32 of the Chalcidic mint at Olynthus (Apollo/Cithara ΧΑΛΚΙΔΕΩΝ), and the *terminus post quem* for all issues of this mint Gaebler put at *ca.* 420 (*Ant. Münz. Nord-Gr.,* III², p. 85).

tinued to be styled Χαλκιδεῖς. Whatever the merit of that suggestion, there is clearly no claim that "the use of Ὀλύνθιοι by Thucydides and in the Peace of Nikias" can be explained by the short-lived appearance of ΟΛΥΝΘΙ on tetrobol anvil-die A32 of the Chalcidic coinage and certainly no suggestion that Ὀλύνθιοι became again, however briefly, the official name of the state.

Footnote 2 is also unhappy in continuing to claim the existence of "evidence of an *alliance* [in connection with the events of 432] . . . in the type of a few coins . . . of the Chalkidians, Bottiaioi, Akanthos, and Arnai . . . ," a proposition taken from West, first stated by Gomme as a fact, and at the end retained as a serious possibility, after a digression on the location of Arnai and notice that "The coin of Arnai is, however, doubtful; and that of the Bottiaioi apparently of the 4th century," with reference to *Olynthus*, IX, pp. 124-125. If the evidence for Arnai is "doubtful" and the evidence for the Bottiaeans "apparently" irrelevant, how can it be possible to retain the hypothesis of an alliance coinage? In point of fact it is of course certain that the Bottiaean bronze in question is all of fourth-century date. And it continues to seem to me reasonably clear that the silver fractions once attributed to Arnai were long ago rightly located at Naretum in Calabria.[12] As for the Akanthos obols, they have been dated by Gaebler part to the middle of the fifth century and part to the first quarter of the fourth; moreover, the young male head on the obverse of the earlier series is not obviously Apollo and the instrument on the reverse of both series is a lyre, not a cithara. The relationship between these obols of Acanthus and the Chalcidic coinage, if ever there was a relationship, remains to me obscure. It is not obscure, I think, that this phantom "alliance-coinage" once raised by West ought now to be left undisturbed to rest in peace.

In conclusion, let it be said, emphatically, that the simple interpretation of the evidence at our disposal is this. In Herodotos, VIII, 127, τὸ Χαλκιδικὸν γένος and Χαλκιδέες are synonyms, "the Chalcidic clan" (or the like) and "Chalcidians." The tetrobol of Attic weight, Horse/Eagle ΧΑΛΚ, must not be taken into the record of evidence until it can be shown that the issue *was struck at Olynthus,* and not elsewhere whether by Thraceward Chalcidians or others. If this is in fact established, then it will indeed be reasonable to claim that Χαλκιδέες in Herodotos, VIII, 127, may be used as the official name of the political unit at Olynthus as Χαλκιδεῖς is used in Thucydides. But this will not affect the evidence for the *terminus post quem* of the Apollo/Cithara ΧΑΛΚΙΔΕΩΝ coinage. For after the unpleasantness of 479 the record of evidence, which begins again in 454/3 with the quota-lists written in Athens, shows that

―――――――――
[12] Bradeen, *op. cit.,* p. 369, ignores the re-attribution and still cites Head's British Museum *Catalogue* of 1879. In *Hist. Num.*², pp. 52-53, Head accepted the attribution to Naretum.

the Athenians called the political unit at Olynthus 'Ολύνθιοι, as they did later, and also shows that the Olynthians themselves with their coinage Horse/Eagle ΟΛΥΝ called their state 'Ολύνθιοι, as they did *not* later. The date of the Olynthians' change of the style is certainly given by the *terminus post quem* of their Apollo/Cithara ΧΑΛΚΙΔΕΩΝ coinage, and that date must lie, I think it can be said with reasonable certainty, towards the middle of the reign of Perdiceas II of Macedon (*ca.* 454-*ca.* 413) on the basis alone of the numismatic evidence newly developed in 1938, namely, the close correspondences in fabric, in style, and in attrition of hoard-coins between issues of the royal mint and coins struck from Chalcidic dies most of which are attested and now arranged, without appeal to comparisons with issues of the royal mint, in a continuous sequence of period-of-use relative to each other on criteria sufficiently certain to assure, not indeed the correctness of the order in the small detail of its arrangement, but surely its general correctness from first to last. The argument from numismatic evidence alone places the *terminus post quem* of the Chalcidic Apollo/Cithara coinage so close to the revolt and synoecism of 432 that it must inevitably be connected with those events and so certify what is, after all, the inherently reasonable interpretation of Χαλκιδείς in Thucydides. Whatever may have prevailed in 479, 'Ολύνθιοι was the official name of the political unit at Olynthos in the period 454-432 (Athenian quota-lists, Olynthian Horse/Eagle ΟΛΥΝ tetrobols) and after 432 Χαλκιδείς (Thucydides, the Chalcidic Apollo/Cithara ΧΑΛΚΙΔΕΩΝ coinage, non-Athenian official documents). The evidence of the coins is doubtless tedious to follow, but it is not confusing.

University of California
Los Angeles

THE PERSIAN BATTLE PLAN AT THE GRANICUS
Eugene Wood Davis

I

The battle of the Granicus, Alexander's first great set-piece battle and his first battle in Asia, is far less complicated than Issus or Gaugamela, but even here there are problems which admit of no easy solution. As with all battles, there are three basic questions which must be answered: why the battle was fought, why it was fought where it was fought, and why it was fought as it was fought. The first of these questions, whether to engage at all, is largely strategic; the second, involving the choice of the field, is a question of the "larger" tactics; while the matter of the actual deployment and use of troops is a purely tactical question.

As must inevitably be the case given the nature of our sources,[1] the principal uncertainties revolve around the activities of the Persians, and most scholars have concerned themselves with this aspect of the problem. The resulting studies developed, during the late years of the nineteenth and the early years of the present century, what may loosely be described as an orthodox view: namely, that the Persians were wrong in deciding to fight and that, though they chose the field of battle wisely, they blundered very badly in their tactical dispositions.[2] In relatively recent years, however, at least four scholars, Tarn, Schachermeyr, Fuller, and Beloch, have questioned the validity of this interpretation. Tarn attempts to justify the Persians, and Schachermeyr and Fuller to explain them; Beloch contents himself with rewriting the entire battle. It will be the purpose of this paper to scrutinize the merits of these more recent solutions.

II

The first question, whether to fight or delay, was one that the Persians faced directly. At their council of war the Greek mercenary commander, Memnon, advocated that they avoid battle and retire before Alexander, scorching the earth in his path and meanwhile sending the fleet to Greece to stir up trouble in his rear. It was a possible policy, but the Persians rejected it. Swayed by the appeal of Arsites, the satrap of Hellespontine Phrygia (whose satrapy would be the one to be scorched), they decided

---

[1] The principal sources are Arrian, *Anabasis* 1, 12, 6-16, 7; Diodorus 17, 18, 1-21, 6; and Plutarch, *Alexander* 16.
[2] For the older bibliography on the Granicus, cf. Kromayer-Veith, *Antike Schlachtfelder* and *Schlachten-Atlas*. In relatively recent periodical literature are articles by Judeich, *Klio* 8 (1909) 372 ff; Lehmann, *Klio* 11 (1911) 340 ff; and Keil, *Mitteilungen des Vereins klassischer Philologen in Wien* 1 (1924) 13 ff.

to fight. The decision was a wrong one as events clearly proved, and modern scholars have in general held that the satraps should have followed the advice of their hired military expert.

While this view is no doubt correct, it is insufficient without a consideration of the factors impelling the Persians to battle. Sir William Tarn suggests that the Persians intended "to strangle the war at birth by killing Alexander."[3] This, of course, is possible, but there is no evidence for it, and the fact that they did undoubtedly try to kill Alexander during the battle is no proof of it. The Persians not unnaturally tried to kill him in every battle. Schachermeyr, who envisions the Persian satraps as a sort of feudal nobility, holds that the Persians rejected Memnon's plan because it was simply unthinkable. They would have been false to their feudal loyalty (*Lehenstreue*) to Darius and would have violated their own knightly code had they retired without a fight.[4] The difficulty with this explanation is that Memnon's proposal should not in fact have been so unthinkable, for it was not even very original; the Persians had actually employed a very similar strategy against Agesilaus little more than half a century before, and there is no evidence that Persian standards of knightliness had risen noticeably in the interval. General Fuller largely ignores this problem, apparently considering that Arsites' plea is enough of an explanation for the Persian decision to fight.[5] Beloch also seems to consider Arsites' appeal sufficient, adding only that the other Persian commanders were led to agree with Arsites because of their trust in their cavalry.[6]

[3] Tarn treats the battle three times: *CAH* 6, 361-2; *Alexander the Great* (Cambridge 1948) 1, 15-17 (identical with the account in *CAH* save for one half-sentence); *Hellenistic Military and Naval Developments* (Cambridge 1930) 70. His suggestion has received some acceptance: cf., A. R. Burn, *Alexander the Great and the Hellenistic Empire* (New York 1948) 90; M. L. W. Laistner, *A History of the Greek World from 479 to 323 B.C.* (London 1936) 295-6. C. A. Robinson, Jr., *Alexander the Great* (New York 1947) 80, dismisses Tarn's thesis by saying that the Persians may have intended to kill Alexander but that if so they chose "a poor way to go about the business." Tarn believes (*CAH* 6, 361 = *Alex* 1, 16) that Memnon did propose to lay waste the country but not to carry the war into Greece because later, when he had the power, he did not do so. It is, however, very much to be doubted whether Memnon did ever have it in his power to carry the war into Greece. After Alexander's campaigns in Greece, especially the destruction of Thebes, the Greeks might have thought twice before revolting with only the support of a rootless navy deprived of its bases. Memnon had to show some successes before approaching the Greeks, and he was in the process of acquiring island bases in the Aegean when he died.

[4] F. Schachermeyr, *Alexander der Grosse*, 141-2; for his full account of the Granicus, 140-6. That the Persian nobility did have some sort of code can hardly be questioned; all nobilities do. It is also true that Arsites gave as his reason for rejecting Memnon's proposal that he would not let a single house in his satrapy be burned, but to say that Memnon's proposal was unthinkable is much too strong.

[5] Major General J. F. C. Fuller, *The Generalship of Alexander the Great* (London 1958, New Brunswick, N. J. 1960) 89; for his full account of the battle, 88-91 and (especially) 147-54.

[6] K. J. Beloch, *Griechische Geshcichte*, 2d Ed. (Berlin, Leipzig 1924) 3, 1,

Though naturally we cannot know with certainty what factors led the Persians to decide to fight, there are certain things which can hardly have failed to figure in their deliberations. One of these was Darius III. He is a dim figure to us, but we can be sure that these satraps knew him,[7] and it is certainly not unknown in history for generals to risk battle even against their better judgment rather than gain a reputation for cowardice in the mind of an absolute monarch. And a craven withdrawal before the first onslaught of a beardless youth would almost certainly have appeared like cowardice to Darius, who was a thousand miles away and inevitably somewhat ill-informed on local conditions. And here it may be well to remind ourselves of something which most certainly was *not* in the minds of the satraps—that they were offering battle to Alexander the Great. This was not the invincible conqueror whom a despairing Darius fled after Gaugamela; this was merely the new young king of Macedon. He had, it is true, his father's very formidable army, and he had already shown himself well able to use it, but he was not yet Alexander the Great. The difference is immense.

A thing, on the other hand, which the Persians surely did take into account was the attitude of the Ionian Greeks, who had a long history of revolts and, of course, a natural sympathy with the other Greeks. Whatever may have been the assurances of Memnon, the Persians must have asked themselves some such question as this: if they let it appear that they dared not face Alexander, would not most or all of Ionia revolt, and with Ionia in revolt, would there be the slightest prospect of success for the fleet even if it should sail over and try to raise the Greeks?

Whatever may have been the factors which finally impelled them, the Persians did decide to fight, and took up a position on the East bank of the Granicus. There has never been any question that they chose their battlefield well. The steep banks of the stream afforded them an excellent defensive position, and their location was such that they were astride Alexander's best route into Asia Minor. Furthermore, Alexander would not dare to by-pass them even if he could, for should he try to ignore them and advance south, they could instantly have cut his communications at the Hellespont.

623-5. Beloch does note that Memnon's plan was the same that was used earlier against Agesilaus. Arrian, incidentally, offers his own explanation (1, 12, 10), that the satraps agreed with Arsites because they suspected Memnon of deliberately trying to prolong the war in order to gain credit with Darius. Modern scholars have largely ignored this suggestion—rightly, it would seem, since it is not easy to see how Memnon could gain credit by being unnecessarily slow in driving Alexander from Darius' territories. One is reminded that Arrian was writing during the Roman Empire and that this suspicion that a general would deliberately drag out a war was one that *did* occur to the Romans, as Metellus against Jugurtha and Lucullus against Mithridates.

[7] One of the Persian leaders was his son-in-law.

III

The most difficult and most discussed problem connected with the battle is that of the tactical disposition of the Persian troops. To summarize the preliminaries of the battle according to the "orthodox" modern view: when Alexander approached the Granicus, he found the Persians already formed up with their cavalry posted along the top of the steep bank and their infantry massed some distance to the rear. It was already rather late in the day, and Parmenio advised him to put off the attack until the morrow, for the Persians, who were outnumbered in infantry, would not dare remain so close, and the crossing could be made unmolested in the early morning. Alexander, however, making his famous remark about shaming the Hellespont should he fear the Granicus, ordered an immediate attack.

The actual details of the battle as it developed need not at the moment concern us, but rather the exchange between Parmenio and Alexander. Parmenio's advice is perfectly good: do not attack a strong position at the end of a day's march. It reads like a maxim from a sound, conservative military text book. But Alexander is supposed to have shown here the brilliance of his tactical insight, for—according to our orthodox version—despite the lateness of the hour and the difficulty of pushing home a charge through a river and up a high, steep bank, Alexander saw that the Persians had blundered very badly. Cavalry must charge to be effective, and by lining up along the top of the bank the Persians had condemned themselves to standing and awaiting the charge of Alexander. Furthermore, by placing their infantry behind their cavalry, they were in effect offering battle to Alexander's whole army with only a part of their own. Accordingly, Alexander determined to attack at once before the Persians could rectify their errors.

The trouble with this account is that it makes the Persians appear too incredibly stupid. Either error is bad enough, but both together seem almost too much. Under these conditions it becomes extremely tempting to try to puzzle out some rational explanation as to what could have been the Persians' purpose behind this apparently mad act of folly, and this is what the scholars we are considering have done.

Tarn believes the Persians actually set a trap with themselves as bait; in *CAH* (6, 361) he says:

> The Persian leaders had in fact a very gallant plan; they meant if possible to strangle the war at birth by killing Alexander. They massed their cavalry on the steep bank of the lower Granicus, put the Greeks behind them, and waited. It has often been explained since that this was not the way to hold a river-bank; but that was not their intention.

Tarn's fullest but also most puzzling statement of his views is given in *Hellenistic Military and Naval Developments* (p. 70):

... The type of this battle was dictated, not by Alexander, but by the Persians. The Persian leaders had the first rule of war clearly in sight—to destroy the main force of the enemy; but as they had not nearly enough men to defeat the Macedonian army, they decided to risk everything on striking at the brains and will of that army, that is, on trying to kill Alexander himself, which would have ended the war. The extraordinary formation they adopted was to induce Alexander himself to charge, and their concentrated attack on his person only failed of success by a fraction of a second.

Tarn here seems to be telling us that the Persians thought that only by the adoption of a faulty formation could they lure Alexander into risking his person, but this is pure nonsense, for the Persians can hardly have thought that, should they adopt a better formation, Alexander would have sent his troops forward while he himself skulked behind in safety. Quite aside from the fact that they must already have learned something of Alexander's dashing impetuosity, the Persians must have known that it was standard practice for both Greek and Macedonian commanders to charge at the head of their troops. Not until Hannibal does the general remain outside the battle. Since Sir William Tarn was not in the habit of writing nonsense, I will assume that the thought is merely mis-phrased, and that what he meant was that the Persian formation was intended to induce Alexander to attack them at once in their apparently strong position rather than to wait for them to attack him.[8]

At first sight the suggestion begins to look persuasive—the Persians did know what they were doing after all—but it in fact merely replaces one stupidity with another. No sensible commanders would deliberately adopt a formation which, failing the death of one particular individual, would not merely deprive them of even the slightest chance of winning but would also make virtually certain the destruction of their whole army—not unless compelled by extreme necessity, and there was in fact no necessity at all. There is another rule of war which says that the invader cannot refuse the offer of battle. Once the Persians had thrown themselves across Alexander's path, he had absolutely no choice but to attack. As we have seen, he had not even the freedom of marching round them, for they could have cut his communications. Had the Persians adopted a better formation, Alexander might have taken Parmenio's advice, but sooner or later he would have had to attack.

To sum up: attempting to kill or capture the enemy general is too standard a feature of both ancient and modern tactics to allow us with no direct evidence to single out the Granicus as the time when killing Alexander was definitive for the whole of the Persian tactics. Tarn thus

[8] The difficulty is with the word "himself." If Sir William had written "to induce Alexander to charge," instead of "to induce Alexander himself to charge," there would have been no problem. Is it possible that Sir William was given to saying "I myself" and "he himself" instead of simply "I" and "he"? It is a very academic failing.

fails to prove that killing Alexander *was* the sole Persian battle plan, and
—even worse—he fails to show that there was any connection between the
plan and the tactics adopted. There was no need whatever for the
Persians to employ this particular formation to accomplish what they
could not fail to accomplish—to make Alexander attack—or to enable
them to do what they would be able to do anyway—to try to kill him
when he did attack.

Schachermeyr's account is closer to the standard one in that he does
not attempt to make clever plans out of the Persians' tactical blunders,
but his view of the Persian nobles as a sort of feudal chivalry introduces
a new element. By refusing to fight, the satraps would not only have
betrayed their feudal loyalty to Darius; they would also have broken
their own knightly code: they would have lost virtue in their own eyes
by basely retiring before a mere peasant phalanx. Accordingly, they
withdrew their infantry to the rear and, lining up the cavalry on the
river bank, offered Alexander "combat in knightly style."[9] Alexander
responded in kind to this chivalrous offer and charged with his cavalry
alone, aided only by some of the light-armed troops. By thus inviting
close, man-to-man combat the Persians had thrown away even the advantage
their javelin-armed troops would have derived from distance,
and the Macedonians of course prevailed.

The difficulty with Schachermeyr's additions to the battle is that all
of them are unprovable and some of them are improbable. We have
already noted that Memnon's proposed delaying action should not have
been so very unthinkable. The case is similar with the suggestion that
Darius himself enjoined a cavalry action. (See above, n. 9). Darius,
who certainly knew that the chief strength of his empire lay in its
cavalry, may very well have ordered his commanders in Asia Minor to
make that their chief reliance, but it is surely unnecessary to invoke
Darius to cause the Persians at the Granicus to see that they outnumbered
the Macedonians in cavalry but were themselves outnumbered
in infantry. Even so, this does not explain why, if the Persians did not
intend to use their infantry, they had it on the battlefield at all.

The element of knightliness also fails to add anything. If it explains
the decision to fight a purely cavalry battle, it completely fails to explain
why the Persians lined up along the river bank.[10] Not even the knightliest
of codes demands of its practitioners that they go into battle using
alien tactics, and these must have been very odd Persians indeed if it

---

[9] "Kampf im ritterlichen Stil" (p. 143). The section dealing with the Granicus
is entitled "Junker gegen Junker." Schachermeyr also suggests (p. 143 and notes)
that it was at the instance of Darius himself that the Persians determined upon a
purely cavalry action. There is, of course, no suggestion that Darius was responsible
for the exact tactical dispositions of the battle.

[10] Actually, Schachermeyr admits that this was an error (p. 142), but the more
we insist on the Persians' knowledge of cavalry, and the more we insist that the
cavalry was to fight the whole battle, the worse the error becomes.

was a sense of shame which made them face the Macedonians toe to toe instead of keeping their distance and skirmishing with javelins as their own ancestors would have done. Surely, also, there is little to be said for the picture of Alexander deliberately accepting the offer of a knightly combat. Whether he would have recognized the peculiarity of the Persian formation as constituting such an offer, I have no idea, but the fact that Alexander charged cavalry with cavalry is certainly no proof of it. It is impossible to picture him charging the enemy cavalry with his phalanx. As for the knightliness of his behavior, Alexander engaged his light-armed along with his cavalry, and a good part of their function was to kill the horses out from under the enemy.

Schachermeyr, thus, in making the battle into a sort of Mediaeval tournament has in fact merely made it more difficult to understand. Bravery there was in plenty, but any element of chivalry is very hard to find, and it is easier to believe that the Persians made a mistake in the placing of their infantry than that they exposed them to capture without any intention of using them.

General Fuller, though usually a close follower of Tarn, recognizes that Tarn's account of the Granicus is wrong and points out that even though the Persians did undoubtedly intend to kill Alexander, they were going about it the wrong way. A hedge of spearpoints at the top of the bank would have been far more effective than a line of cavalry armed with javelins. Here is the general's own explanation (p. 149), which is close to but not identical with that of Schachermeyr:

Throughout history the cavalry soldier has despised the infantryman, and to have placed the Greek mercenaries in the forefront of the battle would have been to surrender to them the place of honour. Military etiquette forbade it; pride of rank is sufficient to explain this particular tactical folly, as it also explains the conduct of the Gothic horsemen at Taganae (A. D. 552), of the French cavalry at Creçy, and the arrogance of the mounted soldier in scores of battles up to the First World War.

This pride of rank of the cavalryman certainly did exist, and General Fuller's explanation is a possible one, but there is one element in the picture which very seriously weakens his case—the fact that these Greeks were mercenaries. Military etiquette does not in fact require the citizenry, mounted or dismounted, to expose themselves to danger to spare the mercenaries hired for that very purpose. If the Persian cavalry placed themselves on the river bank and the mercenaries behind, it is far more likely to have been in pursuance of some mistaken tactical idea than for any reasons of mere punctilio.

Beloch's view of the battle need not detain us long.[11] It has already

---

[11] *Gr. Gesch.* 3, 1, 623-5. Beloch is here following an argument of Konrad Lehmann (see Note 2 above), but he is doing it in his own way, and his presentation of the case is to be found in a still standard general history of Greece, while

been answered by Keil[12] and is totally unacceptable. Relying on a passage in Diodorus, (17, 19) Beloch transposes the whole battle to the following morning and allots the principal part in it to the Thessalians. The Arrian-Plutarch version of the battle he dismisses as merely a romantic picture designed to exhibit Alexander in the light of a Homeric hero. What he is doing here is not merely preferring the poorer to the better authority; he is also setting the Granicus against the evidence of Alexander's whole career. He is making Parmenio out of Alexander the Great. Why should this be the one occasion when Alexander chose the more cautious over the bolder course? And it is impossible to explain either the rest of Alexander's career or the history of the years after his death if Alexander is reduced to a mere colorless competence.[13] Alexander *was* a Homeric hero.

What is of interest here is Beloch's historical method, for it is not his alone. He is here not merely showing his infallible instinct for the duller story; he is also giving evidence of his tendency to believe "only the parts of Greek history he invented himself." Probability is his touchstone, and he freely abandons the better author to substitute a more "probable" bit from somewhere else,[14] but in producing a probable Granicus he has produced the greater improbability of an un-Alexander-like Granicus.

There is still another difficulty inherent in the Lehmann-Beloch version of the battle which, though in itself no more than a difficulty, renders their account yet the more unlikely. It is that in order to accept Diodorus' timing for the battle we really need also to accept his figures for the Persian strength. According to Arrian, though the Persians outnumbered Alexander in cavalry, they were themselves outnumbered in infantry, and Parmenio's advice was predicated on the assumption that the Persians with their smaller force would fear to remain so close to Alexander overnight, and by withdrawing would allow him an uncontested crossing of the river the following morning. Now though Parmenio was certainly no Alexander, he *was* a sound and experienced commander (so, for the matter of that, was Arrian himself), and his opinion cannot be simply ignored. Would the Persians in fact have stayed so near that the battle could be fought through the same riverbed the next day? True, this difficulty disappears if we accept Diodorus' figures of 10,000 Persian cavalry and 100,000 infantry, but

---

Lehmann's is in a periodical of half a century ago, where it is unlikely to be found except by those who deliberately look for it.

[12] See Note 2 above.

[13] The career of Eumenes of Cardia, for example, is impossible except in light of a highly charged and emotional memory-image of Alexander.

[14] While no one would suggest that the sole duty of the historian is to determine the best authority and then transcribe him blindly, it is possible to go too far the other way and, by picking and choosing at will, to produce a totally probable account which is in fact a mere mosaic according to the author's fancy.

no modern historian I know of is willing to allow the Persians anything like that strength in actual military effectives,[15] and no commander I know of, ancient or modern has tried to hold a dangerous position emboldened merely by the number of his camp followers.

None of these four explanations, then, really helps to solve the problem of the Granicus. Tarn is right in saying that the Persians tried to kill Alexander but has failed to prove that this was the basis of their battle-plan and has totally failed to prove that the "plan" in any way necessitated the tactical formations adopted. Schachermeyr is doubtless right in saying that the Persians decided to place their chief reliance on their cavalry, but his introduction of a Persian chivalric code seems merely an unnecessary complication. And while the determination to fight an exclusively cavalry action does explain the placing of the cavalry forward, it fails to explain why it should have lined up along the river bank. Fuller's point of military etiquette is out of order when applied to mercenaries. Beloch, of course, does succeed in solving the problem as far as the Persians are concerned (except for their numbers), but he raises a much greater difficulty with regard to Alexander himself.

Must we, then, give up the problem of the Granicus as insoluble? In the last analysis, of course, the answer must be, "Yes," for with only the information at our disposal we cannot read the minds of the Persian leaders. We can, however, with all due caution, at least notice certain things which have not been noticed and keep in mind certain others which have not received sufficient attention.

IV

As to the strategical question, it is by no means clear that the decision to force a battle was a wrong one. Memnon's scorched earth plan was no doubt excellent, but it, too, involved risks, and there were certain obvious advantages to a bolder strategy. We must not forget that Alexander was under no compulsion to trail hungrily about after Memnon; suppose he had made a sudden dash at one of the nearer cities.[16] Might not his very appearance beneath the walls have sparked a revolt in spite of Memnon's garrison, and might not this have triggered a chain reaction of revolution down the whole Ionian coast? Possibilities such as these will make us hesitant to assert too positively that the Persians ought not to have offered battle. Furthermore, defeat was by no means a foregone conclusion. Had the Persians handled their troops better,

---

[15] Certainly Beloch does not do so; he allows the Persians a mere 5,000 cavalry and 20,000 infantry (3, 1, 625 n. 1).

[16] Arrian, indeed, tells that Memnon advised the Persians even to destroy the cities before Alexander (1, 12, 9). If so, it is small wonder the Persians rejected his advice. Such an operation, involving as it would the flight of the whole population of northwest Asia Minor would have been impossible, or if not actually that, at least fantastically slow. Memnon must surely have envisioned no more than wasting the open country and withdrawing the population behind walls.

and had they not been facing Alexander the Great, the battle of the Granicus might have had a very different outcome—and even a drawn battle would have been a Persian victory.

It was only in the tactical disposition of their forces on the field that the Persians blundered badly, and even here the error, though serious, was by no means obvious. The orthodox account, by reciting the two mistakes together—placing the cavalry where it could not charge and the infantry where it could bring no aid—makes it seem as though no one possessed of his senses could fail to be struck by what Wilcken calls this "glaring" error.[17] Yet not only did the Persians fail to see it when they set it up; but Parmenio, if we may believe Arrian, also missed it when he looked over the field. It took an Alexander to realize the implications of the Persian formation. Also, there is another curious point: the ordering of the Persian troops at the Granicus was not so very unlike that of Darius himself at Gaugamela; he too had his forward division composed almost entirely of cavalry, with his infantry lined up to the rear. It did not work at the Granicus and it did not work at Gaugamela, but can this have been at least a familiar Persian order of battle—or can it have been some Persian theoretician's "answer" to the Persians' acknowledged weakness in infantry?

There is, however, one difference between Darius' practice at Gaugamela and that of the satraps at the Granicus; though Darius had only 2,000 Greek mercenaries with him, he placed them in his forward line, not back in the rear. Yet the satraps, with a far greater number,[18] put the mercenaries back with the local levies. In a way, this is the decisive problem. Why did the satraps treat their Greek infantry on a level with the Asiatics, who probably really were militarily negligible? There is also what just may be another oddity here: Memnon was separated from the main body of his troops; he was in the front ranks along with his cavalry squadrons, which surely were not numerous, not with his infantry. It is impossible to know, but it is tempting to speculate that the Persians may have withdrawn their Greek infantry and separated Memnon from them out of some latent feeling of distrust. This of course could not have been from any general distrust of Greek mercenaries, who had over and over proved themselves loyal to their Persian paymasters, but here there were special circumstances. Memnon had formerly been in overall command on this front but was so no longer; furthermore the Persians were fighting this engagement against his express advice; was it of Memnon himself that the satraps were a little

[17] U. Wilcken, *Alexander the Great*, tr. G. C. Richards (London 1932) 84.

[18] Since 2,000 survived the battle to be sent back to Macedon in chains, it is obvious that there were more to begin with. Arrian tells us (1, 14, 4) that there were almost 20,000, but since none escaped and there were only 2,000 survivors, this figure seems obviously far too high; Memnon may have had 20,000 mercenaries, but some were doubtless off with the fleet, on garrison duty, and the like.

doubtful, for of course his troops would have followed his orders, not theirs, had he decided out of pique to change sides? It is permissible to wonder, no more.

There is one more thing which is not stressed often enough, but which we should never forget. We do not know who was the Persian commander. It is one of the most singular things about the Granicus that, as far as we can tell from our sources, the Persian army seems to have been commanded by a committee. If this was really true, then it may be that we do not have a Persian battle-plan at all, only a botched compromise between several rival plans.

On the whole, the "orthodox" assessment of the battle—though it is too severe in its judgment of the Persians' strategic decision to offer battle—is preferable to the various alternate explanations which have been offered. It is even possible to make too harsh a judgment of the Persian tactics, for while their plan was undoubtedly faulty, it took an Alexander to see it, and we must remember that these satraps, with an inferior army, were trying to halt the greatest military genius of antiquity at the outset of what is still the most remarkable continuous campaign in the annals of warfare. After all, to be less brilliant than Alexander the Great is not proof of total incompetence.

Trinity College
Hartford, Connecticut

CICERO AND HIS HOPED-FOR TRIUMPH

B. L. ULLMAN

When a mere boy Petrarch loved to read Cicero aloud for the sound and rhythm of the words, though he did not understand their meaning.[1] Cicero remained his favorite author, his idol, in fact, though he had a rude shock when he discovered the collection of letters to Atticus in 1345 and learned that his idol was just a human being, with the same frailties the rest of us have. We are, of course, extremely glad that Atticus preserved the letters and that they were ultimately published, but we must admit that he did his lifelong friend a disservice in doing so. Who would not suffer from having his most intimate thoughts revealed to the world? Today no doubt many have learned a lesson from the experience of Cicero and of others and are less frank in their letters, even to close friends and members of the family.

In the year in which he came upon the epistles to Atticus, Petrarch wrote two letters to Cicero.[2] He criticized his beloved preceptor for his feuds with some of his contemporaries and for being lured out of an honorable retirement by the false gleam of glory to engage in war, the business of young men. It was madness, he maintained, to challenge Antony, inconsistent to be friendly to Octavian. It is Cicero's life and character, not his talents as philosopher and orator, about which he complains.

Ever since Petrarch's day Cicero has been the butt of criticisms and ridicule for one reason or another, and the letters have played their part in the denigration of the famous orator, philosopher, statesman, and man of letters. In the nineteenth century the greatest harm to Cicero's reputation was done by Mommsen, under whose spell we still are. It has always seemed strange that the liberal-minded Mommsen should take an anti-Ciceronian and pro-Caesarian position.[3] Yet we must not forget that dictatorships such as Caesar's have often arisen out of popular movements.

No wonder that Carcopino concludes:

"Cicero's Correspondence passed under the political steam-roller. Fascinating though we find the detail in which it abounds, the intense vitality it exhales, the information it brings us is nevertheless only a residuum of truth. Steeped in partisan passion, a passion fundamentally hostile to Cicero, we cannot invariably trust its evidence uncritically or

[1] *Sen.* 16, 1.
[2] *Fam.* 24, 3 and 4.
[3] See the interesting discussion by W. Rüegg, *Cicero und der Humanismus* (Zurich, 1946), VII ff.

without verification. Though ostensibly introduced to us by a friend [Atticus], it was edited by Cicero's murderer [Octavian] in conformity with his designs and should therefore be used only with caution and regarded with distrust."[4]

Carcopino's explanation of the large amount of material in the letters that puts Cicero in a bad light is that the favorable letters and portions of letters were edited out by Cicero's son and by Atticus at the direction of Octavian. At the same time everything favorable to Caesar and Octavian was left in, as well as all that was unfavorable to Pompey, to the optimates, and to Antony. Whether Carcopino is right or wrong (and most critics seem to think he is wrong), it is interesting to note that he is trying to explain the phenomenon that we have been discussing. He holds that the price Octavian paid for Atticus' infamous betrayal of his intimate friend was the betrothal of his stepson and sucessor Tiberius to Atticus' granddaughter Vipsania when she was one year old.

One of the epistles which did Cicero the most harm was the one addressed to Lucceius, in which he asked that minor historian to write up his consulship in a favorable way (*Fam.* 5, 12). Modern historians have been aghast at the thought. Is it not the objective of history to achieve the truth? Does not Cicero himself say so? But truth is elusive, and the best-intentioned historians have their prejudices. Years ago I tried to make the point that there was a difference between universal history and monographic history, that the latter was not so rigidly bound by regard for absolute truth, and that this distinction was widely recognized and influenced the work of many respectable historians.[5]

Even the highly regarded factual historian Polybius wrote a particular, or monographic, history of the Numantine War, and Cicero mentions it specifically to Lucceius as a precedent. That war involved many incidents capable of embellishment. Polybius admits that writers of particular history are forced by lack of facts to make much of trifles (7, 7, 6). The difference between the embellished monograph and the more sober history was not so great as between the historical novel and objective history today, but it was of that order. If I am right in this, we must judge Cicero by the standards and conventions of his day and must grant that his contemporaries would see nothing out of the way in his suggestion to Lucceius.

Another factor deserves consideration in judging Cicero's letter to Lucceius. It was very carefully written and Cicero liked it himself, calling it *valde bella* (*Att.* 4, 6, 4). This fact has led many to suggest

[4] Jerome Carcopino, *Cicero, The Secrets of His Correspondence* 2 (London, 1951) 564.
[5] "History and Tragedy," *Transactions of the American Philological Association,* 73 (1942) 25-53, especially 44 ff.

that Cicero gave it wide circulation. In any case, he clearly had no objection to its being read by others, in contrast to some of his confidential letters, such as, for example, the letter in which he asks Atticus to denounce as spurious the speech he, Cicero, wrote against Curio (*Att.* 3, 12). If Cicero could visit us, he might be much surprised and amused at our attitude towards the letter to Lucceius.

Another episode in the life of Cicero referred to in a number of his letters has been responsible for much ridicule of the orator. Petrarch alludes to it at least twice. Once he says that it would have been much better for Cicero to have grown old in the peaceful countryside rather than to have kept his fasces and to have dreamed of triumphs.[6] The allusion, of course, is to Cicero's keeping his lictors and fasces with him at all times after the beginning of the Civil War in the hope of winning a triumph for his successes during the governorship of Cilicia. Petrarch's remarks set the pattern for succeeding centuries, and ever since historians have not failed to make fun of Cicero for expecting a triumph when far greater issues were at stake. With our hindsight we can, of course, see that Cicero's pathetic concern was a very minor thing as compared with the Civil War, with its world-shaking results. Neither Cicero nor anyone else could have fully foreseen its significance, though at times he comes very close to it.

The point I wish to make, however, is a different one. I grant that Cicero was not averse to personal glory, that, in fact, he may have been fonder of it than many men. Still I do not feel that glory was the chief motive in retaining the lictors. Rather, he had in mind his political rehabilitation. That point, has, I believe, not been sufficiently stressed. I can point to one bit of evidence—if the reader will accept it as evidence —in one of Cicero's letters to Atticus (8, 3, 5) written February 18, 49 B.C. He was worrying whether to follow Pompey if the latter should leave Italy before the advancing Caesar. He, of course, was still considering the possibility that Pompey would eventually defeat Caesar. His foresight is not as good as our hindsight, a point which the historian should never forget. Politically he favors Pompey, but everything Pompey has done has been wrong and contrary to Cicero's advice. A cynic would say that Pompey's actions were wrong in Cicero's eyes because Pompey ignored Cicero's suggestions. Personally, Caesar had been very friendly. What will Caesar do if Cicero, who wanted to be a peacemaker, left Italy to join Pompey? Then follow the key sentences:

"Qui autem impetus illius [Caesaris] erit in nos absentes fortunasque nostras? Acrior quam in ceterorum, quod putabit fortasse in nobis violandis aliquid se habere populare. Age iam, has compedes, fasces, inquam, hos laureatos efferre ex Italia quam molestum est."

[6] *Fam.* 24, 3, 7; 18, 11, 4.

It is quite clear from this and other passages that Cicero had lost his popularity with the voters, that Caesar might harm Cicero and his interests to gain popular support. Cicero's great longing was to regain his popularity so that the reputation he had gained might be refurbished and the *concordia ordinum* which was the chief plank of his political platform might be restored. The real significance I see in this passage is in the sentence that follows *populare*. Why should this word lead him to think of the laurel-wreathed fasces (shackles he calls them) and the nuisance of carrying them about outside of Italy? Because, in my opinion, he wanted the triumph, not for its own sake, that is for glory, but to restore a bit of his previous popular favor. The *supplicatio* (thanksgiving) and the triumph had become part of the political game. Is it not significant that the last sentence in Caesar's *Gallic War* mentions the *supplicatio* of twenty days voted at Rome for Caesar's victories? In the same general category was the politicians' custom of attending theatrical and other performances to see how the popular wind was blowing (*Att.* 2, 19, 3). "Keep in the public eye" must have been familiar political advice in Ciceronian Rome, as it is today in present-day America.[7] A study of the adaptation of Roman customs to political purposes would seem to be desirable. So far as I know, no full-scale study has been made. Included, among other matters, would be the use of augury and other forms of divination for political ends, though this has been thoroughly examined by itself.[8] As early as the third century B.C. Fabius Maximus has the courage to declare that whatever was done for the welfare of the state was done under good auspices.[9] In Cicero's time augury had degenerated into purely political maneuvering.

But to return to the fasces. Cicero himself called the attention of posterity to the absurdity of his situation, and that fact should have reduced, if not ended, the boisterous laughter and sneering at his pompous predicament. In one letter he says he will leave Rome before daybreak so as not to be seen or gossiped about, especially since his lictors still wore the laurels.[10] He calls them *molestissimos*—a great nuisance (*Att.* 8, 1, 3). They are a nuisance in another sense too: If Cicero stays in Italy and Caesar is friendly to him, Caesar will offer

---

[7] Though this advice is not given in so many words, it is implicit throughout the *Commentariolum petitionis*, especially in the long passage on how to make friends and influence people (16-40), more specifically where mention is made of *salutatores, deductores*, and *assectatores* (34-40). Note *certis temporibus descendito*, i.e., go to the Forum as often as possible with a large escort.

[8] A. S. Pease, edition of Cicero's *De divinatione*, 1 (Urbana, 1920) 10, has something to say about politics and cites some literature on the subject. See also J. D. Denniston's edition of Cicero's First and Second Philippics (Oxford, 1926) 180, with reference to the older literature. Wissowa in Pauly-Wissowa, *RE*, *s.v. augures* and *auspicium*, barely touches on the political phase. See also W. Warde Fowler, *The Religious Experience of the Roman People* (London, 1911) 304-306.

[9] Cicero, *De sen.* 11.

[10] *Att.* 7, 10; cf. 12, 4; 20, 2.

a triumph. To refuse it would be dangerous, to accept it would be offensive to the optimates (*Att.* 8, 3, 6).

When Cicero wrote to Atticus on February 18 (*Att.* 8, 3, the last of the letters thus far mentioned in connection with the lictors), he assumed that Pompey would send help to Corfinium and put up a fight in Italy, though he might later abandon it. No further mention is made of the lictors until March 6 (*Att.* 9, 1, 3), when Pompey was already in Brundisium and Cicero planned to join him there. He says that he will either leave behind his lictors (*remotis*) or dismiss them completely (*omnino missis*). The latter act would mean abandonment of any hope of a triumph, since there would be an all-out war and no further hope of a peaceful settlement. On March 8 (*Att.* 9, 2A, 1) Cicero quotes Atticus as advising him to stay in Italy and telling him that the matter of the triumph would be unimpaired (*integrum*). In the same letter Cicero repeats what he had said before about the danger of refusing a triumph if Caesar offered one. Atticus then suggests a meeting between Caesar and Cicero, to which Cicero assents. He approves Atticus' suggestion about the triumph should Caesar offer one: He will readily and gladly reject it (*Att.* 9, 7, 5). Caesar stops to see Cicero at Formiae on March 28 (*Att.* 9, 18). He asks Cicero to come to Rome; Cicero wants to remain neutral and has the courage to stand up to the victorious Caesar. This does not sound like a man who coveted a bit of glory from a minor triumph. By the way, nothing more was said about the lictors after March 8 until April 14, when he told Curio he desired to stay in a quiet place because he still had the lictors (*Att.* 10, 4, 10). In early May he writes to Caesar's follower Caelius:

"Accedit etiam molesta haec pompa lictorum meorum nomenque imperi quo appellor. Eo si onere carerem, quamvis parvis Italiae latebris contentus essem. Sed incurrit haec nostra laurus non solum in oculos sed iam etiam in voculas malevolorum" (*Fam.* 2, 16, 2).

The word *pompa*, "parade," is very well chosen. It suggests the *pompa* of the triumph. Once again the word *molesta* is used. He would like to get rid of the burden but will not, he implies, except in the proper fashion. People are beginning to take notice and to talk; so he wishes to stay in his little villa and not move about with his lictorian display. On May 3 he repeats that he does not want to be constantly on the run with his lictors (*Att.* 10, 10, 1). On June 7, 49, Cicero finally left Italy to join Pompey, apparently taking with him lictors, laurels, and fasces. No letters written by him during the rest of the year are extant, and only two written during the first five months of 48. In August of that year, while Cicero was ill at Dyrrachium, Pompey was defeated at Pharsalus, and the war was practically over. In October Cicero returned to Brundisium, and his letters begin to be more numerous.

Earlier, in May, Dolabella had written from Caesar's camp in Epirus offering to intercede with Caesar on Cicero's behalf, saying that it would be easy to get Caesar to grant Cicero anything that pertained to the status (*dignitate*) of the latter (*Fam.* 9, 9, 3). That this is a reference to the triumph would seem to be indicated by a letter Cicero wrote from Brundisium on November 27 (*Att.* 11, 6, 2-3). It is a nuisance, he says, to stay in Brundisium, but he cannot come closer to Rome, as Atticus urges, because he cannot abandon the lictors legally assigned to him (*quos populus dedit*). They cannot be taken from him as long as he is safe and sound (*incolumi*). This recalls the word *integrum* in *Att.* 9, 2A, 1: "Et de triumpho erit, inquis, integrum," i.e., the possibility of a triumph is safe and unimpaired. Cicero goes on to say that Oppius and Balbus guarantee that Caesar will see to it that Cicero's status (*dignitate*) will not only be preserved but raised. Tyrrell and Purser rightly take this to refer to a triumph; they might well have made the same suggestion in *Fam.* 9, 9, 3, with its similar language. The only other reference to the lictors is in Cicero's speech for Ligarius (7), of the year 46: Though Caesar himself is the one and only *imperator* in the Roman Empire, he allowed Cicero to be a second *imperator* and permitted him to retain the laureled fasces as long as he wished. We may note that *Imperator* as applied to Caesar adumbrates its later use in the sense of emperor. Probably the allusion is to the period of eleven months during which Cicero remained in Brundisium, waiting for the invitation to return to Rome. Presumably he gave up his "precious lictors," as Tyrrell and Purser, among Cicero's best modern friends, sneeringly call them, on his return to Rome in October of 47 B.C. He had them with him in Italy and Epirus for more than a year and three-quarters. And at the end—no triumph nor, of course, any political rehabilitation. *Sic semper tyranni.*

University of North Carolina
Chapel Hill

CICERO'S CONCORDIA IN HISTORICAL PERSPECTIVE

HENRY C. BOREN

Practically every textbook or general work dealing with the late Roman Republic has something to say about Cicero's *concordia ordinum*. However, it is ordinarily treated as a thing in itself, a frail bark launched by the orator in 63 B.C., the year of his consulship, and driven on the shoals a short time later by the ill winds that accompanied the formation of the so-called first triumvirate of Caesar, Pompey, and Crassus. This totally inadequate view is represented even in so responsible a work as the Cambridge Ancient History, where M. Cary calls the *concordia ordinum* a "panacea," declares that Cicero had no thought for needed reforms such as might, for example, bring new blood into the senatorial aristocracy, and, finally, pronounces a benediction over its grave: "Thus in 60 B.C. died the Concordia Ordinum."[1] This essay will attempt to draw a broader and historically more accurate view.

Prior research has already established much that is needed for proper perspective.[2] Of the following points which will be emphasized here, the first would seem not to require substantiation; the next three are made by Strasburger, Lepore, and Hill (though additional information is presented in this essay); the last two points have not been sufficiently noted. 1. In general, the ideal concept underlying the aristocratic government in all times and places is that of the rule of the "best" men (as Cicero's optimates) supported by all "good" men (in Cicero these two terms are sometimes identical in meaning). 2. The concept of *concordia* was historical in Rome of the middle first century B.C. both in the sense that it had been long considered the chief cohesive force of the state and in the sense that historians of the period recognized this and incorporated it into their histories (though not always using the precise terminology.) 3. Cicero's total concept of the *concordia* was broader than the specific measures which he advocated after his consulship and referred to as necessary to a *concordia ordinum*. 4. Cicero himself recognized that his policy was a part of the *mos maiorum* (at least in a general sense) and so presented it. Thus Cicero's thinking cannot be classified into chronological phases as is so often done, i.e., from *concordia ordinum* to *concordia totae Italiae* to *consensus omnium*

[1] In 9. 506 and 515.
[2] The most important single work is H. Strasburger, *Concordia Ordinum, eine Untersuchung zur Politik Ciceros*, (Amsterdam, 1956; first pub. 1931); see also E. Lepore, *Il Princeps Ciceroniano e gli Ideali Politici della Tarda Repubblica* (Naples, 1954), and H. Hill, *The Roman Middle Class in the Republican Period* (Oxford, 1952), esp. 161 ff. Other references to work bearing on the topic will be found in the notes to these works.

bonorum (or sometimes in the case of the last two in reverse order). 5. Changed conditions had made the older formulation of the *concordia* largely ineffective. 6. Cicero at least partially understood the nature of these changes and deliberately modified the traditional policy to meet the new situation.

No completely satisfactory historical survey of the concept of *concordia* in the Roman Republic has yet been done. Strasburger has an introductory chapter of a historical nature. However, he is too preoccupied with the use of the term itself, or of connection with the Greek *homonoia* to notice other important allusions to the concept. It has been remarked that government of the "best" is the aristocratic ideal. The Roman concept of *concordia* recognized not only that the ruling circle must function in the interests of all classes, but also that in an expanding state the ruling clique itself must be broadened; individuals and groups must, at times, be admitted to the exclusive company of the "best." This sort of concord was a fundamental doctrine of state during much of the Republic. No complete historical sketch will be presented here, but as examples of an attitude which certainly is as early as Cicero and likely much earlier, see Dionysius Halicarnassus 2. 11; there *homonoia* among the classes is regarded as basic to the great success of the Roman state, and it is traced back to Romulus. Later the author attributes to Numa Pompilius the same policy. By making concessions to poor plebeians and to the newest citizens he "attuned the whole body of the people like a musical instrument."[3] Similar views are expressed in Livy, notably in 2. 33, where, speaking of the establishment of the office of tribune of the plebs, the historian remarks that through this concession steps were taken toward *"concordia."* Cicero himself—though not always using the term *concordia*—implies that the concept is an element of the *mos maiorum* in *De Re Publica* 3. 41. It is most probable that these views were not new to him at the date of the writing.

Nor was this late view of Roman history a distorted one. Until the second century B.C. political crises nearly always produced Roman leaders whose attitudes were surprisingly tolerant; their proposals sanely permitted a gradual broadening of the ruling classes, invigorating infusions of new blood which prevented excessive factional strife and built a constitutional structure so sound that it could withstand even the centrifugal forces of Hannibal's victories.

The struggle of the orders in the early Republic should be so interpreted. The patricians, unwillingly, no doubt, but with excellent judgment, step by step conceded an approximately equal position to prominent plebeians (chiefly from areas annexed by Rome rather than from rising new classes), thus bringing together all the "best" men in mutual support of the broadened oligarchy. Not only do later historians

---

[3] See 2. 62.

use the term *concordia* in connection with the crisis of 367 B.C., for example,[4] but the early Romans actually deified the concept and built a temple to Concord in that same year, as well as in 304 and again in 121 B.C.[5] Some cynicism regarding the nature of the "concord" established by Opimius, the builder of the temple of 121 B.C. is certainly justified, for he achieved it by suppression and not by concession and amicable accord. Nevertheless, down to this period the policy had served well. The patrician nobility was enlarged not only in the fourth century settlement, but also through admission to its ranks of men of merit like M. Porcius Cato. By Cato's time, however, the *nobilitas* was already becoming a closed group; it is well known how few of these "new men" were able to break into the ranks of those recognized as the "best." Not only in numbers, but in attitude, the nobility had become more rigidly oligarchical than in earlier days. A Marius or a Cicero would be welcomed into the fold only with cold and uncooperative hostility.

The nobility was only guarding its many privileges. For Rome's acquisition of an empire as the consequence of the Punic and later wars meant vastly expanded career opportunities for the ruling class. High office no longer meant merely high honor—though there was also more of glory than ever before. It meant power and material wealth, in an age which had begun to value material things and the gracious life. Perhaps only a minority were corrupted, actually, by the new opulence and the rarefied atmosphere of the elevated position in which the Roman magistrates now found themselves, the dominant class not merely of Rome and Italy but of the world. However that may be, the Roman oligarchs did not wish to share their new-found status and their lucrative offices with anyone.

By the Gracchan period any real harmony at Rome should have allowed for three left-out groups. First, there were the Latins and Italians, who resented the fact that most of the power and much of the wealth devolved upon a relatively small group in a single city. After the Hannibalic war these allies of Rome were expected to furnish unending levies of men whose duty it became, not to defend from attack Italy and the federation of which Rome was the head, but to fight in far-off fields the battles which would add to the power of Rome and to the glory and wealth of Roman officials. And these demands came at a time when Rome was restricting the right of Latins and Italians to become Roman citizens and when Roman officials were increasing their control over the whole of Italy; moreover, not even war booty nor land in veteran colonies was distributed on an equal basis. New opportunities for traders, men not connected with the government, opened for the favored Roman citizens more than for others. Resent-

[4] See the references in Strasburger, 2 ff.
[5] *Ibid.*, 4 f.

ment smouldered. We read in our Roman sources only bits of information—as, for example, the glimpse given us of allied soldiers marching sullenly in the normally joyous parade of a triumph of 177 B.C. because the commander had allotted them only half the booty given the legionaires. Four years later we hear of a colonial commission which assigned ten iugera of land in the Po valley to Romans, but to the allies only three each.[6] Such incidents must not be overplayed; however, the outbreaks of allied protest in the Gracchan period and after to the final rebellion surely reflect feeling which had long been repressed. Our point here is that any real *concordia* after, say, 146 B.C., should somehow have included the leaders of Latin and Italian states.

Secondly, a moneyed middle class arose, in part the consequence of expansion and imperialism. Too wealthy to be ignored and useful, indeed necessary, to the functioning of the military and political machinery, these equestrians demanded favored posts in the provinces and in the courts. They were not, it appears, particularly interested in holding political office. Still they must needs exercise political power more indirectly, and their financial contributions by Cicero's day sometimes made careers. As early as the Gracchan period there could be no concord without them.

The third group demanding attention was the Roman proletariat; it comprised the landless and the veteran, the freedman-citizen and the seeker for opportunity or excitement. Concentrated in growing numbers in Rome, ill housed and ill fed, these poor soon complicated every social, economic, and political problem. The economic depression which hit after 140 B.C., leaving many of them desperate, helps to explain the work of the Gracchi.[7] They were Romans, these men, and yet they had nothing—except votes in the assemblies!

In the years before the Gracchi, where were those who would back a new concord? Where were the "liberal" nobles farsighted enough to recognize that the time was upon them when the ruling class must be broadened to include Latins, Italians, and middle class, who could understand that even optimates must give some sort of consideration to the Roman mob? One looks in vain. Efforts toward harmony were limited to attempts to reconcile factions within the senate, as, for example, when the daughter of Scipio Africanus married the rival of the Scipionic group, Tiberius Sempronius Gracchus, father of the reformers, and the daughter of this pair married the younger Scipio (who was really an Aemilius). This effort at reconciliation came to nothing when Gracchus became a reforming tribune, and in fact it was designed only to close ranks more

[6] Liv., 41. 13; 40. 11. It has been argued that these are atypical incidents, that during this period the allies were generally well treated and not dissatisfied. See J. Göhler, *Rom und Italian* (Breslau, 1939) passim, esp. 97.

[7] See the author's article, "The Urban Side of the Gracchan Crisis," *American Historical Review* 63 (1958) 890 ff.

firmly, somewhat like the similar cooperation between the Claudian group and the rising family of the Metelli, about 140 B.C.[8]

No aristocrat wanted to take any politically risky step, in this decade of the 130's B.C. there was an empire to run, a war in Spain, a terrifying slave revolt in Sicily, pirate activity, economic depression. It was no time to be adding to men's woes with plans for reform of the state. If Gaius Laelius, the close friend of Scipio Aemilianus, hoping to stem the flow of farmers to the city, offered an agrarian law,[9] he could be persuaded, in the interest of harmony, to withdraw it. As for Scipio Aemilianus himself, he knew the value of the Latins and Italians and would defend their interests when Tiberius Gracchus' agrarian law somehow threatened what they conceived to be their rights. He was capable of supporting liberal measures,[10] but he was no real reformer. Still, Cicero made Scipio his chief exponent of harmony among the classes in his *De Republica* (notably 2. 69).

What of the Gracchi? By no stretch of definition could they be conceived of as supporting a *concordia*. They rejected the very nucleus— the traditional aristocracy—about which a real *concordia* might have been formed. On the part of Tiberius this was simply the consequence of his program and of his determination and self-assurance. For Gaius it was deliberate policy.[11] The Gracchi did first try to function within the existing framework of law and custom, but they were rebuffed. So, alas for *concordia*, they did not hesitate to erect a new system, which required a strong paternalistic leader at the top and support of the masses. The result was a new kind of factional strife which (as we now see) could be resolved only by civil war and the principate.

Only one person appears in the Gracchan age whose program, conciliating and relatively enlightened, if too limited, was in the tradition of true concord. Livius Drusus, the tribune who opposed Gaius Gracchus in 122 B.C., appears to have recognized that Rome owed concessions to her allies and that the ruling aristocracy must accept responsibility for improving the lot of the Roman poor.[12] He offered to the Latin not, indeed, the Roman citizenship, but one of its most desired privileges, the *provocatio*, or right of appeal. This right had been granted to Romans early in the century and to Romans serving in the army more recently.[13] It was perhaps in response to this that Gaius

[8] See F. Munzer, *Römische Adelsparteien und Adelsfamilien* (Stuttgart, 1920) 269.

[9] Plut., *Ti. Gr.* 8.

[10] Such as the bill giving the secret ballot in comital trials; Cicero, *De Leg.* 3. 37.

[11] Though he may at first have intended to strengthen the senate, rather than strip it of power, by adding equestrians to it; Liv. *Epit.* 60.

[12] See the author's article, "Livius Drusus, t. p. 122 B.C., and his Anti-Gracchan program," *Classical Journal* 52 (1956) 27 ff.

[13] Plut. *C. Gr.* 9; cf. A. N. Sherwin-White, *The Roman Citizenship* (Oxford, 1939) 28, and A. H. McDonald, "Rome and the Italian Confederation (200-186 B.C.)," *JRS* 24 (1944) 19.

offered a sweeping citizenship proposal. The genuineness of Drusus' concern for Latins and Italians is indicated by family marriage connections[14] and by fragmentary inscriptional evidence which shows that Drusus later granted privileges to the allies in respect to Roman *ager publicus*.[15] It was understood that Drusus had the general support of the nobles. To the Roman poor he offered recognition by the senate of land distributions already made, with rentals to be abolished and the land given to the individual possessors in full title (so making the land saleable). In addition he proposed a generous colonial scheme.

A true *concordia* should have tried to bring together the equestrians and nobles, to heal the wounds which Gaius Gracchus had deliberately inflicted. Was any such effort made? Perhaps it would be safe to make an *argumentum ex silentio*. The nobles made no effort, either in 122 nor in the years immediately following the demise of the younger Gracchus, to recover control of the extortion courts nor to change the tax-collecting system in Asia introduced by Gracchus and so highly profitable to the equestrians. The senators did not even try to extend Gracchus' judiciary law to make the equestrian jurors liable to prosecution for bribery. Does not this strange inaction in matters affecting the equestrians indicate that the nobles had achieved a working accord with this upper middle class group? Surely it is safe to postulate something of this nature and even to work into the accord Opimius and his temple to Concord, outrageous to true harmony as his vindictive actions may have been.

The instrument of "harmony" created by Drusus produced many a cacophonous chord after a few years of peace, for the senatorial aristocracy could not agree as to who should pipe the tune. Equestrian control of the extortion courts came under attack, and new men like Marius had to storm the inner fortress of nobility without invitation and without welcome after the fact.

It is possible that Marcus Aemilius Scaurus may have professed the liberal and compromising attitude necessary to harmony in these years, though the evidence is not complete enough to permit a confident statement.[16] Himself of an undistinguished branch of his family, he seems nevertheless to have been the leader of a senatorial faction. Cicero puts himself distinctly in the political lineage of Scaurus.[17] In fact, Scaurus knew Cicero's father, encouraged the son and may have been something of a sponsor for him, as Cicero in his turn encouraged other po-

---

[14] See the evidence in *CJ* 52 (1956) 28 f. Cf. Münzer's article in *RE* 13, 855.

[15] Along with Romans. See Lex Agraria of 111 B.C., *CIL* 1¹. 200, line 29. This interpretation has been challenged (see E. Badian, *Historia* 11 (April, 1962) 214) but for reasons too complex to explain here the author thinks Badian wrong.

[16] For Scaurus' career see G. Bloch, "M. Aemilius Scaurus, Etude sur L'histoire des partis au VIIe siécle de Rome," *Mélanges d'histoire ancienne* 25 (1909) 1-81.

[17] *Pro Scauro* 32.

tential new men in a speech discussing concordia.[18] Scaurus was the colleague of the elder Drusus in the censorship (109 B.C.) and in late life was prosecuted for supporting the younger Drusus,[19] who will be presented as a supporter of concord in his father's steps. Another bit of evidence is found in Cicero; dwelling upon his own views of the state —including basic harmony—Scaurus is cited with approval as one who *seditiosis omnibus restitit* from Gaius Gracchus to Quintus Varius.[20] Surely Cicero meant that Scaurus championed harmony among responsible citizens in the same way that he himself did when opposing Catiline. Scaurus' actions in the Jugurthan war, as well as Sallust's contempt for him, become more explicable if Scaurus, like Cicero, found himself obliged to overlook or even defend a degree of corruption among the nobles for the sake of general concord.

Support for the ideal of concord can be seen rather more definitely in the younger Livius Drusus, tribune of the plebs in 91 B.C.[21] Drusus is often considered the political descendant of Gaius Gracchus, but despite the considerable similarities of their programs, there is no doubt that Drusus acted as a champion of the senate and with the support of most senators in the early passage of his laws and for most of his year in office. Cicero calls him *senatus propugnator,* adds that he worked in support of the *auctoritas* of that body, and lists several of the senators who supported him, at least initially.[22]

Drusus realized well that the senate could not function effectively without general support; moreover he had maintained the family connections with influential Italians and was prepared to support their demands for citizenship. For the purposes of this essay it will be sufficient merely to list the measures which Drusus' rather extensive program embraced. There was, first, a judiciary measure which both returned to the senate the juries of the extortion courts and made equestrian jurors liable to accusations for bribery. Since there would be no equestrians in future juries, the intent of the latter clause must have been retroactive, as indeed Cicero states.[23] A major element intended to maintain concord provided for the enlargement of the senate by inclusion of many

[18] *Pro Sest.* 136 ff.
[19] See Cicero, *Pro Font.* 38.
[20] *Pro Sest.* 101.
[21] Strasburger, p. 9, note; Münzer, "Livius Drusus," *RE* 13. 868.
[22] *Pro Milo.,* 16, *De Or.* 1, 7, 24 ff., 96 f., *De Domo Sua* 50; see also Asconius, *In Scaur.,* 19. Among useful modern treatments of Drusus and his program are P. A. Seymour, "The Policy of Livius Drusus the Younger," *English Historical Review* 29 (1914), 417-425, and Rudi Thomsen, "Das Jahr 91 v. chr. und seine Voraussetzungen," *Classica et Mediaevalia* 5 (1942) 13-47).
[23] *Pro Cluen.* 153; *Pro Rab. Post.* 16; Appian, *Bell. Civ.* 1, 35. Hugh Last, in *CAH* 9. 179 n. 6 rejects the view that Drusus meant his law to be retroactive; however, Last overlooked the statement of Cicero in *Pro Cluentio.* Further, since all jurors were now to be senators (some think this incorrect) there was no other reason for the provision regarding equestrians. Rutilius Rufus, recently railroaded so blatantly by an equestrian court, was an uncle of Drusus.

equestrians—perhaps enough to double its size to 600.[24] This effort to broaden the base of the ruling class was in the best traditions of the past. But in this period—at least since the Gracchi—no *concordia* was possible which did not conciliate the Roman proletariat. The intention was not so much to obtain their support as to neutralize them, and to neutralize possible *popularis* leaders in opposition as well. And so Drusus got the senate to back several measures of the sort *popularis* tribunes might demand: there were a *lex frumentaria* (this depends on a single word—*frumentariisque*—in the Livian epitome), possibly a *lex colonia* (Appian is the sole source for this), two *leges agrariae* (One a *Lex Saufeia*; this appears most clearly in an inscription, an *elogium*, CIL 6.[1] 1312) presumably providing viritane allotments of land to poor citizens. Drusus is said to have declared cynically that he had left nothing for anyone else to distribute except the mud or the sky![25]

The tribune carried a majority with him in the senate, but there was surely factional opposition right from the first. The makeup of senatorial factions for this period remains obscure and needs to be worked out; certainly the older groups had been mixed in an extraordinary way.[26] But when Drusus now advocated the citizenship for all Italy, and perhaps the extent of the Italian conspiracy began to be suspected, he lost his most powerful supporters. This latter measure he had at first kept secret in order to gain support. This is not specifically stated in the sources. However, Drusus had the backing even of Licinius Crassus and Mucius Scaevola, who as consuls four years before had arbitrarily withdrawn citizenship from many Latins and Italians by their *Lex Licinia et Mucia*[27] and this would appear to have been impossible if Drusus had presented his program as a unit. It is well known that the senators generally feared "that a free state is changed into a monarchy when large numbers are given the citizenship through the efforts of one man."[28] Further, there were stories of Drusus' high-handed behavior and the propaganda against him even included copies of an oath by which Italians were supposed to have sworn solemn fealty to Drusus personally. This oath has sometimes been accepted as genuine, but the arguments do not seem convincing.[29] It would have been out of

[24] I have here followed Appian (*Bell. Civ.* 1. 35); the terse statement in the biography in the *De Viris Illustribus* (66) seems to give support, while the remark in the Livian epitome (71) is rather ambiguous. For a different view see Seymour, *loc cit.*
[25] Florus 2. 5. 6; *De Vir. Illus.* 66.
[26] The work of W. Schur, "Das Zeitalter des Marius and Sulla," *Klio* 46 (1942) attacks the problem but not very satisfactorily.
[27] Cicero *De Off.* 3. 47; *Pro Sest.* 13. 30; *Brut.* 63.
[28] Sallust (or pseudo-S.) *Epis. ad Caesarem* 6.
[29] E.g., by Lily Ross Taylor, depending chiefly on Carl Koch. See *Party Politics in the Age of Caesar* (Berkeley, 1949) 46 f., with notes. For a recent rejection of Koch's views see H. J. Rose, "The Oath of Philippus and the 'Di Indigites,'" *Harvard Theological Review* 30 (1937) 165 ff. See also R. Syme's comments in a review of Schur (*op. cit.*) in *JRS* 24 (1944) 108.

character for Drusus to demand it, and certainly out of character for a man like Pompedius Silo to take it. It is called the "Oath of Philippus," which indicates that it was Drusus' worst enemy who "revealed" it. Finally, it is mentioned only by Diodorus. Appian, not to mention Cicero and others, must have known of it, but make no mention of it.

In any event the general pattern is clear. Drusus presented his program piecemeal. Perhaps the judicial measures came first; last was the citizenship bill, on which he lost support in the senate. One law was somehow invalidated on the ground that it violated the *Lex Caecilia et Didia,* which forbade omnibus bills. After a period of disorder Drusus was assassinated and the Italians rebelled.

Before we come to Cicero's own *concordia,* it may be remarked in passing that even Sulla's reactionary constitutional enactments did not lack an element of the traditional methods of achieving harmony. His vastly enlarged senate and the larger number of magistrates, especially quaestors, must have brought into the senate many equestrians who would never have achieved this status under the former order of things. It goes without saying that other elements of concord were lacking.

The failure of the younger Drusus and the dissatisfaction with Sulla's new order illustrate well two obstacles to any real harmony; the illiberality of many senators and the truculent demands of the lower classes in Rome. But there is another important cause of the failure of Drusus, and this was a failure to recognize the needs and aspirations of the equestrian order. Cicero understood this order, and it was precisely in this connection that Cicero's specific plan for a concord broke with tradition and met more realistically the existing situation. Incidentally, Cicero's expressed disapproval of the program of Drusus —because of the *ex post facto* intent of Drusus' measure against corruption of equestrian jurors, as we have seen—does not mean that Cicero was not essentially in agreement with Drusus' aims.

Cicero apparently did not speak specifically of a *concordia ordinum* before his consulship. However, it can easily be shown that the basic views encompassed in his policy were formulated early in his career. In a speech of 80 B.C. (*Pro Sex. Roscio Amerino*), the young orator warned the nobility that they must prove they are the *boni* (139) ; those truly the *optimi,* the *nobilissimi,* he said would approve his arguments for justice for equestrians like Roscius (142). Why had many citizens, himself included, been willing to support the Sullan side? Because they fought for a certain type of noble who like young Messala stood for justice (Messala was aiding Roscius), and protected the innocent (149). The nobles were further warned that the support of the citizens might be withdrawn unless they changed their ways. Do we not have here an argument for a concord between the nobles and the equestrians (represented in Roscius), and also the idea of the *consensus omnium bonorum?*

There are several passages in the *Pro Cluentio* of 66 B.C. which in effect advocated a basic working arrangement between noble and equestrian. All except the most factious of the senators, the praetor argued, "are anxious that the order of knights should occupy a position second only to that of their own order and most firmly allied to it by the bond of unanimity (152)." What is this if not the *concordia ordinum*, three or four years ahead of its often presumed birthdate in Cicero's consulship? In a speech made in the year of his consulship, Cicero (defending Rabirius) spoke of what amounted to a consensus of all orders, indeed of all good men, referring to the affair of Saturninus in 100 B.C.[30] He quite clearly mentions the *consensio bonorum* as a feature of senatorial government *a maioribus traditum*, emphasizing that the accusation against Rabirius was an attempt to abolish the *consensio*.[31] Cicero's use of Scipio Aemilianus as a defender of the traditional *concordia* in the *De Republica* (especially 2. 69, as previously noted) indicates Cicero's historical view of the subject. Surely these passages show that Cicero from his early career considered an accord between senate and equestrians as essential to good government; moreover, the consensus of all good men was clearly part and parcel of the same general concept, and therefore did *not* develop only secondarily, some time after Cicero's consulship, as a kind of broadened *concordia*.[32]

Cicero chose to drive for a new *concordia* in his consulship and immediately after for several reasons. First, his own election to the consulship, the first equestrian, new man for a long time, put him in a unique position. He was a man who had gained the support of powerful groups of nobles; by suppressing the conspiracy of Catiline he had (so he thought) obligated to himself all responsible classes, including the nobility. Although now a member of that group himself, he considered himself still a representative of the equestrian class, a spokesman for it, even a kind of patron of it.[33] He saw himself as the logical man to resolve the disputes which inevitably arose between the two orders. Finally, Cicero possessed a complete understanding of the equestrian order which he everywhere demonstrated, and especially in connection with his *concordia*.

A key passage in the *Pro Cluentio* (153 ff.)[34] shows Cicero's comprehension of equestrian wants and needs and demonstrates well why the old schemes for enlarging the senatorial nobility could not satisfy their aspirations. The orator contrasts the life of the senator-politician

---

[30] *Pro Rab.* 6. 18 ff.
[31] In 1. 2; see also 2. 4, where the charge is repeated.
[32] As is so often stated; e.g., in Strasburger, 12 (although S. does recognize a prior period of development).
[33] *Phil.* 6. 13. For remarks on Cicero's relationship with the equestrian order, see the author's article, "The Sources of Cicero's Income: Some Suggestions," *CJ* 57 (1961) 17 ff.
[34] Cf. the equally clear and emphatic passage in *Pro Rab. Post.* 16 f.

with that of the equestrian businessman. He describes the difficulties peculiar to the senatorial class, emphasizing political prosecutions, and remarks on the compensatory honor and dignity. Then he speaks for the equestrians: "[We are] satisfied with our own order . . . we have preferred to pursue the life it offers . . . sheltered from the storms of popular prejudice and legal actions such as this . . . [it is] unfair that we . . . should be debarred from public recognition and yet not be free from the danger of political prosecution in the courts." In reality, legal restrictions tended to make it impossible to be both business man and politician.

There is a modicum more of justice in this plaint of the equestrians than is usually granted. While it may, indeed, seem wholly unreasonable for them to demand some political power via the extortion court juries and at the same time to insist on exemption from prosecution for corruption in that connection, it is also true that most prosecutions in Rome were for political ends; only occasionally, the cynic might say even incidentally, did the trials involve clear-cut efforts to improve public morals or magisterial ethics. It *was* somewhat unreasonable to expose to such political harassment men who basically were not politicians and who did not want to become involved in politics—except to protect their own interests.

Knowing so well that the equestrian businessmen did not want to participate fully in government, and knowing too that men so powerful must not be alienated, Cicero did not propose in traditional style to induct some of them into the senatorial oligarchy. Rather he envisioned a ruling class which would safeguard equestrian interests and so gain their support and cooperation. To be sure, Cicero hoped also to see a continuing influx into this ruling class of highly talented new men like himself. Moreover, he had ideals, too, despite his recognition of the need for compromise.

Parenthetically, the author would like to remark that modern scholars who condemn Cicero because he was a compromiser are themselves politically naive and a little ridiculous. Even a shallow investigation of the workings of the United States Congress today would do much to enlighten them. Politicians who stand rigidly on principle accomplish little; they may be praised for their ideals, but to be unbending is to be politically ineffective, even stupid, like the man who did most to wreck Cicero's *concordia,* Cato.[35] The first duty of a politician is to get things done, to make the ponderous machinery of government function—now, this day, this month; he does this through give-and-take, striving for the best possible settlement, and not through oratorical pontificating in favor of something impossible of achievement. He should, naturally, work for something still better for the future.

[35] See Cicero's own fair estimate of Cato's short-sightedness in *De Off.* 3. 88.

It is not within the purpose of this essay to discuss the specific measures which Cicero advocated as part of his policy in 63 B.C. and after, nor to evaluate his failure. But perhaps the Orator's *concordia ordinum* and *consensio bonorum* or *totae Italiae* will be better understood when viewed in this rather sketchy historical setting.

University of North Carolina
Chapel Hill

THE UNITY OF PROPERTIUS 2.34 AND 3.20

Ronald E. White

This is the last in a series of three papers supporting the unity of six poems by Propertius and illustrating this poet's use of a technique which has been called "dramatic development."[1]

2.34

This discussion might best commence with a paraphrase of the poem. "My sweetheart was almost stolen from me by Cupid, who has always been a source of strife amongst men (1-8). Lynceus, how could you dare to make advances toward my beloved! Take anything I own, but leave her alone (9-18)! Though I fear everything as a threat to my love, I forgive your transgression because you were tipsy; but I know that even old fellows like you appreciate love (19-24).

"Now that you are in love, Lynceus, your studies in philosophy, epic poetry, and tragedy are useless; follow instead the slender muse of love poetry (25-46). Take me as your guide, for I have already won success through my love poems (47-58). Love is the life for me; let Vergil undertake the great Roman epic (59-66). Pastoral poems on the loves of shepherds are also in your sphere, Vergil (67-76). Even your didactic poetry charms its reader (77-84). Other distinguished erotic poets are: Varro, Catullus, Calvus, Gallus, and myself, if my reputation will warrant my inclusion in this list (85-94)."

Despite the fact that this poem is undivided in the manuscripts, Ribbeck has held that a new elegy begins at line 23 and Otto, followed by Butler and Barber, suggest that a new elegy begins at line 25. Butler, Enk, and Abel have argued in favor of treating the entire poem as a unit. An additional break after line 58, has been suggested by Damon and Helmbold. No other scholars have recommended this second division. In this paper, the unity of the elegy will be defended.

Let us consider Ribbeck's arguments for division:[2]

Wie sollte der fein empfindende Dichter, der eben erklärt hat, dass er nur in dem berauschten Zustande des Freundes, in einer vorübergehenden Anwandlung von Sinnlichkeit eine Entschuldigung für dessen frechen Angriff auf sein Mädchen finden könne, in demselben Athem nicht nur anerkennen, dass derselbe ernsthaft in dasselbe verliebt sei (*insanit amores* 25), sondern

---

[1] The first two papers were: R. E. White, "The Structure of Propertius 2.28: Dramatic Unity," TAPA 89 (1958) 254-61; R. E. White, "The Unity of Three Poems by Propertius: 1.8; 2.29; 2.33" (to be published in CP).

[2] O. Ribbeck, "Zur Erklärung und Kritik des Properz," RhM 40 (1885) 486.

sich auch darüber freuen und ihm Anweisung geben, wie er zum Ziel gelangen könne!

Ribbeck points out the inconsistency between lines 1-22 in which Propertius is angry with Lynceus and excuses his overtures toward Cynthia only because he was drunk, and the following lines in which the poet rejoices over Lynceus' falling in love and offers him advice. Butler and Barber make a similar objection:[3]

The tone of the poems [lines 1-24, 25-94] is different. In the first he reproaches Lynceus for attempting to steal Cynthia from him. The attempt has failed and, though the offender is pardoned (21), the resentment remains. In the second there is no trace of anger; the offender is wholly forgiven.

Notwithstanding these objections, no one can deny that both sections are addressed to Lynceus (9 *Lynceu*, 22 *tua verba*, 25 *Lynceus*, 26 *te*, 31 *tu*) and stem from the same event, his flirtation with Cynthia. Furthermore, if a new elegy is begun at line 25, the result is that two successive poems are dedicated to the same person, and it is not Propertius' custom to dedicate consecutive poems to the same person, except Cynthia, though it is not inconceivable that this be an exception. How then are we to explain the relationship between lines 1-24 and 25-94?

Otto believes that the two sections are separate elegies; but he says of lines 25 ff. that they comprise one of a class of peculiar Propertian elegies which presuppose the immediately preceding poem for their understanding and continue the same theme.[4] He admits that the manuscripts usually do not separate these "independent" poems. It may be answered that what is "peculiar" is not Propertius' poems, but the theory which favors separation in spite of all the evidence to the contrary. Butler, in his earlier edition, apparently recognized the framework of this poem:[5]

The poem is rambling: it begins as a remonstrance to a friend, and by a series of gradual transitions ends as a defence of erotic poetry. But there is no definite break in the poem, and there is no necessity . . . to regard the order of the lines as hopelessly disturbed, or . . . to divide the poem into several elegies.

Butler's point that the poem becomes a defense of erotic poetry is well taken and will be discussed below. Furthermore, as Abel has pointed out, the use of the third person in line 25 with reference to Lynceus

---

[3] H. E. Butler and E. A. Barber, *The Elegies of Propertius* (Oxford 1933) 255.
[4] A. Otto, "Die Reihenfolge der Gedichte des Properz," *Hermes* 20 (1885) 558.
[5] H. E. Butler, *Sexti Properti Opera Omnia* (London 1905) 252.

is prepared for by the *omnes norunt* of line 24;[6] moreover, *ipse* in line 25 is an illustration of *omnes iam* in line 24—"everyone, even my friend Lynceus!"

As of line 24, then, Lynceus has been forgiven. Nonetheless, we are not prepared for the almost congratulatory tone of lines 25-26:

> Lynceus ipse meus seros insanit amores!
> solum te nostros laetor adire deos.

The rapid changes from anger to forgiveness (21) and from forgiveness to congratulations (26) seem to lead Enk to believe that the poet was never seriously angry:[7]

Vehementer errant, qui inde ab hoc versu . . . novam incipiunt elegiam . . . Postquam enim poeta iocose amicum perstrinxit, quod suam puellam amare coepisset, dicit unum se didicisse: Amori ne severos quidem homines resistere posse; coram formosa puella omnes praecepta moralia oblivisci. "Si quis mihi dixisset, inquit poeta: caveas amicum tuum Lyncea, noli ei tuam puellam committere, risissem neque tam turpi calumniatori credidissem; ecce autem severus ille sui oblitus meae puellae blandiri est ausus. Iratusne es, inquies; immo vero ignosco tibi; unum gaudeo te iam desiturum esse Amorem despicere; quid nunc tibi severa illa studia prosunt? Quam felix esses, si carmina amatoria legisses."

According to Enk's interpretation, the rebuke in the first section is jocose rather than serious, and there is therefore no inconsistency with the tone of the second. But it is difficult to consider lines 1-18 as spoken jocosely; they appear rather to be a sincere expression of anger at his friend's disloyal conduct. This is not to say that Propertius fails to prepare us for the changed mood in lines 25 ff. He begins to calm himself in lines 19-20:

> ipse meas solus, quod nil est, aemulor umbras,
> stultus, quod stulto saepe timore tremo.

This is an admission that he himself is too inclined to jealousy and it constitutes a softening of his rebuke to Lynceus, preparing the reader for the complete pardon in the next couplet:

> una tamen causa est, cur crimina tanta remitto,
> errabant multo quod tua verba mero.

Lynceus is fully forgiven on the grounds that he was tipsy when he transgressed. There is no evidence to support the contention of Butler and Barber that the resentment remains. Lines 23-24:

---

[6] W. Abel, *Die Anredeformen bei den römischen Elegikern* (diss. Berlin 1930) 61.

[7] P. J. Enk, *Ad Propertii Carmina Commentarius Criticus* (Zutphen 1911) 193-4.

> sed numquam vitae fallet me ruga severae:
> omnes iam norunt quam sit amare bonum

show no sign of resentment or anger; their only message is that the poet understands that everyone, old men included, appreciates love.

It is surprising to me that no one, in discussing Propertius' change of attitude toward Lynceus in this poem, has mentioned the closely parallel situation in 1.5. The opening lines of that poem make clear that it, like 2.34, is motivated by a friend's desire to usurp Cynthia's affections or favors:

> Invide tu tandem voces compesce molestas
> et sine nos cursu, quo sumus, ire pares!
> quid tibi vis, insane? meos sentire furores?
> infelix, properas ultima nosse mala.

For the first twelve lines, he angrily warns of the dangers involved in loving Cynthia. But as of line thirteen, there is a distinct change of tone from anger to sympathy:

> ah, mea contemptus quotiens ad limina curres,
> cum tibi singultu fortia verba cadent,

and as of line twenty-seven, there is not a vestige of ill-feeling:

> non ego tum potero solacia ferre roganti,
> cum mihi nulla mei sit medicina mali,
> sed pariter miseri socio cogemur amore
> alter in alterius mutua flere sinu.

As bosom comrades, they will weep together over their incurable love. The last couplet commands Gallus, the friend, to leave off wooing Cynthia, but there is no bitterness and no harsh words as there were at the beginning (1 invide, molestas; 3 insane; 4 infelix).

A further development occurs between lines 24-25. Now that his anger has cooled and he has forgiven his friend, Propertius realizes the humor of scholarly old Lynceus falling in love, and proceeds to lecture him on amatory success. To comprehend the transition from line 24 to lines 25 ff., we must realize that the poet is employing what has previously been labeled "dramatic development."[8] The reader is to understand an unexpressed passage of time, perhaps only a slight pause, between lines 24-25. It is during this pause that the full humor of the situation finally occurs to Propertius, causing him to suppress any further expression of resentment. It might be well to indicate this pause by a horizontal line between lines 24-25, but there is no justification for treating the sections as independent poems.

We may take up now the relationship of lines 59-94 to lines 1-58.

[8] R. E. White, "The Structure of Propertius 2.28..." (above, note 1) 260.

Damon and Helmbold have argued that lines 59-94 must be considered independent of what precedes.⁹ They have presented these reasons: (1) that there is an essential difference in tone; (2) that Lynceus has disappeared; (3) that lines 59-94 comprise a σφραγίς poem, advertising, in an unusual way, the author and his connections with the literary world. Butler and Barber had earlier rejected this separation:¹⁰

55-8 provide a less definite conclusion, and harmonize so well with 59-60, that such partition is a very dubious expedient. It is true that Lynceus disappears from the poem and is no longer addressed directly by Propertius. But 50-94 are still appropriate enough as indicating that erotic poetry is the true line which should be followed by the love-sick poet if he desires to win real fame.

The point that lines 55-58 and 59-60 harmonize is well taken, but Butler and Barber did not explain Lynceus' disappearance. Rothstein had previously offered this explanation:¹¹

So ist die Person des Lynceus am Ende der Elegie ganz vergessen; der Dichter lässt ihn fallen, nachdem er seinen poetischen Zweck erfüllt hat, ganz wie er es mit dem Freunde in den Gedichten II 8 und III 11 und dem Fremden in der Elegie IV 1 macht. Er ist eben nur eine Kontrastfigur, der Typus eines unpraktischen, dünkelhaften Stubengelehrten, der sich wohl einmal im Rausch an ein Mädchen wagt, aber mit so wenig Erfolg, dass selbst der verletzte Nebenbuhler noch Mitleid mit ihm empfindet und ihm seine Führung auf dem neuen Wege anbieten kann.

It may be objected that 2.8, 3.11, and 4.1 are not acceptable parallels since the persons spoken to and later dropped in those poems do not receive such specific emphasis as that given to Lynceus in 2.34, 1-24. But concerning lines 25 ff., Rothstein is quite correct in his explanation that Lynceus is used as the prototype of the arrogant scholar with whom Propertius contrasts himself, the successful writer of erotic poetry. The emphasis of the poem is transferred from Lynceus' transgression to a defense of love poetry which includes a eulogy of Vergil. The poet addresses lines 25-58 to his friend in order to link together smoothly the two themes. Thus we hear no more of Lynceus after line 58 because he is of no further use in the poem. The fact is that Propertius has used the Lynceus affair as a springboard from which to leap into the larger theme of a defense of poetry, especially love poetry.

There is no noticeable change of tone in lines 59-94 from lines 25-58; from the general argument that girls are won by erotic poetry rather than scholarly studies, the poet passes to a praise of specific

[9] P. W. Damon and W. C. Helmbold, "The Structure of Propertius, Book 2," *University of California Publications in Classical Philology* 14 (1950-52) 238.
[10] Butler and Barber (above, note 3) 255.
[11] M. Rothstein, *Die Elegien des Sextus Propertius* (Berlin 1920) 1².434.

poets.[12] As for the charge by Damon and Helmbold that this poem advertises the author and his connections in the literary world, it can be answered that in listing the several famous poets, Propertius makes no mention whatsoever of personal connection with any of them; he mentions himself only in the closing couplet, and even then his inclusion in the list is conditional. If anyone objects to this interpretation on the ground that it proposes two different subjects for one poem, there can be cited the following elegies which have twofold themes: 2.1; 3.5; 4.1; 4.6.

The ninety-four lines of this poem, then, are a unit, and this elegy manifests a recurrence of Propertius' skillful use of abrupt transition as a dramatic device to indicate to the reader that some aspect of the situation has developed further. In this case, the development is the change in the poet's mood from one of forgiveness to one of good-natured advice. The reader is not told directly of this change, but must gather for himself what has happened from the poet's own reaction to this change in the second section (lines 25 ff.).

3.20

Let us first consider the contents of this elegy.

"Forget your inconsiderate lover, who has saddened you thus by sailing away to Africa in search of profit; he very likely has a new sweetheart (1-6). You are lovely, talented, and noble; accept me as your lover, and my devotion will make your blessings complete (7-10). And you, Phoebus, shorten the long summer daylight, for the first night of my new love is nigh; Luna, extend the time of your beaming during this first night of love (11-14). Pacts must be drawn up and signed first—Cupid himself makes these binding, with the constellation Ariadne as witness—then how many hours of love's sweet talk will pass before Venus' warfare is begun (15-20)! For when there are no bonds, nothing restrains either party from deserting the sweetheart through lust; may this not happen in our case (21-24)! Let him who is unfaithful suffer all the pangs of an unsuccessful love affair (25-30)."

Although the manuscripts make no division after line 10, Scaliger, Butler and Barber, and Schuster have held that lines 11 ff. be separated from lines 1-10 and considered a different poem. Rothstein, Butler, Enk, and Bailey have argued in favor of the poem's unity. The view of the latter group will be supported in this discussion.

The first point to be discussed is the identity of the girl in this

---

[12] W. Abel (above, note 6) 58, takes lines 1-94 as a unit. He argues that it is a closing defense of amatory poetry as opposed to epic poetry, and complements the introductory poem, 2.1, which was on the same theme. I agree with this interpretation.

poem. O'Neil believes that she is Cynthia, since:[13] "... the description in verses 7 ff. is so similar to that of Cynthia that there can be little doubt about the identity." Butler and Barber seem inclined to the same view:[14] "... the lady's accomplishments are surprisingly like those of Cynthia (cp. 7, 8 with I. ii. 25-30; II. iii. 9-22)." But against this theory we may object, as Butler and Barber themselves admit, that:[15]

... the poem, if the new mistress is Cynthia, must refer to the very opening of the liaison. But it is clear that the poem itself does not belong to that period, since it is emphatically not in Propertius' early manner. It would be strange for him at this date to publish a poem celebrating his first joys with Cynthia, without a hint that years had elapsed since those days, and still stranger that he should place it so close to the poems whose theme is his final breach with her.

Furthermore, there is no objection to the explanation that the lady in question was a new love. It is generally agreed that the affair with Cynthia was cooling during the period in which Book 3 was written (cf. 3.24; 3.25). It is therefore reasonable to suspect that our poet, a man of passionate nature, would seek for solace in a new love. As to the argument that this girl's accomplishments sound very much like those of Cynthia, it can be answered that Cynthia did not hold a monopoly on such qualities, and further, that, were Propertius seeking another sweetheart, his preference would probably be one endowed with the same qualities he so admired in Cynthia.

Butler and Barber believe that a new poem begins at line 11:[16]

It may be argued ... that at line 11 there is a break in the sense. He suddenly assumes that his invitation has been answered and that she is with him ... On the whole, the case for division seems slightly the stronger, and we have consequently made a new elegy begin at line 11.

In his earlier edition, however, Butler judged differently:[17]

There is a slight break in the sense. He assumes that his invitation in line 10 has been answered and that he has won her ... The contradiction between the two parts is so slight that the division is not absolutely necessary.

Rothstein, on the other hand, finds the development employed in this poem natural and pleasing:[18]

Was hier [in lines 7-10] noch Wunsch und Bitte ist, wird im weiteren Verlaufe des durch frische Natürlichkeit der Gedankenentwicklung und lebendige Wärme des Empfindens ausgezeichneten, offenbar unmittelbar aus dem Leben geschöpften Gedichtes schon als erfüllt vorgestellt.

[13] E. O'Neil, "Cynthia and the Moon," CP 53 (1958) 5.
[14] Butler and Barber (above, note 3) 312.
[15] *Ibid.*
[16] *Ibid.*
[17] Butler (above, note 5) 316.
[18] M. Rothstein, *Die Elegien des Sextus Propertius* (Berlin 1924) 2^2.156-7.

Elsewhere Rothstein comments on the coherence of lines 1-10 with lines 11-30 thus:[19] "Den inneren Zusammenhang der beiden durch den Gedanken *fidus ero* verbundenen Teile glaube ich oben deutlich gemacht zu haben."[20] This is an important argument in support of unity. In his efforts to persuade the girl, Propertius has employed the first six lines of the poem to accuse her absent lover of thoughtlessness, avarice, and even infidelity. With this picture, he carefully contrasts his own eagerness to provide against the uncertainties of the incipient love affair, formal agreements to be signed beforehand by both parties (lines 15-24). The invective of the opening six lines is neatly balanced by the thinly-veiled reference to the absent lover in the last six lines; in these, the poet curses all who break love pacts and indulge in infidelity.

The fact that both sections concern the poet's exhortation to a new sweetheart is clear, but what of the fact that his success, not even hinted at in lines 1-10, is suddenly assumed in line 11? The answer to this question is that the poet has here employed once more that type of development which has been labeled "dramatic." The reader is to understand between two lines (10-11) an unexpressed passage of time during which some unexpressed event has occurred. In line 10, Propertius asks the girl to become his mistress. In line 11, he is already making arrangements for the love affair. The reader is to understand from what the poets says in lines 11 ff. that the invitation extended in line 10 has been accepted. The acceptance could have consisted of a nod of the head or even an embrace, but clearly some such occurrence must be understood to link together the two closely related sections.

One result of the attempt to divide this elegy in two has been the suggestion that lines 13-14 be transposed before line 11. The reason for this is that, according to the proposed division, line 11 would begin a new elegy, and *quoque* would become completely unclear. Thus Butler and Barber argue:[21]

13, 14, 11, 12. This transposition (Scaliger) is necessary, since without it *tu quoque* is meaningless. With the transposition *quoque* introduces a second appeal, this time to the Sun. The dislocation may be explained by the homoeoteleuton *toros . . . toro*.[22]

It may be answered that *tu quoque* becomes meaningless only when one insists upon beginning a new poem after line 10. When the poem is left as it stands in the manuscripts, *quoque* is understandable without the harsh expedient of transposition. The reader has only to imagine

[19] *Ibid.*, 375.
[20] This same observation had been made by Guil. Ad. B. Hertzberg, *Sex. Aurelii Propertii Elegiarum Libri Quattuor* (Halle 1843) 1.89.
[21] Butler and Barber (above, note 3) 313.
[22] The view that this transposition is necessary to explain *quoque* is held also by P. J. Enk (above, note 7) 270.

Propertius depicting himself here as the general marshalling his troops in war, the war of love. Thus he first commands the girl to run to his couch (line 10); next he turns to the sun (line 11), bidding it to hurry and complete its course; finally, in a perfectly natural sequence, he instructs the moon to shine longer in order that he and his beloved may accomplish all the necessary arrangements. Thus Bailey, rejecting the suggested transposition, defends the coherence of the lines as they stand in the manuscripts:²³

But *quoque* may fairly be understood as linking *tu* with *puella* of 10, persons and things being so linked, not only when alike in themselves, but also when their activities are similar in kind or tendency (4. 8. 45 is an instance) . . . Furthermore, to call upon the moon before the sun is a reversal of natural order.

Bailey's argument that *quoque* links together *tu* and *puella* is supported by the fact that his *quoque* is used in a weakened sense with the meaning "and."²⁴ Enk attempts to overcome the objection that transposition results in a reversal of natural order by interpreting that the request to Phoebus [in lines 11-12] has reference, not to the same day, but rather to the following morning, and so the time sequence is logical.²⁵ But I suggest that the text does not permit this interpretation. For, if lines 11-12 were to have reference to the following morning, their meaning should be something of this sort: "Let the sun not rise too early." The idea would be that the sun, by rising late, would allow the moon to remain longer, thereby affording the lovers more time for their activities. But as it is, the poet speaks of the sun as being already in its course (*qui aestivos spatiosius exigis ignes* in line 11), and his command is that the night time, which is more appropriate to amatory affairs, may come more quickly.

²³ D. R. S. Bailey, *Propertiana* (Cambridge [England] 1956) 313.
²⁴ One parallel for this use of *quoque* is found in 2.13, 39. Propertius has instructed Cynthia as to the arrangements for his own funeral, and he goes on in lines 37 ff. to say:

>nec minus haec nostri notescet fama sepulchri,
> quam fuerant Phthii busta cruenta viri.
>tu quoque si quando venies ad fata, memento,
> hoc iter ad lapides cana veni memores!

He claims that his tomb will be as famous as that of Achilles, and he asks Cynthia to return to it when she is old and near death. It would be senseless to translate this *quoque* as "also." Clearly the meaning here is: "And you, Cynthia, when you..." Another example of *quoque* meaning "and" is that in 4.1, 144. The astrologer, Horus, tells Propertius that he is fated to be enslaved by love for one woman, and that (lines 143-4):

>illius arbitrio noctem lucemque videbis,
> gutta quoque ex oculis non nisi iussa cadet.

Quoque makes no sense when translated "also"; the obvious meaning is: "And you will not weep, except at her command." For two other instances in which *quoque* does not mean "also," see 2.21, 17 and 2.25, 21.
²⁵ Enk (above, note 7) 271.

The final point to be discussed is the proper order of lines 15-22. Here are the lines as arranged in the manuscripts:

> 15 foedera sunt ponenda prius signandaque iura
>   et scribenda mihi lex in amore novo.
>   haec Amor ipse suo constringet pignera signo:
>   testis sidereae torta corona deae.
>   quam multae ante meis cedent sermonibus horae,
> 20 dulcia quam nobis concitet arma Venus!
>   namque ubi non certo vincitur foedere lectus,
>   non habet ultores nox vigilata deos.

Enk argues that Lachmann was right in transposing lines 19-20 before line 15 because only thus is the force of *namque* in line 21 brought out, by its following immediately upon line 18.[26] It is my opinion, on the other hand, that the force of *namque* is brought out sufficiently when lines 19-20 are left in place. The *namque* explains the necessity for the arrangements described in lines 15-16. The objection of those who suggest transposition seems to be based on the feeling that the idea of a pact expressed in lines 15-16 is too far removed from the explanation in lines 21-22 as to why there must be a pact. But what is said in lines 17-18 is clearly parenthetical, in that it serves only to enforce the idea expressed in lines 15-16. When we interpret thus, only two lines (19-20) intervene between the statement (in lines 15-18) and the conclusion based on that statement (lines 21 ff.). Greater respect should be paid to the order of lines as found in the manuscripts, and greater efforts should be made to understand their meaning as they stand.

The poet has employed, in this poem, that dramatic technique which he used earlier in 1.8; 2.28; 2.29; 2.33; and 2.34. This elegy in particular is a clear example of the fact that the purpose of Propertius' abrupt transitions is to indicate vividly a further development of a situation. It is quite clear from the poet's reaction in lines 11 ff. that the girl has accepted his invitation. What the poet accomplishes by using this device, instead of saying directly, "She has accepted me!", is an exciting sense of immediacy and movement.

McMaster University
Hamilton, Ontario

[26] *Ibid.*

LUCAN AND CAESAR'S CROSSING OF THE RUBICON

Robert J. Getty

Quintilian's description of Lucan as "ardens et concitatus"[1] could be equally well applied, as the action of the *De Bello Civili* begins, to Caesar's onrush across the Alps and plans already formed for war:

> iam gelidas Caesar cursu superaverat Alpes
> ingentisque animo motus bellumque futurum
> ceperat.[2]

At the Rubicon he was checked by the nocturnal apparition of his *patria* who, in her sorrowful attempt to dissuade his army from crossing the river, is thus described:

> ingens visa duci patriae trepidantis imago
> clara per obscuram voltu maestissima noctem
> turrigero canos effundens vertice crines
> caesarie lacera nudisque adstare lacertis
> et gemitu permixta loqui.[3]

Her remonstrance made no distinction between Caesar and his men who were carrying her standards and whom she called her citizens, provided that they came no farther:

> "quo tenditis ultra?
> quo fertis mea signa, viri? si iure venitis,
> si cives, huc usque licet." tum perculit horror
> membra ducis, . . .[4]

The horror-stricken general was deterred for an unspecified time. Then (*mox*) he addressed Capitoline Jupiter, the Phrygian Penates of the Gens Iulia, the mysteries of Quirinus who had been snatched from earth, Jupiter Latiaris on the Alban Mount, Vesta's hearths, and finally *Roma* whom he hailed as "summi numinis instar" and begged to be propitious towards what he had begun:

> "summique o numinis instar
> Roma, fave coeptis. non te furialibus armis
> persequor."[5]

---

[1] *Inst.* 10. 1. 90. I hope that this article on a poet's view of a historical occurrence will not be out of place as a tribute to the memory of a scholar who was so much in sympathy with the close relationship of literature and history.
[2] 1. 183-85. Lucan had previously called Caesar *inter alia* "acer et indomitus" (vs. 146) in contrast to Pompey. The juxtaposition "Caesar cursu" recalls the "ὁρμὴ Caesaris" of Cic. *Att.* 7. 11. 5.
[3] 1. 186-90.
[4] 1. 190-93.
[5] 1. 199-201. In the preceding lines "rapti secreta Quirini" and "Vestales foci"

So with the assertion that he was coming, not as an enemy, but as her loyal soldier, he unloosed war and swiftly bore his standards through the swollen river. Having thus disregarded her warning, he then thought fit, as Cicero wrote at the time, to seize loyal cities and thus make his way to his *patria* with greater ease.[6]

To Cicero in this and other letters, as to Lucan in retrospect, the *patria* was in danger such as she had faced in the days of Catiline.[7] Now that the threat was Caesar, the poet recalled the words of the orator who to him was

> Romani maximum auctor
> Tullius eloquii, cuius sub iure togaque
> pacificas saevus tremuit Catilina securis,[8]

and who thus described her in his fourth Catilinarian oration:

obsessa facibus et telis impiae coniurationis vobis supplex manus tendit patria communis, vobis se, vobis vitam omnium civium, vobis arcem et Capitolium, vobis aras Penatium, vobis illum ignem Vestae sempiternum, vobis omnium deorum templa atque delubra, vobis muros atque urbis tecta commendat.[9]

It was Lucan's sense of irony as much as of history that made him endow Caesar with the effrontery of invoking the religious heritage which, along with the lives of her citizens and her walls and buildings, Cicero had pictured the *patria communis* as entrusting to the conscript fathers of the threatened republic.

In an interesting and important article which discusses *res publica, patria,* and other terms in their historical and literary relationship to *Roma,* Ulrich Knoche has pointed out that equations in Cicero and his contemporaries of the *patria* with *Roma* do not mean that the latter was more than a personification in the time of the Republic.[10] Knoche has

---

have been translated literally but probably mean "Quirinus snatched mysteriously from earth" and "Vesta the hearth-goddess." Thus Caesar invoked deities throughout.

[6] *Att.* 7. 11. 1: "honestum igitur . . . occupare urbis civium quo facilior sit aditus ad patriam." According to *Att.* 8. 3. 6 (a letter written just as news came that Caesar had reached Corfinium), Q. Mucius Scaevola used to say during Cinna's reign of terror that he would rather see himself dead than march in arms against his *patria*.

[7] Cf. *Fam.* 16. 12. 1 (a letter to Tiro): "quo in discrimine versetur salus mea et bonorum omnium atque universae rei p. ex eo scire potes quod domos nostras et patriam ipsam vel diripiendam vel inflammandam reliquimus." Cicero was now unable to do what had been done against Statilius, Gabinius, Cethegus, Lentulus, and Catiline. Cf. Luc. 2. 541-43 (Pompey's comment):
> "nec magis hoc bellum est, quam quom Catilina paravit
> arsuras in tecta faces sociusque furoris
> Lentulus exertique manus vaesana Cethegi."

[8] 7. 62-64.

[9] 18.

[10] "Die augusteische Ausprägung der DEA ROMA," *Gymnasium* 59 (1952),

also shown that *patria,* a noble word with a noble history in poetry and oratory,[11] became a political catchword of Cicero and the opponents of Caesar, particularly after the latter's death when his murderers became the *conservatores patriae* and his avengers the *proditores patriae.*[12] Events to the end of the Republic continued as they had been when Lucretius wrote the introduction to his poem, for they succeeded one another "patriai tempore iniquo."[13]

But Vergil spoke for the Augustan age when he made the ghost of Anchises rebuke both Caesar and Pompey for the violence they did to their *patria*:

> ne, pueri, ne tanta animis adsuescite bella
> neu patriae validas in viscera vertite viris.[14]

The *patria* was their *patria communis,* and such was the spirit of the *pax Augusta*. Furthermore Vergil used the great speech of Anchises, not only to establish in literature the association of *Roma* and *Augustus*,[15] but also to confirm *Roma* as the synonym in the new age for the *res Romana* and indeed for something more. The "moribus antiquis stat res Romana virisque" of Ennius was expressed anew in the *Aeneid* by a *Roma* "felix prole virum" which would "bound her reign / With earth's wide bounds, her glory with the heavens" under the auspices of Romulus:

> en huius, nate, auspiciis illa incluta Roma
> imperium terris, animos aequabit Olympo,
> septemque una sibi muro circumdabit arces,
> felix prole virum.[16]

Of these and the following lines, in which Vergil expressed a novel

---

324-49, esp. 333: "ein Zusammenschiessen der einzelnen Gedanken zum Bilde einer *Roma-patria* zeigte sich nur in ganz seltenen, hochpathetischen Augenblicken, und an eine echte Vergöttlichung der ROMA in der Hauptstadt selber kann vollends in dieser Zeit durchaus nicht gedacht werden." The "patria communis" of *Cat.* 4. 18 had been amplified earlier in 63 B.C. to the "Roma, communis patria omnium nostrum" of *Leg. Agr.* 2. 86, but the personification of *Roma* was still more celebrated when Cicero chose to glorify that year in verse. For the possible or probable phrasing of his hexameter see Walter Allen, Jr., " 'O fortunatam natam...,' " *TAPA* 87 (1956), 130-46.

[11] Cf. the lament for Romulus after his death, Enn. *Ann.* 111-12 (Vahl.): "O Romule, Romule die, / qualem te patriae custodem di genuerunt" and, in Carbo's defence of L. Opimius, his judgment on the death of C. Gracchus as reported by Cic. *De Or.* 2. 106: "id iure pro salute patriae factum esse dicebat."

[12] Cic. *Fam.* 12. 3. 2: "(M. Antonius) ea dixit de conservatoribus patriae quae dici deberent de proditoribus." Knoche (above, note 10), 329, exclaims: "Kein Wunder, dass der ehrwürdige Begriff der *patria* auf diese Weise vollständig ausgehöhlt und wertlos wurde."

[13] Lucr. 1. 41.

[14] *Aen.* 6. 832-33.

[15] See my article, "Romulus, Roma, and Augustus in the sixth book of the *Aeneid*", *CP* 45 (1950), 1-12, esp. 8-10.

[16] Enn. *Ann.* 500 (Vahl.); Milton, *Paradise Lost* 12. 370-71; Verg. *Aen.* 6. 781-84.

idea of *Roma* and which Knoche rightly calls "den schönsten Ausdruck für seinen ROMA-Glauben,"[17] more will be said presently. But if the poet of the *Aeneid* revived with his "felix prole virum" and transferred to *Roma* the Ciceronian concept of the *patria* "quae communis est parens omnium nostrum,"[18] Horace with his "dulce et decorum est pro patria mori" echoed not only Tyrtaeus but Cicero in the *De Legibus*: "sed necesse est caritate eam [patriam] praestare, qua rei publicae nomen universae civitatis est; pro qua mori et cui nos totos dedere et in qua nostra omnia ponere et quasi consecrare debemus."[19]

It was in another "Roman" ode that the captured soldiers of Crassus, disgracefully married to Parthian wives and growing old in the service of the enemy, were said to have forgotten the symbols of their heritage, although Jupiter and the *urbs Roma* still endured:

> milesne Crassi coniuge barbara
> turpis maritus vixit et hostium
>   (pro curia inversique mores!)
>   consenuit socerorum in armis,
>
> sub rege Medo Marsus et Apulus,
> anciliorum et nominis et togae
>   oblitus aeternaeque Vestae,
>   incolumi Iove et urbe Roma?[20]

The exclamation of pain and disgust, "pro curia inversique mores," with which Horace passed judgment on this defection to the Parthian foe, cannot have failed to remind his contemporaries of another incident, more recent but similarly discreditable, which is told briefly by Appian, Plutarch, and Florus, and more fully by Lucan.[21] The last-mentioned devoted two hundred lines to narrating how the defeated and retreating Pompey recommended at Syhedra in Cilicia that he and his followers should turn to Parthia for support, and how Lentulus in an impassioned speech poured such scorn upon this remarkable proposal that it was defeated. If Caesar on the bank of the Rubicon showed effrontery with his "Roma, fave coeptis" at the end of his invocation of a number of Roman deities, what of Pompey who asked the blessing of *Roma* in the same words and on the startling assumption that the gods could grant her no greater joy than to annihilate the Parthian nation by having it brought as a combatant into her civil wars and thus involving it in his own misery?

[17] Above, note 10, 335.
[18] *Cat.* 1. 17, cf. *De Or.* 1. 196.
[19] Hor. *Carm.* 3. 2. 13; Tyrt. 6; Cic. *Leg.* 2. 5: and cf. *Fin.* 2. 60 and 76.
[20] Hor. *Carm.* 3. 5. 5-12.
[21] App. *BCiv.* 2. 12. 83; Plut. *Pomp.* 76; Flor. 2. 13 (4. 2) 51; Luc. 8. 256-455. Dio 42. 2. 5-6 found the story incredible. Its scene was placed in Cyprus by Plutarch.

"Roma, fave coeptis; quid enim tibi laetius unquam
praestiterint superi, quam, si civilia Partho
milite bella geras, tantam consumere gentem
et nostris miscere malis?"[22]

Earlier, before Pharsalia, Pompey besought his soldiers to imagine the supplications of dishevelled matrons, aged senators, and even *Roma* in her dread of a master:

"credite pendentes e summis moenibus urbis
crinibus effusis hortari in proelia matres;
credite grandaevum vetitumque aetate senatum
arma sequi sacros pedibus prosternere canos
atque ipsam domini metuentem occurrere Romam."[23]

To Pompey before and after his defeat *Roma* was still a personification of the city which could fear a human master or be the recipient of a doubtful boon from the gods.[24] To Caesar on the eve of his success she was the vision of *Dea Roma,* in her hour of distress it is true, but a goddess whose favor he could invoke at the end of an enumeration of deities which began with Capitoline Jupiter himself.

In addition to "Roma, fave coeptis," the employment of *instar* by both speakers is illuminating. Pompey commenced his speech at Syhedra thus to the numerous senators who had gathered around him in his flight:

"comites bellique fugaeque
atque instar patriae."[25]

Caesar addressed *Roma* as "summi o numinis instar." In its regular meaning, "the equivalent of,"[26] *instar* enabled Pompey to describe his senatorial comrades in war and exile as the equivalent of the Re-

[22] 8. 322-25.
[23] 7. 369-73. The matrons and senators of Rome were as dishevelled ("crinibus effusis" and "sacros ... prosternere canos") as the *patria* herself in 1. 188: "canos effundens vertice crines." For *Roma* letting her hair down in grief cf. Prop. 2. 15. 46; "lassa foret crines solvere Roma suos." As for "ipsam domini metuentem ... Romam," Lucan seems to have aimed this and similar barbs at Nero, cf. 5. 385-86: "namque omnis voces per quas iam tempore tanto | mentimur dominis, haec primum repperit aetas." Nero may have allowed himself to be called "dominus," cf. Suet. *Vitell.* 11. 2; Mart. 7. 45. 7.
[24] Personification of *Roma* in poetry goes back to Ennius, who had represented Scipio as "cum patria loquens" and as beginning a speech to her with "desine, Roma, tuos hostes" (Cic. *Fin.* 2. 32. 106; cf. *De Or.* 3. 167). For the personification in Pompey's mind see J. P. Postgate's revised edition of Book 7 (Cambridge 1913) and O. A. W. Dilke's revision thereof (Cambridge 1960) on vs. 373. Postgate more wisely than Dilke did not cite 1. 185 ff. as a parallel.
[25] 8. 262-63.
[26] So J. P. Postgate in his edition of Book 8 (Cambridge 1917) *ad loc.* See also K. Alt, "instar (Verg. *Aen.* 6. 865)" *MH* 16 (1959), 159-162 ("Beiträge aus der Thesaurus-Arbeit XI").

publican *patria* for which he had fought. But Caesar's use for the word was to leave no doubt concerning the godhead of *Roma*, "the equivalent of the highest *numen*."

This ambivalence of *Roma* (personification or deity) in the *De Bello Civili* was seen by W. E. Heitland, who remarked of Lucan:

> He attributes to her a divine character I 199—200 *summique o numinis instar Roma, fave coeptis*. He also personifies her in other places as VII 373 *atque ipsam domini metuentem occurrere Romam*, VIII 322 *Roma, fave coeptis*. Less striking instances I omit: but I conceive that I have shewn ground for believing that *Roma* was in Lucan's time recognized as a divinity, though her formal worship had not as yet been established in the city itself.[27]

Later scholars would deny *Roma* the divine character which Heitland inferred from her appellation in 1. 199-200, e.g. the Budé and Loeb translators render it by, respectively, "toi, l'égale des plus grandes déesses" and "thou, O Rome, as sacred a name as any."[28] However "summi numinis" is too precise an expression for this phrase to be so inadequately translated from serious poetry.[29] Ovid could adjure his mistress with "perque tuam faciem, magni mihi numinis instar" and make Aeneas say to the Sibyl "numinis instar eris semper mihi."[30] But the qualification "summi" warns the reader of the *De Bello Civili* to look higher.

The Vergilian description of *Roma* in the sixth book of the *Aeneid* provides the clue. Immediately after acclaiming her as the blest mother of heroes, "felix prole virum," Anchises proceeded to compare her with Cybele or the Magna Mater:

> qualis Berecyntia mater
> invehitur curru Phrygias turrita per urbes,
> laeta deum partu, centum complexa nepotes,
> omnis caelicolas, omnis supera alta tenentis.[31]

My chief argument concerning this whole passage in an earlier article was that the parallelism of "felix prole virum" with "laeta deum partu" suggested an equation of Augustus, the greatest son of *Roma*, with Jupiter, the greatest son of Cybele, Rhea, or the Magna Mater.[32] No doubt is left in this passage concerning what J. W. Mackail called "the canonization of Rome."[33] Vergil had personified *Roma* previously in

---

[27] *M. Annaei Lucani Pharsalia* ed. C. E. Haskins with an Introduction by W. E. Heitland (Cambridge 1887), p. l.

[28] A. Bourgery (1926) and J. D. Duff (1928).

[29] Serious poetry is specified because of *Priapea* 40. 4, but the meaning is sufficiently precise there too.

[30] *Am.* 3. 11. 47; *Met.* 14. 124.

[31] 784-87.

[32] Above, note 15. For Jupiter as the son of Cybele see *Aen.* 9. 80-103 and cf. 10. 252.

[33] In his edition of the *Aeneid* (Oxford 1930), p. xiv.

the first *Eclogue* and in the second book of the *Georgics,* but she now became a goddess like the turreted Berecyntian Mother, and Lucan went a stage farther in portraying her too as endowed "turrigero vertice."[34] In thus describing *Roma,* both Vergil and Lucan passed from personification to deification.[35]

In assigning a turreted crown to *Roma* for the first time in literature, Lucan was thus indebted to Vergil, just as Vergil himself had an original or at any rate a Roman inspiration on the part of Lucretius in mind for his turreted Cybele:

> muralique caput summum cinxere corona,
> eximiis munita locis quia sustinet urbis;
> quo nunc insigni per magnas praedita terras
> horrifice fertur divinae matris imago.[36]

It would seem, too, that Lucan as well as Vergil remembered these Lucretian lines, with "horrifice" suggesting Caesar's "horror" to him and "divinae matris imago" the "patriae trepidantis imago." For "caput summum" Bailey's (and the usual) translation is "the top of her head"; but this gives a facile and otiose meaning to "summum." A true parallel is provided by Lucretius elsewhere: "capitis summi praeclarum insigne," which means "the glorious emblem on a sovereign head."[37]

[34] For the Vergilian personifications see *Ecl.* 1. 24-25 and *Georg.* 2. 534-35. The line which Vergil slightly adapted from the latter context, "septemque una sibi *muro* circumdedit arces" was now reinforced in the simile by the suggestion of Cybele's mural crown. See *Proc. Camb. Philol. Assoc.* 172-174 (1939), 3-5, and my edition of Lucan 1 (Cambridge 1940 and 1955) *ad loc.* for my belief that the Vergilian comparison of *Roma* with the *Berecyntia mater* was Lucan's literary source for the turreted head of 1. 188. An artistic source is by no means so likely. Coin-types depicting turreted heads which can be identified for certain with that of *Dea Roma* are not to be found before Imperial times. In the first and second centuries A.D. they are not infrequent in the province of Asia, but in the West a noteworthy example appeared three years after Lucan's death, i.e. that of a denarius minted in Gaul in A.D. 68 with obv. ROMA and bust of *Roma* wearing a turreted and crested helmet, as she does four centuries later in the poems of Sidonius (2. 391-92; 5. 13-15), himself a native of Lugdunum. See *BMCRE* I, 294; pl. 50, no. 7; Mattingly and Sydenham, *RIC* I, 184, no. 6; pl. xiii, no. 206; J. M. C. Toynbee, *The Hadrianic School* (Cambridge 1934), 18, n. 6; 136; pl. ix, no. 17.

[35] F. Richter in Roscher's *Lexikon,* s.v. "Roma," 132, 53-57, introduces his citation of both passages, as well as of others concerning *Martia Roma,* with the words: "Bei Betrachtung des literarischen Materiales werden natürlich nur solche Stellen für uns in Betracht kommen, wo durch eine Personifikation deutlich gemacht ist, dass es sich um die *dea* Roma handelt." Knoche (above, note 10), 335, says of the Vergilian context: "ROMA, gleichsam eine *Troia renascens,* ist hier ganz Gestalt geworden; ihr Lobpreis ist uneingeschränkt der eines göttlichen Wesens."

[36] Lucr. 2. 606-9. J. Perret, "Le 'Mythe de Cybèle' (Lucrèce II, 600-660)," *REL* 13 (1935) 332-57, esp. 348-57, thought that Lucretius' source for the cult and attributes of Cybele was Roman and not Greek. At any rate this is the first appearance of a turreted Cybele in literature.

[37] 5. 1138. See the commentaries of Cyril Bailey (Oxford 1947) and W. E. Leonard and S. B. Smith (Madison 1942) *ad loc.* It is typical of Vergil that, in his first personification of *Roma*:

Thus "caput summum" provides an exact and important parallel for Lucan's "summi numinis instar" in its true sense of "the equivalent of the sovereign deity."

Those who are reluctant to believe that "summi numinis" in this passage denoted Cybele are best answered by Alexis of Thurium: τοῖς γὰρ ὀρθῶς εἰδόσι | τὰ θεῖα, μεῖζον Μητρὸς οὐκ ἔστιν ποτέ.[38] The Homeric Hymn to the Mother of the Gods began by calling her Μητέρα πάντων τε θεῶν πάντων τ' ἀνθρώπων. As Rhea she was described by Pindar as πάντων 'Ρέας ὑπέρτατον ἐχοίσας θρόνον and by Apollonius Rhodius as πολυπότνια whom all the other immortals revered.[39] But Vergil's successors thought of her mainly as the mother of the gods, e.g. Ovid in what Erato said:

> "illa deos," inquit, "peperit. cessere parenti
> principiumque dati Mater honoris habet."[40]

Silius Italicus too, no doubt with Lucan in mind, emphasized her "numen" as Claudia addressed her on her arrival in Italy at the mouth of the Tiber:

> "caelicolum genetrix, numen, quod numina nobis
> cuncta creas, cuius proles terramque fretumque
> sideraque et manes regnorum sorte gubernant."[41]

Thus "summum numen" was applied as naturally to the Magna Mater as to the "magnus pater," concerning whom Lucan elsewhere has a phrase corresponding to "summi numinis instar."[42] In his description of Pompey's grave he asked what visitor will not prefer it to the temple of Jupiter on the neighboring Mount Casius: "et Casio praeferre Iovi." Two lines later he added "nunc est pro numine summo | hoc tumulo Fortuna iacens," thus implying that, as an attraction, Pompey's "fortuna" in its tomb was the equivalent of Jupiter on his height.[43]

---

verum haec tantum alias inter caput extulit urbes
    quantum lenta solent inter viburna cupressi (*Ecl.* 1. 24-25),
"tantum" would appear to mean both "as high" and "as sovereign." Henceforward Augustan and later poets thought of *Roma* as "magna," "maxima," "maxima rerum," "caput orbis," "caput rerum," etc. See Franz Christ, *Die römische Weltherrschaft in der antiken Dichtung* (Stuttgart-Berlin 1938), esp. 83-89 on "Rom als Personifikation (Weltherrscherin) + Epitheta." The duality of meaning which Vergil gave to "tantum" in *Ecl.* 1. 24 is spelled out in Prop. 3. 11. 57: "septem urbs alta iugis, toto quae praesidet orbi."

[38] Stobaeus, *Florileg.* 79. 13. Cf. C. J. Fordyce, *CR* 54 (1940) 97.
[39] Pind. *Ol.* 2. 77; Ap. Rhod. 1. 1101-2, 1125.
[40] *Fast.* 4. 359-60.
[41] 17. 36-38.
[42] Jupiter was called "magnus pater" in Verg. *Aen.* 4. 238; Ov. *Met.* 7. 615-17; Val. Flacc. 5. 644, etc. Cf. H. Graillot, *Le Culte de Cybèle, Mère des Dieux* (Paris 1912), 195: "Elle est la Dame suprême, Despoina, Domina, comme Zeus est le suprême Seigneur; et seule elle a le droit de porter ce titre."
[43] 8. 851-61. *Summus* is again the epithet of Jupiter in 2. 34; 4. 110; and 9. 177-78; cf. Verg. *Aen.* 1. 380, 665; 6. 123; etc.

But, to return to the crossing of the Rubicon, Plutarch reports that Caesar on the previous night dreamed that he was having incestuous intercourse with his mother.[44] This was the dream which Suetonius ascribes in effect to 67 B.C., when Caesar was quaestor in Spain.[45] The interpretation offered to him was that his mother "non alia esset quam terra, quae omnium parens haberetur." It is an easy conjecture that Lucan, knowing this story, decided to invest it with epic decorum and therefore, as a republican sympathizer, introduced the "imago" as that of the *patria* which Cicero had described as the "communis parens omnium nostrum."[46]

Be that as it may, such was Lucan's artistry, or, more precisely, his sense of historical drama,[47] that he made the invader pause before ambition triumphed over fear. Then Caesar saw before him, not the *patria* of Cicero and the Republic of the past, but the *Roma* of Vergil and the Empire of the future.[48] So it was that he fortified his resolution, broke down the barriers of war, and crossed the Rubicon.

University of North Carolina
Chapel Hill

[44] *Caes.* 32.
[45] *Div. Iul.* 7.
[46] Knoche (above, note 10), 328, finds the image of the "mütterlichen, schutzbedürftigen, oft bedrohten und immer wieder sorgenden römischen *res publica*" very different from the Greek impressions of 'Ρώμη, e.g. that of a youthful and appetitive Amazon. "Ich fürchte," he adds, "ihre Kinder, die römischen Quiriten, hätten sich einer so leichtgeschürzten Mutter im tiefsten Herzen geschämt, wenn sie sich zu ihr in diesem Bilde hätten im Ernst bekennen sollen, wie sie da einherschritt, *non modo suris apertis, sed paene natibus apertis ambulans* (Varr. *Men.* [*Meleagri*] 301 B)." If there was a story afoot of any such *mater* appearing to Caesar in his dream, Lucan's desire to alter her appearance can be understood.
[47] For which Petronius, *Sat.* 118, would have criticized him: "non enim res gestae versibus comprehendendae sunt, quod longe melius historici faciunt." Later writers who allude to Lucan as a historian rather than a poet are mentioned in my edition (above, note 34), xxvii.
[48] An epic poet who had an eye to the mythological background of his subject, and with Vergil's example regarding Aeneas before him, might have brought about the intervention of Caesar's divine ancestress Venus (or Dione). See Suet. *Div. Iul.* 6 and cf. Petron. *BCiv.* 266-67: "primumque Dione / Caesaris acta sui ducit." But, with the *Roma*-passage in the sixth book of the *Aeneid* before him, the choice of the City, first personified and then deified as a truly Roman divinity, was most happy for a poet who virtually abandoned the traditional mythology of epic. As for *Roma*, Lucan and Vergil were followed, in language which recalls Cybele, by Martial 12. 8. 1-2: "terrarum dea gentiumque Roma / cui par est nihil et nihil secundum." But here the story of *Dea Roma* in Latin poetry must close for the present.

SPECULUM CAESARIS*

Robert E. Wolverton

According to Seneca the Younger (N. Q. V.18.4), Livy questioned whether the birth of Julius Caesar had been a blessing or an evil for Rome. Succeeding centuries have tended to reinforce Livy's doubt as men have found Caesar worthy of praise or worthy of blame for his efforts in creating what came to be called the Principate. It is the aim of this study to investigate what some of the earliest writers of the Principate thought or wrote about Caesar, the man and the god. The writings of five authors—the two Senecas, Velleius, Valerius Maximus, and Lucan—will be considered, in order to determine the nature of the legend of Caesar.

These five were selected because they are the better-known writers of the first half of the First Century A.D. and because they do indicate something of their own feelings about Caesar. Three types of references are employed: those dealing with Caesar's career, those which offer some glimpse of the author's own opinion of Caesar, and the titles or names by which the author refers to Caesar. We cannot, of course, know how accurately these authors reflect the over-all opinion of their own times, but from their writings it is possible to discern a sort of image or pattern of Caesar evolving. It is this literary image with which we shall concern ourselves.

Four conclusions emerge from these considerations: first, the authors, while they do give individualized judgments, tend to concentrate on certain facets of Caesar's life and career. Second, they seem to exercise some discretion in applying titles to Caesar. Third, interest in Caesar's civil war activities tends to increase, with a corresponding decrease of attention to his earlier campaigns, as the years go by. Finally, the absence of direct quotations from Caesar's works and the numerous discrepancies with what Caesar himself wrote are evidence that the authors made use of secondary source material available to them; this, in turn, suggests that Caesar's own attempts to make clear his actions and positions either proved unsuccessful or that, in the interval, his works had been allowed to slip into relative obscurity.

Seneca the Elder, although he is somewhat noncommittal with regard to Caesar, is included here, since he is a representative of the generation which witnessed the transition from Republic to Principate. His extant works reveal that he could see both good and bad features

* Based on a paper presented at the C. A. N. E. meeting, Wellesley College, March 25, 1960.

in the new era: in Republican times, men were more independent and courageous (*Suas.* 6,7), yet the new age had brought the benefits of peace and prosperity (*Con.* II.4,13; VI.6; X. *Praef.* 5). His considerations of Caesar indicate esteem for his clemency (*Suas.* 6.13; 7.1; *Con.* VI.8; X.3.1,5) and censure for his union with Pompey and Crassus (*Suas.* 6.12-13; 7.2). He refers to Caesar, the man, as *princeps* in two passages (*Suas.* 7.1,5) and to Caesar, the god, as *divus Iulius* in three (*Suas.* 2.22; *Con.* VII.3.9; X, *Praef.* 16).[1]

Velleius Paterculus in his *Historiae Romanae* presents a much fuller account of Caesar and his acts, beginning with a statement about Caesar's family and character (II.xli.1-2):

"Sprung from the most noble family of the Julii and tracing his descent from Anchises and Venus—a claim which is agreed upon by all scholars of antiquity—he was the most outstanding of all citizens in his personal appearance, the sharpest in vigor of mind, the most lavish in his generosity, beyond human nature and belief in courage, and much like Alexander the Great in the magnitude of his thoughts, his speed of fighting and his endurance of dangers . . . Caesar used food and sleep always for life, not for pleasure."

In tracing the career of Caesar,[2] Velleius, himself an ex-soldier, discloses profound respect for Caesar as a military man; the very words employed by Velleius give evidence of his admiration: *celeritas, festinatio, vigor, fulgor, virtus, vires, valentia, fiducia militum, industria*—all these are attributes of the brilliant and successful general. As remarkable as the energy of Caesar, however, was his clemency: *clementia, voluntas, misericordia, mitis, clementer, ignovit, ignoscere*—all these words are used to indicate Caesar's clemency, the greatest use of which was made after the battle of Pharsalia: "There was nothing more marvelous in that victory, nothing more magnificent, nothing more renowned than the fact that the country lost not a single citizen except those who had fallen in battle" (II.lii.6). Another attribute of the successful general is *fortuna*, which Caesar alternately followed (II.lv.1) and possessed (II.li.2; lv.4); *fortuna*, however, can arouse jealousy in others (II.lx.1), and it must yield to fate (II.lvii.3).

Velleius describes Caesar's position as one of power, *potentia*, while he was a triumvir and consul (II.xliv.1, 5; xlvii.2), and of pre-eminence,

[1] Of Caesar's acts, Seneca mentions his restoration of Laberius to the equestrian order (*Con.* VII.3.9), his creation of senators to replenish the ranks thinned by civil wars (*Ibid.*), and his possession of property (*Suas.* 7.5).

[2] II.xxxvi.2; xli-lix, *passim*; with the account found here, one may compare the two ancient Lives of Caesar (Suetonius and Plutarch), the modern biographies, *e.g.* M. Gelzer, *Caesar der Politiker und Staatsman* (2nd. ed., 1941), and the recent first-person works of Rex Warner, *The Young Caesar* (1959) and *The Imperial Caesar* (1960).

principatus, after the civil wars (II.lvi.3; lvii.1; *cf.* II.1.3).[3] In only three instances does the author suggest disapproval of Caesar's acts: his participation in the triumvirate (II.xliv.1-3), his possible involvement in Cicero's exile (II.xlv.2), and his possible bribery of Curio (II.xlviii.4-5). In stating the reasons for the Civil War, Velleius places the responsibility squarely upon Pompey and then upon Curio; throughout the pre-war negotiations, Caesar is recognized as the one trying to maintain peace at all costs, and, once the war has begun, as still hoping to effect a truce before anyone is killed (II.xlviii.1).

The deification of Caesar is never directly mentioned, although some of his accomplishments are put in the realm of the super-human: "The affairs carried on around Alesia were as great as a man would scarcely dare and no one but a god would complete" (II.xlvii.1).

To conclude, then, Velleius considers Caesar a man rather than a god, but a man swift and energetic in war, clement after battle, and interested both in his own and the state's welfare—in short, *tantus vir* (II.xlii.1; lvi.3).

Quite a different picture emerges from the *Facta et Dicta Memorabilia* of Valerius Maximus: Caesar was really a god incarnate. Witness these passages: "The heavenly will avenged itself; at once he crucified the captured pirates" (VI.9.15); "divine Julius, the most perfect peak of both heavenly will and human talent" (VII.8.3); "this bent the perseverance of the divine spirit" (II.10.7); "Caesar stretched his heavenly hands to the British island" (III.2.23);[4] "the safety of Cato was no small part of the divine works of Caesar" (V.1.10); "Flaccus, with insane pertinacity, resisted the divine power" (IX.2.4); "if the divine strength of Caesar had not checked the reddening blast . . ." (IX.15.1); "the very great clemency of the divine spirit was being separated from his mortal body, let down his toga and said, 'Mortal men do not die in this way, but the immortal gods seek again their abodes'" (IV.5.6); "You had not killed Caesar, Cassius, nor can any divinity be extinguished; but, by injuring him while he was still using a mortal body, you earned for yourself such a hateful god" (I.8.8); "then at once you, divine Julius, exacted just revenge for your heavenly wounds" (VI.8.4); "divine Julius, formerly the ornament of arms and the toga and now also of the stars" (III.2.19). In addition to being himself a god, Caesar was also under the protection of the gods (I.6.12; IX.8.2).

As a climax, what could Valerius do but pray? "Revering your altars and your most sacred temples, divine Julius, I pray that by your

[3] Caesar is also referred to as *imperator* (II.lv.4), and he and Pompey are called "the two heads of state" (II.liii.3) and "the greatest generals" (II.liv.1).
[4] Valerius also asserts that Caesar was not content to enclose his works with Ocean's shore and went to Britain (III.2.23) and that Caesar conquered all foreign and domestic foes (V.7.2).

propitious and favoring will you allow the misfortunes of such great men to be softened by their consideration of your example. For, on that day when you sat on a golden chair, dressed in a purple cloak—lest you appear to have scorned an honor which the senate had so zealously requested and offered—before you presented the desired sight of yourself to the citizens, we learned that you were accessible to the worship which you were already anticipating. We learned, also, that when a fat ox was sacrificed, no heart was found in the entrails, and that the seer Spurinna told you that this sign pertained to your life and counsel, both of which the heart represents. Then occurred the parricide committed by those men who, intent upon removing you from the number of men, added you to the council of the gods" (I.6.13).

Valerius cites the living Caesar as an *exemplum* in the categories of *vis eloquentiae* (VIII.8.3), *temeritas* (IX.8.2), *fortitudo* (III.2.19), *mansuetudo* (VI.2.11-12), *humanitas et clementia* (V.1.10), *verecundia* (IV.5.6) and *neccessitas* (VII.6.5). The dead Caesar appears in the section dealing with miracles; Cassius, at the battle of Philippi, saw Caesar, larger and more majestic than life, charging at him (I.8.8). Valerius also considered Caesar an outstanding soldier: "He taught those ready to be conquered how to conquer" (III.2.19), and he was himself an "unconquerable general" (VII.6.5). Valerius ascribes the Civil War to a rupture of the harmony between Pompey and Caesar, a break brought about by Pompey (I.6.12; 8.10) and by the death of Julia (IV.6.5).

The title most frequently applied to Caesar is *divus*; others include *princeps* (V.1.10; 7.2), *dux* (VII.6.5), *imperator* (IX.2.4), and *parens patriae* (VIII.11.2).[5]

The rather well-defined judgments of the foregoing authors are in contrast with the opinions of Seneca the Younger and Lucan, both of whom experienced difficulty in reconciling Caesar as a representative of the Stoic doctrines of government and humanity with Caesar as a staunch opponent of Cato, the Stoic saint.

Seneca's Caesar possesses clemency (*De Ira* II.23.4; III.30.4; *De Ben.* III.24.1; V.16.5), fortune (*De Cons.* 14.3), ingratitude toward Pompey (*De Ben.* V.16.5), love of glory and fear of a superior (*Ep.* 94.65), a desire to own the state (*Ep.* 14.12-13), hostility toward Bibulus

[5] The following events of Caesar's life are mentioned by Valerius: his capture by pirates (VI.9.15), accusation of Dolabella (VIII.8.3), two consulships (II.10.7; VIII.3.2), war with Pompey (I.6.12; I.8.10; IX.8.2; IX.11.4), defeat of Pompey at Pharsalia (I.5.6; IV.5.5), weeping over Pompey's head and reciprocal concern with Cato's glory (V.1.10), besieging of Flaccus at Ategua, Spain (IX.2.4), battle at Munda (VII.6.5), admitting of people into his gardens (IX.15.1), the episode with Caesetius (V.7.2), the omens before his death (I.6.13; VIII.11.2), death in the Curia (IV.5.6), and funeral (IX.9.1).

(*De Cons.* 14.1-2), wealth (*Ep.* 95.70) and property (*Ep.* 51.11).[6] When he speaks of the part of Brutus in the killing of Caesar, Seneca clearly reveals the difficulty mentioned above; he says that Brutus feared the name of king, yet he goes on to point out that the best state is that under a just king (*De Ben.* II.20.1-3).

Two passages indicate one of Seneca's reasons for disliking or distrusting Caesar, namely, that Caesar was a leader of the masses: "Caesar transferred war from Gaul and Germany to Rome, and that worshiper of the plebeians, that favorite of the people (*ille plebicola, ille popularis*) pitched camp in the Flaminian Circus, closer than Porsena had been" (*De Ben.* V.16.5). "Cato's whole life-time was spent in civil wars or in an age planning civil wars, and you could say that he, no less than Socrates, had reared himself for slavery, unless by chance you think that Pompey, Crassus and Caesar were the allies of liberty. . . . If you wish to imagine that period, you will see on one side the plebeians and the whole mob incited to revolution and, on the other, the optimates and the equestrian order, whatever was sacred and fine in the state; two things were left in the middle, the Republic and Cato" (*Ep.* 104. 29-31).

In Seneca's analysis of the causes of the Civil War, both Pompey and Caesar were culpable; he states that it was a struggle for *dignitas* (*Ep.* 14.13; *cf.* Caesar, *B.C.* I.4.4), and he lists Caesar's motives as fame, ambition, and no limit of excelling all other men (*Ep.* 94.65).[7]

Seneca refers to Caesar as *princeps furens* (*Ep.* 14.12), *imperator* (*De Ben.* V.24.2), and, in five instances, as *divus Iulius* (*De Ira* III.30.4; *De Ben.* II.20.1; V.24.1; *N.Q.* VII.17.12; *Ep.* 98.13). There may be some significance in the fact that the title, *divus Iulius,* never occurs in the nominative case. For the first time in this group of authors, *dictator* is employed to describe Caesar's position: Seneca says that Antony was ungrateful toward his dictator, when he proclaimed that Caesar had been justly killed (*De Ben.* V.16.5). Finally, mention is made of the comet which appeared at the time of the worship of Venus Genetrix and was believed to represent the soul of Caesar as it was received into heaven (*N.Q.* VII.17.2).

[6] There are also references to Caesar's campaigns in Spain, Africa and Egypt (*Con. ad Hel.* 9.7-8), his crossing to Britain and loss of Julia (*De Con.* 14.3), his alliance with Pompey and Crassus (*De Prov.* 3.14; *Ep.* 104.29-30), battle at Pharsalia (*De Ira* II.23.4; *Ep.* 71.8), and his death (*Con. ad Marc.* 14.1-3). For a more complete account of Seneca's Caesar, see W. H. Alexander, "Julius Caesar in the Pages of Seneca the Philosopher," *Transactions of the Royal Society of Canada, Series* III, XXXV (1941), Sec. II, 15-28.

[7] Two instances of criticism of Caesar are mentioned by Seneca: Pompeius Pennus, forced to kiss Caesar's shoe, expressed his outraged feelings (*De Ben.* II.12.1); and, when, in a play of Laberius, this line was spoken, "He must fear many whom so many fear," it caught the fancy of the people as though it expressed the national feeling (*De Ira* II.11.3).

The last author to be considered, the poet Lucan, reveals opinions somewhat akin to those of Seneca the younger but phrased in more ringing tones. Throughout the *Bellum Civile,* he roundly condemns Caesar's motives and most of his actions, even his granting of clemency (*e.g.,* I.183-5; II.519-21). On the other hand, Lucan seems more fascinated by Caesar than by any other figure in the period of which he is writing.[8] Like Velleius earlier, Lucan emphasizes the speed and energy of Caesar: *moras solvit, inpiger, ocior, nescia virtus stare loco, acer et indomitus, inpellens,* etc.; also, Caesar is the only character physically described in the poem (VII.729-60; X.332-495);[9] and again, the similes used to depict Caesar mark him as the most striking man of action (*e.g.,* I.205-12; VI.567-71).

Fortune, considered a deity by Lucan, leads Caesar in one campaign after another, as Caesar himself is made to assert (I.225-7).[10] Fortune is also included in Lucan's expressed causes of the Civil War; others given are the greatness of Rome, the triumvirs, the deaths of Crassus and Julia and the subsequent struggle for first place between Pompey and Caesar, the excessive luxury and greed of the Roman people, with bribery and corruption flourishing and might replacing right. (I.67-182).

The title most frequently applied to Caesar is *dux* or *ductor,* although both *dominus* (VI.234; IX.20) and *tyrannus* (X.343) appear. At one point, Caesar is pictured speaking of his accomplishments to Fortune: "I bore the fasces denied by war; no Roman power will be free from my titles, and no one except you, Fortune, (you who alone know my prayers), will know that I die a private citizen; and yet, I go to the Stygian shades having enjoyed offices, both as dictator and consul" (V.663-7).

Although Lucan never refers to Caesar as *divus,* he twice insinuates that Caesar has acquired status as a god, even as Jupiter. When he introduces Caesar in the poem, he compares him to a lightning bolt slashing its way through the sky, unchecked by anyone or anything, and collecting again its scattered fires (I.151-7). Later, Lucan says, "Mortal affairs are cared for by no gods. Yet for this disaster we have revenge, so far as gods can give satisfaction to countries: civil wars

[8] See, for example, H. C. Nutting, "The Hero of the *Pharsalia,*" *A. J. P.,* LIII (1932), 41-52.

[9] E. C. Evans, "Roman Description of Personal Appearance in History and Biography," *Harvard Studies in Classical Philology,* XLVI (1935), 43-84.

[10] To Caesar *fortuna* stood in contrast to *virtus;* the former he used to excuse or explain mistakes or failures, the latter was responsible for his successes. Lucan, as had Cicero, distinguishes *fortuna* as envisaged by Pompey and Caesar. *Fortuna,* as Cicero's speech *De Prov. Cons.* shows, was an integral part of Pompey's success, while the successes of Caesar were calculated and deliberate, as Cicero implies in the *Pro Marcello.* For a fuller discussion, see Elizabeth Tappan, "Julius Caesar's Luck," *C. J.,* XXVII (1931-1932), 3-14. Velleius Paterculus, by exaggerating the role of *fortuna* in Caesar's battles, contradicts what Caesar himself says: *e.g., B.G.* V.34.2, 44.14; *B.C.* I.52.3.

will create gods equal to those above; Rome will adorn their images with thunderbolts, rays and stars, and, in the temples of the gods, will swear by their ghosts" (VII.454-9). Here too the poet must be thinking of Caesar and his attempts to associate himself with Jupiter.[11] Such oblique references to Caesar have other parallels in the *Bellum Civile*; for example, in relating what Pompey's funeral did not have (VIII.729-35), Lucan clearly foreshadows the account of Caesar's funeral in Suetonius;[12] or again, by his constant criticism of Caesar's exercise of clemency (*e.g.*, II.517-21), he admits to Caesar's use of it.[13]

Two other criticisms of Caesar appear: he is accused of shedding crocodile tears as he gazes upon the head of Pompey (IX.1037-56) and of wasting time with Cleopatra, "the shame of Egypt, the deadly Fury of Latium" (X.59); so great was her beauty, however, that "even the hard heart of Caesar was consumed with flames" (X.71-2; *cf.* X.61; 105). The fact that Lucan is the first Silver Age author to speak of this affair between Caesar and Cleopatra will not seem surprising, when it is realized that Lucan is following through the civil wars in chronological order. Lucan, however, does more than speak of the affair; he denounces it with vehemence. The reason for his denunciation harks back to Book I, where he lists the causes of the wars. There, as it has been noted above, he condemns the Roman people for their love of luxury and the ill effects it has produced. Here, in Book X, he demonstrates that Egypt was a prime source of the evils which beset the Romans: *Explicuitque suos magno Cleopatra tumultu / nondum translatos Romana in saecula luxus* (X.109-10). He then describes in great detail the prevailing luxury of the Egyptian court, ranging from the elaborate architecture to the extravagant dishes served at the banquet (X.111-71). It was in Egypt, Lucan concludes, that Caesar learned to squander the wealth of a plundered world. And, while Caesar dallied in Egypt, the remnants of Pompey's armies were regrouping in Libya (X.78-9).[14]

The portrait of Caesar as the aggressor throughout the Civil War

---

[11] The most cogent arguments for Caesar's identifying himself with Jupiter have been presented by L. R. Taylor, *The Divinity of the Roman Emperor* (1931), pp. 68 ff.; a more reserved account is given by H. H. Scullard, *From the Gracchi to Nero* (1959), p. 154. This book is a most valuable addition to the literature dealing with the fall of the Republic and the emergence of the Empire; the reader will find excellent notes in the back, notes, which for reasons of space, can not be wholly included here.

[12] B. L. Ullman, "Caesar's Funeral in Lucan VIII.729-735," *C.Q.*, XV (1921), 75-77.

[13] C. C. Coulter, "Caesar's Clemency," *C. J.*, XXVI (1930-1931), 513-524. For an excellent discussion of *clementia*, as understood and used by Cicero and Caesar, see M. Treu, "Zur *clementia* Caesars," *Museum Helveticum*, V (1948), 197-217; for *clementia* as one of the virtues of Augustus and his successors, see M. P. Charlesworth, "The Virtues of a Roman Emperor: Propaganda and Creation of a Belief," *Proceedings of the British Academy*, XXIII (1937), 105-133.

[14] *Cf.* Scullard, *op. cit.*, p. 144 and the accompanying note 14, p. 408.

corresponds closely with Lucan's theme, the horrors of civil war (I.1-33). This theme cannot be handled with cool objectivity and logic; because of the extensive and irreparable damages brought on by civil war, the theme demands passionate and emotional treatment: *Quis furor, o cives, quae tanta licentia ferri?* (I.8). Despite the many factors responsible for such madness, there must be one to strike the first blow; the man who did this, in Lucan's mind, was Caesar when he crossed the Rubicon. Caesar is therefore presented as the aggressor from that point on; first Pompey, and then Cato, is the leader trying to stem Caesar's headlong rush. But Caesar's insatiable desire for war, like the lightning-bolt, is not to be checked. It is just this desire which rouses in Lucan such scorn of Caesar. Again and again the theme of the horrors of civil war is juxtaposed to Caesar's passion for civil war (*e.g.*, I.145-50; 184-5; 291-3; 393-4). Thus Caesar is the dominant figure in the *Bellum Civile*, "an essentially great man, capable of great deeds for the state, but turned from them by lust of war."[15]

Such is the literary legend of Caesar for the first half of the first century A.D. Although each author expresses his own judgment of Caesar, all the judgments share some points in common: Caesar was an outstanding military leader, a dispenser of clemency, a triumvir, and a primary cause of civil war. A majority of the authors speak of Caesar as a favorite of fortune and too fond of glory and indicate that Julia was a strong force for good by keeping Caesar and Pompey together in harmony. All accept the fact that Caesar was deified, but their acceptance takes various forms and methods of expression. Many reveal little evidence of any deep knowledge or understanding of Caesar's political career, and most of them express dismay at his assassination.

The assigning of titles to Caesar seems to have been judiciously carried out; *dux, ductor* and *imperator* were perfectly innocuous and appear often. *Dominus* and *tyrannus* may signify the extreme of his actual or desired power, but *rex* never occurs.[16] References to Caesar as *princeps* may denote both the authors' awareness of the title taken by Augustus and their acknowledgement that Caesar was, in some respects, the forerunner of the subsequent heads of the state. Such a designation, however, may be only an *ex post facto* recognition of Caesar's position, an attempt to make that position more prestigious and legal. Nowhere in *De Bello Civile* does Caesar refer to himself as *princeps*; he defines his position only as dictator and consul and points out that he resigned the dictatorship after ten days (II.21.5; III.1.1; III.2.1). The fact that *dictator* is only twice used by our authors, and

[15] E. M. Sanford, "Lucan and the Civil War," *C.P.*, XXVIII (1933), 121-127.
[16] For further discussions of Caesar's titles and/or intended titles, see Walter Allen, Jr., "Caesar's *Regnum* (Suet. *Iul.* 9.2)," *T.A.P.A.*, LXXXIV (1953), 227-236; Taylor, *op. cit.*, 67-74; Scullard, *op. cit.*, 153-158.

in neither case with any hint of objection, shows that the name and powers of that office had been effectively buried or forgotten.

It is of some interest to notice the many facts of Caesar's public and private life not mentioned by the authors; these omissions, in addition to the observation that many of the episodes included in the works mentioned above seem inconsequential to us, point to the existence of a well-established tradition emphasizing certain aspects of Caesar and neglecting others.[17] The tradition tended to produce a rather standardized legend of Caesar, a legend which would present him as an *exemplum* in certain categories. The legend, however, was still broad enough to allow each author to set forth his own evaluation of Caesar, the man and the god. The absence of direct references or quotations from Caesar's own literary works indicates that, even in this relatively short span of time, secondary sources were available for use by the authors.

One further observation may be made, namely, that the tone of the authors writing in the reigns of Augustus and Tiberius is in sharp contrast to that of the authors in the age of Nero. While those of the earlier period stress Caesar's Gallic campaigns more than the Civil War, Seneca the Younger and Lucan are much more preoccupied with Caesar as an instigator of and participant in civil struggles. Perhaps the atmosphere of Nero's reign was more charged with the thought of civil war than later historians have realized. The ill-fated conspiracy of Piso may have been the culminating effort of many months of planning and anticipating. And one can only wonder what effect, if any, the legend of Caesar had upon the known and unknown critics of Nero.[18]

Florida State University
Tallahassee

[17] Alexander, *op. cit.*, argues cogently for the existence of a "regime-tradition." Also see L. R. Taylor, *Party Politics in the Age of Caesar* (1949), 162-182 and R. Syme, *The Roman Revolution* (1939), 459-475; the reader may profit greatly by reviewing Syme's discussions of the new senators created by Caesar, 78-96 (*cf.* Seneca the Elder, *supra*) and the political jargon of the civil war period, 149-161 (*cf.* note 16, *supra*).

[18] How much the philosophical training of the writers in the age of Nero influenced their views on government is still a matter of some debate; see, *e.g.*, B. M. Marti, "The Meaning of the Pharsalia," *A.J.P.*, LXVI (1945), 352-376. Or, the political influence of Seneca the Younger may have encouraged the belief among some that literary opposition to political leaders, especially those safely dead, could be indulged in with impunity. Perhaps the early years of Nero's reign had not witnessed destruction of literary works, a practice which Augustus and his successors had found necessary (Syme, *op. cit.*, 486-489). The whole question of philosophical or Republican opposition, surely based on sentimental rather than logical grounds, is an extremely knotty one; the name of Caesar, however, could be used as a battle-cry for the malcontents, be they students of philosophy or admirers of the Republic. (R. Syme, *Tacitus*, Vol. II (1958), pp. 554-565, offers an illuminating discussion and examples.)

FREEDOM OF SPEECH IN THE EMPIRE—NERO

ROBERT SAMUEL ROGERS

Underlying the study which follows hereunder are two basic assumptions, as the reader may wish to call them, although in our conviction they are facts proven or susceptible of demonstration.

First, the Roman Empire was a rule of law. This we believe was proved beyond a peradventure by Fritz Schulz[1] when he showed that not only were the Emperors bound by every law which did not specifically exempt them, but further they considered themselves morally, even when they were not legally, bound by the laws.

Secondly, the present writer, in a monograph study of *Lèse Majesté under the Roman Emperors,*[2] will set forth that in the Roman juristic literature the definitions and descriptions of what constitutes treason (*maiestas*) include nothing of what the modern world calls *lèse majesté,* that is, criticism, ridicule, contempt, or abuse of the Head of State— with the solitary exception of the *deliberate* mutilation of *consecrated* statues of the Emperor. Now, since the Empire was a rule of law, this evidence of the juristic literature *ought* to be of itself sufficient reason for rejecting the famous dictum of Tacitus that Augustus was the first to prosecute libel and slander under the law of treason.[3] But so strong are prejudices and preconceptions that the Empire was an arbitrary, nay even a capricious, tyranny that this will not actually suffice. Therefore the monograph goes on to show that the overwhelming preponderance of our evidence displays a policy initiated by Julius, established by

[1] *Eng. Hist. Rev.* 60 (1945) 136-176, esp. 153-162.
[2] Pending its publication the reader may find adumbrations and excerpts, together with citation of evidence, in *CJ* 47 (1951/2) 114 f.; *TAPA* 82 (1951) 190-199; *Studies Presented to David Moore Robinson,* St. Louis, 1953, II 711-718; *TAPA* 83 (1952) 279-311; 86 (1955) 190-212; *JRS* 49 (1959) 90-94; *TAPA* 90 (1959) 224-237; *CP* 55 (1960) 19-23. It may be remarked specifically that the passage of Paulus customarily adduced by critics of this thesis needs to be read in conjunction with a passage of Modestinus. *Dig.* 48.4.7.3 f. (Modestinus): "Hoc tamen crimen iudicibus non in occasione ob principalis maiestatis venerationem habendum est, sed in veritate: nam et personam spectandam esse an potuerit facere, et an ante quid fecerit et an cogitaverit et an sanae mentis fuerit. nec lubricum linguae ad poenam facile trahendum est: quamquam enim temerarii digni poena sint, tamen ut insanis illis parcendum est, si non tale sit delictum, quod vel ex scriptura legis descendit vel ad exemplum legis vindicandum est. (4) Crimen maiestatis facto vel statuis violatis vel imaginibus maxime exacerbatur in milites." Cf. Paulus *Sent.* 5.29: "...quod crimen non solum facto, sed et verbis impiis ac maledictis maxime exacerbatur. (2) In reum maiestatis inquiri prius convenit, quibus opibus, qua factione, quibus hoc auctoribus fecerit: tanti enim criminis reus non obtentu adulationis alicuius, sed ipsius admissi causa puniendus est." It is evident that Paulus' radical abridgement has obscured, not to say distorted, the meaning.
[3] Tac. *Ann.* 1.72.4.

Augustus and Tiberius, maintained by their successors through the centuries. This policy was that the Emperor must refute criticism by argument, laugh when the joke is at his expense, ignore ridicule, disrespect, abuse, as beneath his dignity to notice. What the Emperor actually did when he was intolerably offended was, not prosecute for treason, but sever all friendly relations and intercourse with the offender, *amicitiam renuntiare*. This institution, traditional from the *mos maiorum* has already been discussed elsewhere.[4]

The thesis that *lèse majesté* was never prosecuted in the Empire will be to most so revolutionary an idea as will receive only the most reluctant acceptance. It is a large order to ask the present reader to take it on faith. Yet exactly that is asked of him, so that in this article we may look at the more particular evidence that freedom of speech did obtain under Nero, while noting incidentally some of the Neronian evidence of the larger thesis just enunciated.

Seneca in the *de Clementia*, written in 55 or 56, says that there was now complete freedom except only of destroying self, and enjoins that rulers must in self-restraint forgo that free speech which even the humblest citizen enjoys. And he thus admonishes his imperial pupil:

We now advise the *princeps* that when he is evidently injured he hold anger under control and refrain from punishing if he safely can, and if not, be moderate and far more placable regarding wrongs done himself than those done others. For . . . it is magnanimity to endure wrongs when one has supreme power, and nothing is more glorified than a *princeps* wronged with impunity.[5]

Dating so early in the reign this might well be discounted and dismissed as composite of wishful thinking and pious hope, if it stood alone. But it does not stand alone. Supported by evidence, both general and particular, of other sources, it must be reckoned as having validity.

Suetonius writes of Nero:

It is remarkable and if you will especially noteworthy that amid these disasters and misfortunes he bore nothing with greater patience than the curses and insults of men and that he was not more clement toward any persons than toward those who attacked him by spoken word or lampoons. . . . But he did not search out their authors, and certain persons denounced by informers to the Senate he forbade to be punished very severely.[6]

The suppression of the Pisonian conspiracy provoked public attacks on Nero for the numerous executions. He took the attitude dictated by the traditional policy of Augustus and Tiberius, that serious criticism

---

[4] Rogers, "The Emperor's Displeasure—*Amicitiam Renuntiare*," *TAPA* 90 (1959) 224-237.
[5] Sen. *de Clem.* 1.20.
[6] Suet. *Nero* 39.1 f.

must be refuted by serious argument. He met the criticism with a speech in the Senate and an edict to the people, together with publication of the minutes of the trial proceedings in his Court, including testimony of witnesses and confessions of defendants. And Tacitus concludes this account with the comment that there was no question at the time in the minds of those who had a care for the truth, of the fact of the conspiracy, and that exiled convicts, restored after Nero's death, admitted their guilt.[7] Nero's refutation of the criticism had been valid.

We have noticed the evidence of Suetonius that Nero ignored abuse. The occasion which most produced abusive attack was the assassination of Agrippina, and Dio specifically asserts that Nero paid no attention. We read:

When Nero entered Rome after the murder of his mother, people paid him reverence in public, but in private, so long at least as any could speak their minds with safety [Dio never mentions when and how it subsequently became unsafe], they tore his character to shreds. . . . people could even be heard saying in so many words that Nero had put his mother out of the way; for information that certain persons had talked to this effect was lodged by many men whose purpose was not so much to destroy the others as to bring reproach on Nero. Hence he would admit no suit brought on such a charge, either because he did not wish that the rumour should thereby gain greater currency, or because he by now felt contempt for anything people said.[8]

Or, we may add, because it was the traditional imperial policy to pay no attention to abusive attack.

In A.D. 66 Publius Clodius Thrasea Paetus was brought to trial. There is no question in our mind, and we believe we have earlier demonstrated,[9] that the *indictment* was for high treason. But Tacitus *says* that the prosecutor *said* that Nero had long hated Thrasea because:

1) when the Senate voted a *supplicatio* after Agrippina's death, Thrasea walked out of the House;
2) he had neglected the Juvenalia of 59, but had sung a tragic role in a festival at his native Padua;
3) he had moved leniency for a man convicted of libeling Nero in 62 (the case, *as Tacitus reports it,* is not historical) ;[10]
4) he had absented himself from the voting of divine honors to Poppaea, and from her funeral, A.D. 65;
5) he had not taken the oath of allegiance on 1 January, presumably 66;
6) though XVvir he had not attended the undertaking of the *vota*;
7) he had never sacrificed for Nero's health nor for his heavenly voice;

[7] Tac. *Ann.* 15.73.1-3.
[8] Dio 61.16.1, 3.
[9] *TAPA* 8⸱ (1952) 285-291.
[10] Cf. Rogers, "The Tacitean Account of a Neronian Trial," in *Studies ....* Robinson (note 2 *supra*).

8) he had not been in the Senate-House for three years;
9) when Silanus and Vetus were convicted of treason, 65, he was absent serving his own clients in their private suits.[11]

But on none of these earlier occasions has Tacitus in his annalistic narrative given any indication that Nero had said by way of censure or done by way of punishment anything whatsoever to Thrasea. The historian *has*, however, recorded that in 63 Thrasea was forbidden attendance at Antium upon the birth of Poppaea's child, that is, *amicitiam renuntiare*; that a reconciliation followed; that again, in 66, Thrasea was excluded from the reception for Tiridates. It is clear that Thrasea's *reported* offenses went quite unpunished, but that others, undescribed and unmentioned, brought withdrawal of Nero's personal favor.[12]

Mention of Nero's "heavenly voice" (which Juvenal says[13] sounded like a rooster pecking a hen in the barnyard) inevitably recalls the priceless story of Apollonius of Tyana, surely one of the most delightful tales in the whole history of the Empire. The Cappadocian philosopher, like Saint Paul and at almost the same time, with companions came to port at Puteoli and moved on to Rome.

They put up at an inn close to the gate, and were taking their supper, for it was already eventide, when a drunken fellow with a far from harsh voice turned up as it were for a revel; and he was one it seems who was in the habit of going round about Rome singing Nero's songs and hired for the purpose, and anyone who neglected to listen to him or refused to pay him for his music, he had the right to arrest for violating Nero's majesty. And he carried a harp and all the outfit proper for a harpist, and he also had put away in a casket a second-hand string which others had fastened on their instruments and tuned up before him, and this he said he had purchased off Nero's own lyre for two minas, and that he would sell it to no one who was not a first-rate harpist and fit to contend for the prize at Delphi. He then struck up a prelude, according to his custom, and after performing a short hymn composed by Nero, he added various lays, some out of the story of Orestes, and some from the Antigone, and others from one or another of the tragedies composed by Nero, and he proceeded to drawl out the airs which Nero was in the habit of murdering by his miserable phrasing and modulations. As they listened with some indifference, he proceeded to accuse them of violating Nero's majesty and of being enemies of his divine voice; [and now note well the conclusion of the story] but they paid no attention to him.[14]

One of Nero's stage roles, that of Nauplius, evoked an epigram of Lucilius: "A Greek city once emptied, my Lord Caesar, when Hegelochus arrived to sing the part of Nauplius. Nauplius is ever calamity to the

[11] Tac. *Ann.* 16.21-22.1.
[12] Tac. *Ann.* 15.23.5; 16.24.1; cf. *TAPA* 90 (1959) 227 f.
[13] Juv. 3.91.
[14] Philostr. *Apollon.* 4.39 (Loeb).

Greeks, sending great waves against their ships, or having a lyre-singer for his role."[15]

Lucilius wrote also: "You danced the whole programme according to the book, but, omitting the one most important action, you displeased us mightily. For dancing Niobe you stood like stone, and again as Capaneus, you fell, stricken suddenly; but as Canace you were less satisfying, for you had her sword and yet you left the stage alive—which is not according to the book." Both Niobe and Canace, we know, were in Nero's repertoire.[16]

Cichorius, discussing Lucilius' epigrams,[17] concluded that these two must be dated early in the reign and criticize some actor of the period. For it was to him unimaginable that the verses criticize Nero, or even another actor after Nero had taken up those roles. But Cichorius, born in 1863, had lived in a time and place in which *lèse majesté* was a serious matter; he was able to forget or ignore Suetonius' categorical statement that Nero cared not at all about lampoons.[18] We, remembering that evidence, feel very sure that Lucilius' epigrams were directed at the Emperor-Artist himself (one of them apostrophizes him), need not belong to the early years, and document a role, Capaneus, which is not mentioned in our other sources.

Thus we come to the area of literature and the question, perhaps for us the most interesting, the most significant, the most important: Was literature free? There was a very considerable literary production in the years that Nero the Artist and Patron of the Arts occupied the Empire's throne. It seems to have been quite untrammeled.

To be sure, Calpurnius Siculus and the authors of the Einsiedeln fragments wrote in a manner far too gratulatory to provoke a ruler's displeasure; and Columella's subject matter was fairly remote from any criticism of the powers. Whether Persius attacked Nero or not is a debatable and debated question. But Petronius' satire, in general at least, if hardly in particular detail, reflected adversely on Nero, his society, and his times. Yet it was a personal grudge of Tigellinus, according to Tacitus,[19] and alleged connections with one of the Pisonian conspirators, not the *Satyricon,* which brought downfall to Petronius. Seneca's poems, letters, and dialogues contain almost innumerable laudatory references to Cato, the *aetas Catoniana,* and the *libertas* of that age. Tacitus[20] asserts that among the criticisms of Seneca was that he had increased poetical output after Nero became a poet, but has no slightest hint that *what* Seneca wrote was basis of the charges against

[15] *Anth. Gr.* 11.185.
[16] *Anth. Gr.* 11.254.
[17] Cichorius, *Röm. Studien,* 373 f.
[18] Cf. *supra.* n.6.
[19] Tac. *Ann.* 16.18.5.
[20] Tac. *Ann.* 14.52.3.

him. And there was Thrasea's *Life of Cato*; not even Tacitus, rehearsing the past misdeeds of Thrasea, in the purported indictment by Cossutianus Capito, mentions the biography among his offenses.[21]

But the younger Pliny, cataloguing the writings of his uncle, Pliny the Elder, dates the work *Dubii Sermonis* to the last years of Nero "when literary composition of a more liberal sort was dangerous."[22] One might wonder just what Pliny meant by "omne studiorum genus paulo liberius et erectius," for by his own account his uncle's historical work on the *German Wars* and his *Studiosus*, treatise on the training of the orator, would appear to have been composed under Nero, though not in the last years. But whatever Pliny meant, it matters not at all. For he himself has completely damned himself as witness either for or against any Emperor. In the *Panegyric* he writes: "The good citizen's first duty toward an excellent Emperor [*scil.* Trajan] is to attack Emperors unlike him; for he will not love good Emperors enough who does not hate bad ones as much as he should." We are very sure that Pliny did his best to perform the first duty of a good citizen, and will not suppose that his uncle had been inhibited from writing anything he wished.[23]

But the preëminent example, in the period, of the freedom of literature is Lucan's *de Bello Civili*. For not only can Lucan magnify and glorify the Pompeys and Brutus and Cato; he is anti-Caesarian, anti-monarchial, and anti-imperial. He could even write of Cato: "Behold the true Father of his Country, most worthy, Rome, of your altars, by whom you will never feel it shame to swear, and whom, if ever you stand yoke-free, you will exalt to godhead." It is true that all was not published in the poet's lifetime; but doubtless much was delivered in *recitatio*, which amounts to the same thing. Not only was the public reading customary, but Suetonius says specifically that Lucan did read from this epic.[24]

Lucan made his début as a poet at the Neronia in 60 with a "Praise of Nero." Then, visiting and resident in Athens, he was recalled by Nero to the capital, became *amicus Caesaris* in the Emperor's suite, and received the quaestorship before his eligible age. But, Suetonius says, he did not continue in the Emperor's favor—"non tamen permansit in gratia." The phraseology is in the language of *amicitia Caesaris*; this interpretation is made certain by Vacca's more specifically technical wording: "inimicum sibi fecit imperatorem." Suetonius explains the breach between them: Lucan took offense because, when he was giving a public reading, Nero suddenly and with the sole deliberate purpose of throwing cold water on the performance, but pleading a called meet-

[21] Cf. *supra*, n.11.
[22] Pliny *Ep.* 3.5.5.
[23] Pliny *Pan.* 53.2.
[24] Luc. *BC.* 9.601-604; Suet. *Luc. ad init.*

ing of the Senate, walked out: "aegre ferens, *quod Nero se* (Reiff.) recitante subito ac nulla nisi refrigerandi sui causa indicto senatu recessisset. . . ." Now this must certainly be quotation of Lucan's own indignant comment immediately after the incident. Suetonius has accurately repeated a source which preserved the expression of the poet's exasperation. So, Suetonius continues, Lucan thereafter indulged in hostile words and hostile actions, and finally became one of the leaders of the Pisonian conspiracy.[25]

Tacitus, commencing to narrate that conspiracy, says that Lucan brought to it "lively hatreds" stemming from "personal reasons." Explaining the reasons, he wrote, "famam carminum eius premebat Nero prohibueratque ostentare vanus adsimilatione . . ." This could be interpreted as meaning "Nero tried to repress the fame of his poems and had restrained the display of his talent, vaingloriously matching himself with Lucan." But the historian probably intended to be, and he has always been, understood as saying, "Nero suppressed the fame of his poems and had forbidden him to display his talent."[26] So Vacca understood it, writing a biography of Lucan, and elaborating Tacitus' damnation of Nero. "The Emperor with ambitious vanity [echoing Tacitus' 'vainglorious matching'] claimed for himself the principate not only of men but also of the arts and Lucan was forbidden [*interdictum est* reflects Tacitus' *prohibuerat* but without its ambivalence] both the writing of poetry and the pleading of court cases." The last is rather silly, for Vacca himself indicates that the nearest Lucan came to the courts was to compose two declamations, one in defense, one in prosecution of the defendant to an indictment for murder in A.D. 58.[27]

According, then, to Tacitus and Vacca, but *not* according to Suetonius quoting (we believe) Lucan, Nero "suppressed Lucan's fame and forbade him to display his talent." *How* did Nero do that? Exactly, precisely, *what* did he do? What *could* he do? There was no law under which he could indict and prosecute; there is *nothing* in the law of treason which will apply here. If Lucan plans to give a *recitatio* of his work, what can prevent? There will not be available a salon in the imperial palace, but Lucius Calpurnius Piso, or another, will provide. Just clap him in jail! It cannot be done. The Roman Empire is a rule of law, not a twentieth century totalitarian dictatorship. Nero could attend the *recitatio* and ostentatiously walk out in the middle. He did. Nero could say to Lucan, "We are displeased; We terminate Our favor toward you; the doors of the Palace are closed to you." He did that.

[25] Suet. *Luc.*; Vacca *Vit. Luc. med.*
[26] Tac. *Ann.* 15.49.2 f.
[27] Vacca, "Quo [*scil.* imperatore] ambitiosa vanitate, non hominum tantum, sed et artium sibi principatum vindicante interdictum est ei poetica, interdictum est etiam causarum actionibus." Cf. *ibid. ad fin.* "prosa oratione in Octavium Sagittam et pro eo."

Nero could say to the litérateurs, "If you will compare his stuff with the product of Our genius, you will realize that he is nothing but a miserable poetaster." He probably did that too; for Tacitus says he was "vanus adsimilatione." What more, what else, can he do? Nothing. Not until Lucan became an active leader of the Pisonian conspiracy.[28]

There was freedom of speech in the Roman Empire, even when it was ruled by Nero.

Duke University
Durham

[28] Suet. *Luc.*; Tac. *Ann.* 15.49.2; 15.70.1.

EFFECTS OF ROMAN CAPITAL INVESTMENT IN BRITAIN UNDER NERO

MARY FRANCIS GYLES

Buchanan and Ellis point out that the term "underdeveloped area" is relative. They write: "The citizen of first century Rome was materially poorer than today's resident of Copenhagen or Columbo. But he was not poor compared with people living on the outskirts of the then Roman world, for example in Germany or Macedonia."[1] While it might be interesting to argue about the material well-being of the Roman citizen in the light of Petronius and Juvenal, it is presently more important to accept the general truth of the statement and emphasize the fact that Rome, and Roman Italy, represented the "developed" economy in the mid-first century A.D. Fringe areas like Germany, Macedonia and the newly conquered province of Britain must by contrast be labeled "underdeveloped areas."

But did an ancient underdeveloped area share any characteristics which are common to those so labeled in the twentieth century? What common patterns[2]—if any—can be discerned in the economic growth of underdeveloped areas, ancient or modern? Can modern economic theory be successfully used to gain increased understanding of the expanding economy of the early Roman empire? In a short paper only an attempt to answer these questions can be made; an initial experiment to suggest the fruitfulness of such an inquiry to historian and economist alike. To the one it may demonstrate that economic theory may be useful, at least as a guide to thought, in Roman history. To the other it may indicate the possibility of testing general theory in a larger framework.

The area to be explored and the theory to be applied must be selected and rigidly limited. Roman Britain has been chosen because of the evidence readily available from archaeological, numismatic and literary sources, and because its beginnings as a province can be, in a sense, isolated in space and time. Theories dealing with the economic development of underdeveloped areas are several, but Rostow's "stages" (pre-conditions, setting and take-off) seem most useful as an experimental tool to explain the development in Britain from the effective conquest under Claudius through the principate of Nero (43-68 A.D.).

[1] Norman S. Buchanan and Howard S. Ellis, *Approaches to Economic Development* (New York, 1955), 4.
[2] Philip Sheinwold, "Conversation," November 2, 1961 notes that "one cannot talk of *the* pattern of economic growth, but must rather think of a box of tools from which some may be selected to employ in developing the resources within any given area. This is necessary since what constitutes a resource depends on the place, time and popular need."

It must be understood clearly that: (1) Rostow's theory is used as theory—not as a body of accepted principles, but (2) it must be assumed for the purpose of the experiment that its major premises are acceptable. It must also be clear that statistical methods for the measurement of real changes in ancient economic growth (for example in per capita income) are totally lacking or have yet to be devised. Within these limitations it may be said that Rostow's preconditions for sustained[3] growth were met in Britain shortly after the conquest, and the setting was provided in the reign of Nero in whose later years the take-off occurred.

To use Rostow's theory accurately it must first be determined to which of the two "cases" or types of underdeveloped economies Britain originally belonged. To the first case is assigned parts of modern Asia, the Middle East and Africa, where population tends to be large, land area limited and the hand of tradition heavy. To the second case belong the Americas and Australia, where the population was sparse, the land area great and tradition less binding. Britain, at the time of the Roman conquest, may easily be shown to belong to the second case.[4] Of this case Rostow writes:

the process of their transition to modern growth was mainly economic and technical. The creation of the preconditions for take-off was largely a matter of building social overhead capital—railways, ports and roads—and of finding an economic setting in which a shift from agriculture and trade to manufacture was profitable; for in the first instance, comparative advantage lay in agriculture and the production of food-stuffs and raw materials for export.[5]

Conceived, of course, in terms of the developed Roman economy and technological achievement, Roman Britain received the necessary investment of social overhead capital, found the economic setting as a part of the Roman empire and made a remarkable shift to manufacture within the time span given.

Higgins provides a detailed list of criteria, including economic, demographic, cultural and technological characteristics of underdeveloped areas.[6] He makes more specific Rostow's point about the reliance on agriculture, mining and forestry to provide both for local

[3] Economic theorists seem to view the idea of "sustained growth" as infinite, but I shall use it finitely here to refer to the next two centuries of imperial economic expansion. Factors of change in the later empire need separate consideration, though Britain may have suffered less change because of them than many other areas of the empire. See note 42.
[4] R. G. Collingwood, "Roman Britain," *The Economic Survey of the Roman Empire* III, edit. by T. Frank (Baltimore, 1937), 9-10. The density and distribution of population was confined chiefly to areas of lighter soils. The people only "nibbled at" the dense forest cover on the heavy lowland soils.
[5] W. W. Rostow, *The Stages of Economic Growth* (Cambridge, 1960), 17-18.
[6] Benjamin Higgins, *Economic Development* (New York, 1959), 11-13. See also Lyle W. Shannon, edit. *Underdeveloped Areas* (New York, 1957), passim.

consumption and for export. He adds much detail, including: poor housing and inadequate sanitation, little or no savings except among landholders who do not invest them, little trade on a per capita basis, a weak or non-existent middle class, and traditional behavior patterns. Hirschman, concerned primarily with Latin America (which also belongs in Rostow's second case), adds:

It is likely that total mobilizable savings in such an economy exceed total investing capacity. The excess may actually show up in unadulterated forms such as hoarded gold or foreign exchange; more likely an excess of potential over actual savings may be indicated by luxury consumption of the rich, by occasional large-scale spending and gifts even among the poor, and by considerable amounts of time devoted to leisure and similar phenomena ubiquitous in underdeveloped countries.[7]

But whatever the difference in detail, basic agreement has been reached on the characteristics of an underdeveloped area. Agreement is also expressed on the absolute need for social overhead capital to create the preconditions for change, or take-off.[8] It is, too, a matter of common consent that once an area has successfully made the transition, manufacturing and its products increase, new industries appear, per capita income rises and the total volume of trade increases. In other words, a period of sustained growth ensues marked by changes of many types. But change, as Hirschman notes, does not occur without hardship: "it brings disruption of traditional ways of living, of producing, and of doing things, in the course of which there have always been many losses; old skills become obsolete. Old trades are ruined. . . ."[9]

One is inevitably reminded of the words Boudicca is supposed to have used in stirring revolt against the Romans in 61: "How much better is poverty with no master than wealth with slavery" (Cass. Dio 162.3 cf. Tacitus *Ann.* 14.13 and *Agric.* 15).[10] But a view must first be gotten of the Briton's poverty before examining his newfound wealth.

Strabo, a few years before the conquest, wrote that Britain produced grain, cattle, gold, silver, iron, hides, slaves and clever hunting dogs (4.5.2). Tacitus remarked:

The soil can bear all produce except the olive, the vine, and other natives of warmer climes, and it is fertile. Crops are slow to ripen but quick to grow, both facts due to one and the same cause, the extreme moistness of land and sky. Britain yields gold, silver and other metals, to make it worth conquering (*Agric.* 12).

[7] Albert O. Hirschman, *The Strategy of Economic Development* (New Haven, 1958), 37.
[8] *Ibid.*, 86.
[9] *Ibid.*; see also Rostow, *op. cit.*, 46-52.
[10] The causes of the revolt are variously given but sources agree that financial motives play a part. See note 20 and *infra*.

The archaeology of pre-conquest Britain supports this catalog of exports. Richmond accounts for the probable origin of each item on Strabo's list,[11] and C. and J. Hawkes comment on the discovery of iron shackles confirming the sale of slaves.[12] All are raw materials; the products of forest, farm, mine and war.

But areas of Britain differed greatly in the period between Caesar's invasion and Claudius' conquest. The expansion and solidification of Roman control over Gaul sent several groups of war-like refugees to Britain. The newcomers (Belgae, Atrebates and others) hewed out kingdoms for themselves at the expense of the more peaceful, or at least weaker, inhabitants. Perhaps the most powerful leader among the invaders was Cunobelinus, who overcame his neighbors the Trinovantes and established his capital of Colchester (Camulodunum) on their land. His sons warred with one another and with surrounding tribes, and the victims of these wars often ended in the Roman slave market, where they doubtless sold cheaply because of their lack of skills (Strabo 4.5.2).

However, Cunobelinus and his heirs, along with other kings of southern and eastern Britain, coined their own money during these years. Sutherland points out that little or no bronze was current in these issues,[13] and Richmond perceptively notes that the local currencies were of such denominations to be indicative of a foreign trade mostly in luxuries.[14]

Towns were few, and not to be considered true towns in the Mediterranean sense. Colchester was a sprawling agglomeration of scattered habitations within a twelve square-mile area bounded by dikes.[15] Most of the inhabitants of Britain lived on upland farms of small size. The refugees from Gaul introduced improved ploughs, querns and other equipment in the regions they conquered, but peoples of the north and west continued to use cruder tools. At best the crop-yield per acre must have been small, though perhaps Strabo's description of the Briton's poor livelihood may be exaggerated. He wrote:

Their habits are in part like those of the Celti, but in part more simple and barbaric—so much so that, on account of their inexperience, some of them, though well supplied with milk, make no cheese; and they have no experience in gardening or other agricultural pursuits.

[11] I. A. Richmond, *Roman Britain* (Penguin, 1955), 12-13.
[12] Christopher and Jacquetta Hawkes, *Prehistoric Britain* (Penguin, 1937), 160.
[13] C. H. V. Sutherland, *Coinage and Currency in Roman Britain* (Oxford, 1937), 4.
[14] Richmond, *op. cit.*, 11.
[15] *Ibid.*, 12; see also C. F. C. Hawkes and M. R. Hull, "Camulodunum," *Reports of the Research Committee of the Society of Antiquaries of London* XIV (1947).

He adds:

The forests are their cities, for they fence in a spacious circular enclosure, make huts for themselves and also pen up their cattle, not however with the purpose of staying a long time (4.5.2. cf. Caesar *de bell. gall.* 5.14 and Diodorus 5.21).

Overland transportation was poor, though rough tracks existed,[16] and items of Roman trade, plentiful in the south and east, reached the north and west in a very thin stream.

"And they have powerful chieftains in their country," says Strabo (4.5.2). The tribal society permitted the existence of a well defined aristocracy, or group of chiefs, who lived largely on rents collected from their followers. They strove to obtain imported luxuries and, from the evidence of their graves, succeeded. They also displayed the finest native-made weapons and trappings, but as C. and J. Hawkes write (confirming Strabo), the aristocrats

probably passed their everyday lives in squalor. Their houses were of the simplest—round huts lacking in domestic amenities. It was this combination of lavish personal display with graceless living that the Greeks and Romans despised in their barbarian neighbours.[17]

The quantities of wine jars found in chiefs's tombs and in other excavations prove that wine was the largest import. But other luxuries were popular also. Strabo says that the Britons bought ivory, chains and necklaces, amber, glass vessels and other pretty wares of that sort (4.5.3). Archaeologists have found beautiful pottery, silver and other fine metal wares, occasional gem stones, statuettes and medallions. All the evidence confirms the view that pre-conquest Britain exhibits the characteristics agreed upon as typical of an underdeveloped economy. Luxury consumption obtained by foreign trade was high on the part of the rich, except in distant areas of the island. No middle class is to be seen, and the majority of the population lived on poor farms and under miserable conditions.

The Roman legions, entering in 43, battered their way quickly across the island to the edge of Wales. By 47 they were stationed along that border in the west, and at Lincoln in the north.[18] Few troops remained in the rough square of the new province, and only one colony

---

[16] H. Goodwin and E. H. Willis, "Cambridge University Natural Radiocarbon Measurements II," *American Journal of Science, Radiocarbon Supplement* II (1960) 63-64. These tracks date to the late Bronze Age. For trade with north and west Britain see Richmond, *op. cit.*, 16.

[17] Hawkes, *op. cit.*, 134.

[18] R. G. Collingwood, *Roman Britain,* 2nd ed. (Oxford, 1932), 20. Also Bernard W. Henderson, "Roman Legions in Britain," *English Historical Review* (1903), 1-23. Collingwood estimates that about 100,000 soldiers, traders, officials and camp-followers came with the Romans into Britain.

of veterans was placed there—at Colchester. A Roman procurator spent much of his time at the new, but rapidly growing, mart of London.[19] St. Albans, Dover, Hythe, Canterbury, Winchester, Bath and other towns sprang up. Ports were improved and harbor facilities increased. In the wake of the legions, or along with their advance, roads were laid out and constructed. By 49, the Fosse Way, Watling Street, Ermine Street and several shorter routes connecting the growing towns lay smooth and straight. Paving was done with local materials and the natives were required to maintain and repair the highways, an effort which (de Roover has noted[20]) should be considered a form of forced savings.

Mutationes and *mansiones* were constructed for the use of the imperial post and the convenience of travelers. The towns and localities maintained these hostels, but they were built on government order. If not constructed earlier, they were sure to have been built under Nero for he gave orders to his procurator in Thrace (another new province) to build such shelters and relay stations along all the roads in his province.[21] In view of his other policies, Nero could hardly have done less for Britain.

Claudius gave money to British chiefs, and during Nero's early years private capital followed public investment. Seneca lent forty million myriads to the British chiefs. Dio asserts that the sudden recall of this loan in 60, together with the actions of the procurator, Catus Decianus, who tried to reclaim the gifts of Claudius (which Decianus insisted were loans), helped bring about the revolt of Boudicca (42.2.1 and 60.23.3 cf. Tacitus *Ann.* 14.32). It is rather suggested here that the recall of these monies was part of the preparation for Nero's currency reform. It is unlikely that Seneca, whose total fortune is quoted at three hundred million sesterces (Tacitus *Ann.* 14.53-56), had suddenly developed a "liquidity preference." His troubles with Nero began at a later date and there is no other distinguishable reason for his abrupt recall of the British investment. Sutherland points out that after the currency reform under Nero almost no silver coins of preceding periods are found in Britain. He also notes that hoards of coins dating from the reign of Nero are few indeed,[22] which is astonishing when Boudicca's revolt is remembered. Why did not Romans and Britons flying from

---

[19] *Ibid.*, 56-57. See Tacitus *Ann.* 14.32; and E. Birley, "The Epitaph of Julius Classicianus," *Antiquaries Journal* XVI (1936), 207-208.

[20] Raymond de Roover, "Conversation," October 9, 1961, points out that the corveés for road work and other projects probably, or possibly, caused a temporary lowering of the standard of living for the Britons and may have contributed to Boudicca's revolt. But at the same time this investment of forced labor benefited the Britons in following years and for future generations.

[21] CIL, III, 6123. On the *mutationes* and *mansiones* see Richmond, *op. cit.*, 91-92.

[22] Sutherland, *op. cit.*, 6 and 14.

Colchester, London and St. Albans hide their money? Perhaps they had little but bronze to hide.

After suppression of the revolt, a further investment of social overhead capital was made. Extensive drainage was carried out in the Fens. Richmond, noting that the area belonged to the rebellious Iceni, and assuming that they furnished the labor force, describes it thus:

> The Fens were drained by a series of wide canals, the most notable being the Cambridgeshire and Lincolnshire Car Dykes ... In conjunction with the rivers, which in many places followed different lines from those of today, these canals served both for drainage and transport ... The foundation of the system has been shown by excavation to belong to the later years of Nero ...[23]

In the year following the revolt, the severity of the military governor, Suetonius Paulinus, led the new procurator, Julius Classicianus, to complain to Nero. He believed a milder, more relaxed policy necessary for the recovery of peace and prosperity on the island. Nero sent an investigating commission headed by the freedman Polyclitus to look into the complaints, and shortly afterwards an excuse was found to recall Paulinus (Tacitus *Ann.* 14.38-39 and *Agric.* 16). His successor, P. Petronius Turpilianus, cooperated well with Classicianus and helped create the "setting" (in Rostow's words) for the take-off.

London grew up again, says Richmond, like a "boom town." Colchester and St. Albans were rebuilt, and other towns, undamaged by the revolt, continued to grow. New towns and new roads were spreading to the westward.[24] Old industries grew and new ones began. By the end of Nero's reign the take-off had been reached and passed. "In nearly all places where excavation has been undertaken it has been found that the Flavian era marked a great increase of activity ..." writes Charlesworth.[25] The period of sustained growth had begun. Collingwood, studying the pottery and metal wares, says:

> During the first century and a half much Gallic Samian ware was imported into Britain ... But it provoked the British manufacturer to compete, and to put on the market a style of pottery which resembled it in having ornament in relief and a highly glazed surface.

He adds:

> There developed a school of Romano-British metal work,

[23] Richmond, *op. cit.*, p. 129. See also J. G. D. Clark, "Report on the Excavations on the Cambridgeshire Car Dyke," *Antiquaries Journal* XXIX (1949), 145-163.
[24] M. P. Charlesworth, "The Roman Occupation," *The Heritage of Early Britain* (London, 1952), 91-92.
[25] M. P. Charlesworth, *Trade Routes and Commerce of the Roman Empire.* 2nd. rev. ed. (Cambridge, 1926), 210.

and again,

Romano-British sculpture has the beginnings of a style and character of its own, and that is different from traditional Graeco-Roman sculpture . . .[26]

Charlesworth mentions that so strong a tradition of a stone-cutting, masonry and other building techniques grew up in Britain that masons were sent from there to Autun in the third century.[27] Tenney Frank supports the fact of sustained industrial growth from the Roman side, saying: "Britain's imports from Italy were few . . . During the first century Italian metal jugs and candelabra came in quantities by trade, yet by the second century British industry took care of such needs."[28]

Mining took giant strides forward and the metal-working industries became increasingly significant. Lead mines were brought under the ownership of the Roman government, but often were leased to private citizens. Lead pigs, stamped with the names of Roman lessees have been found in huge quantity, and Richmond notes that there is some evidence for the export of Mendip lead.[29] Pliny the Elder commented that "black" lead was so common in surface strata in Britain that "there is a law preventing the production of more than a certain amount" (*H.N.* 34.48.164). The meaning of the latter statement becomes clear when he remarks elsewhere that "white lead yields no silver, though it (silver) is obtained from black lead" (34.46.158). It has been assumed that Rome curbed British production in favor of Spain's already developed industry, but it might be suggested that the law was designed rather to protect the government's prerogative to coin money. The production of silver could not be of disinterest to Rome, and Richmond, though not mentioning this possibility, notes significantly that British lead was extremely important because "the only way of producing silver known to the ancient world was by cupellation from lead."[30]

"The iron mines of Britain were numerous and hardly less productive than the lead mines,"[31] writes Richmond, and continues to describe the mines known to have been exploited, apparently by both natives and Romans. The chief Cogidumnus, whose capital was at Chichester, controlled the mines in the Weald and an interesting inscription of an iron workers' guild (believed to be made up of Britons though organized

---

[26] Collingwood, Roman Britain, *op. cit.*, 101-120.
[27] Charlesworth, "The Roman Occupation," *op. cit.*, 95-96.
[28] Tenney Frank, *Economic Survey of the Roman Empire* V (Baltimore, 1940), 291. See also Collingwood in *Econ. Survey* III, *op. cit.*, 110-111. This section is closely related to the development described by Rostow, *op. cit.*, 49-50.
[29] Richmond, *op. cit.*, 151.
[30] *Ibid.*, 149.
[31] *Ibid.*, 157. Iron production was not restricted. See also Collingwood, *Econ. Survey, op. cit.*, 40, who states: "In the Weald there are 4 pre-Roman furnace sites and about 10 of Roman date, some on a very large scale... Slag heaps are found to contain coins as early as Nero, with those of Vespasian in especially large numbers."

on a Roman model) has been found in that area. The works in the Weald produced so much slag and cinders that the nearby roads were surfaced with these iron wastes. The seven tons of nails found by Richmond on the site of a Roman camp, and dated to 84, furnish dramatic proof of the capacity of British production under the Flavians.[32] Other metal-working industries likewise flourished and, as Collingwood has indicated, there is abundant evidence that native Britons were largely concerned in their development.

Charlesworth, following Pliny the Elder and searching the archaeological sources, lists the plant and animal introductions into Britain under the Romans. The cherry tree came by 50, and the walnut and chestnut soon followed. Herbs and vegetables such as dill, coriander, beetroot, beans, peas, cabbage and others; and fruits such as the apple, plum, raspberry and strawberry were perhaps introduced at this time (Pliny *H.N.* 15.102 and 42.6). Charlesworth supposes also that laurel, box, roses, violets and the poppy were Roman gifts to Britain. Finally, new breeds of sheep and cattle were brought to the island by the Romans.[33]

Indeed, change was everywhere apparent as culture and industry evolved under the stimulus provided. But nowhere were purely Roman methods imposed. Roman styles and designs tended to dominate briefly but, as Collingwood noted, British taste and craftsmanship reasserted themselves to produce a hybrid style.[34] Wheeler, speaking specifically of Wales, writes:

The policing of Wales by Roman troops may have accelerated rather than diverted the natural evolution of native culture ... We are confronted ... with the paradox that the intrusion of the foreigner coincided with and perhaps contributed indirectly towards the culmination of a prehistoric native culture.[35]

Agriculture reflects the same phenomenon. Roman field systems were not adopted, though the villa system grew slowly and came to flourish exceedingly in the fourth century. Yet it never displaced entirely the native villages and small farms. It is interesting to note with Richmond that the reclaimed land in the Fens was not laid out by the Romans. He says: "It becomes clear that, while the canals and main roads across the area bear the systematic imprint of the Roman engineer, the farms, fields and lanes are no less characteristically native."[36]

Tacitus, writing near the end of the first century, notes: "The Britons themselves submit to the levy, the tribute and other charges of the empire with cheerful readiness provided there is no abuse. That,

[32] *The New York Times,* October 11, 1961. So huge a quantity of nails indicates a vast construction industry in wood.
[33] Charlesworth, "The Roman Occupation," *op. cit.,* 94.
[34] Collingwood, *Roman Britain, loc. cit.*
[35] R. E. M. Wheeler, *Prehistoric and Roman Wales* (Oxford, 1925), 215.
[36] Richmond, *op. cit.,* 130.

they bitterly resent, for they are broken in to obedience, not to slavery" (*Agric.* 13). Richmond assumes the tax rate to have been high, saying that the canal-side granaries in the Fens "indicate the stage at which the Roman tax-collector entered into the giant's share of the produce."[37] But an opposite view might be drawn from Tacitus' account (*Ann.* 14.39) of the relaxed and easy policies of Julius Classicianus and Petronius Turpilianus. Tacitus mentions no abuse until the time of Domitian. Undoubtedly the canal-side granaries served the tax-collectors, yet they may have been equally useful to the farmer in transporting his crop to market. Here, as in the case of Wales, the prosperity of Roman Britain was not due to an "indirect" contribution by Rome, but rather to the direct investment of social overhead capital.

An over-all increase in per capita income (though statistics are lacking to measure it) is evident from the growth of towns, villages and villas,[38] and from the improvement of living conditions everywhere except in the most isolated villages. In towns and villas water was supplied by channels sometimes above, sometimes below, ground[39] and other amenities were common. Literacy increased amazingly. Collingwood writes that in the towns literacy "was not confined to the upper classes but was common among the industrial population."[40] Evidence of literacy is less common at the villas and quite rare in the small villages—though not entirely absent. Moreover, inscriptions and graffiti are in Latin, not Celtic. Martial may have been correct in saying: "Even Britain is said to recite my verses" (11.3.5), and surely Juvenal was half-serious when he wrote: "eloquent Gaul has instructed British pleaders, now Thule talks of hiring teachers of rhetoric" (*Sat.* 15.110-112); for with certainty Demetrius the Grammarian went to Britain under the Flavians (Plutarch *de Def. Orac.* 2.410).

Even poor farms and farming villages benefited a little from the general prosperity, though they remained strongly bound to conservative, traditional patterns. Still, their inhabitants learned to burn coal which was extensively mined and widely used as fuel. Evidence of its use has been discovered in poor farmhouses twenty to thirty miles from the nearest mines.[41] Many scholars hold the opinion that the Britons, if left to their own devices after the withdrawal of the Roman legions, would have carried on and continued to develop the patterns of life to which they had become accustomed. And this view, based on the Romano-British fusion together with the widespread decentralization of industry in the late Empire period,[42] has much to support it.

[37] *Ibid.*
[38] Collingwood, *Econ. Survey, op. cit.*, 12-13.
[39] *Ibid.*, 51.
[40] *Ibid.*, 65.
[41] *Ibid.*, 37.
[42] *Ibid.*, 88-107; and Richmond, *op. cit.*, 170-185 et al. In the fourth century

The investment of social overhead capital in Britain by Rome had important and rapid effects. The work of the legions in keeping the peace, the work of the engineers and governors in building roads, harbors, and town facilities, and in reclaiming waste lands all combined to establish the "preconditions." New products, new skills and new techniques were introduced. New markets were made available in the Empire and in Britain itself through the resident armies and growing towns. Some Roman private capital was supplied and the native Britons were mobilized to invest through a form of forced savings. British investment capital soon followed and poured into the pottery industries, furniture-making, and stone industries. Metal-wares increased in production under both Roman and native hands. The "setting" was thereby provided and the "take-off" followed with astonishing rapidity. From the beginning of Vespasian's reign, the British economy is marked by a steady, sustained growth which remains undisturbed by the renewed Roman expansion to the north. Indeed, the same economic effects followed the Roman legions wherever they succeeded in the firm establishment of peace and order. The existing highways were carried into the new areas and the drainage of the Fens extended into Lincolnshire. New mines were opened and new towns sprang up. Britain changed from an underdeveloped area to a province with a healthy economy capable of supplying both needs and luxuries for its own population, and able to export desirable goods beyond its boundaries.

But it remains for the future to test Rostow's theory in greater detail[43] and in a broader framework, and perhaps to contrast it with alternative economic theories. The present experiment seems to justify the use of these theoretical tools in exploring Roman economic development. And, at the least, it has clarified the essential role of social overhead capital investment in an ancient, underdeveloped economy.

Brooklyn College of the
City University of New York

there was a population shift and an industrial shift from the towns to the villas—a sort of decentralization. But there is no clear evidence of overall decline in productivity. Rather, as Collingwood notes, the villas flourish at the expense of the towns. When the Saxons came in, destruction was terrible. Gildas wrote of it thus: "fragments of human bodies...looking as though they had been squeezed together in a wine press; and with no chance of being buried save in the ruins of the houses." *The Works of Gildas.* edit. by J. A. Giles (London, 1848), 311-312.

[43] No attempt has been made to isolate and identify each positive factor contributing to the preconditions for take-off, nor have the conditions involved in the take-off itself (e.g. percentage of investment rate) been identified. Obviously the relationship of primary growth sectors to secondary growth sectors remains to be explored. And, finally no comparison between Roman and "modern" colonialism has been made, nor has its significance as a factor in the stages of growth been so far considered.

AMBER
AN HISTORICAL-ETYMOLOGICAL PROBLEM[1]

JOHN M. RIDDLE

Millions of years ago, amber forests grew near the shores of Denmark and Germany, where coniferous trees secreted large amounts of resin. In the geological ages following, many of the trees became victims of a creeping ocean. Time and the sea hardened their resin into a fossil called amber. During the eons when man evolved, he came to use amber as an ornament, as a medicine, and, because of its peculiar electrostatic qualities, as a magic amulet. It is still used both decoratively and medicinally.

As an element in man's life, amber is mentioned in early literary works. In the *Odyssey* (18.296), Homer tells of a servant giving Eurymachus a gold necklace "strung with amber (ἠλέκτροισιν) beads, bright as the sun."[2] Elsewhere (4.73), Telemachus in describing Menelaus' palace says "observe . . . the flashing of bronze, of gold, of amber, of silver, and of ivory." In still another place (15.460), the swineherd Eumaeus tells Odysseus of an amber necklace strung on gold thread.[3]

If the Homeric works, then, are the first to mention amber in Greek, they are also the beginning of a philological problem of large proportions. Strabo (*Geog.* 3.2.8), Pliny (*H.N.* 33.23-80-1), and Pausanias (5.1.12.7) speak of a mixed residuum or alloy of gold and silver which is called *elektron* in Greek and *electrum* in Latin. This is the same Homeric word which is translated "amber." This study will deal with the modern research on the problems involved in translating the word "amber" in ancient writings.

A quantitative analysis of the use of *elektron* in Greek literature is a formidable undertaking. In some cases the reference obviously concerns amber, in others an alloy of gold and silver. Sometimes the term

[1] For his supervision of this paper, I am deeply indebted to the late Loren C. MacKinney, Kenan Professor of History at The University of North Carolina. Mr. Thomas Herndon and Mr. Gordon Mueller also made helpful suggestions. I am also indebted to the School of Medicine of the University of North Carolina for a grant which enabled me to spend two years of research on amber and its medical uses.

[2] Unless otherwise indicated the Greek originals for "amber" in our quotations are some form or the other of ἤλεκτρον.

[3] In the *Homeric Epigrams* (15. 10), a rich bride is "standing on a floor inlaid with amber." In *Hymn to the Delian Apollo* (103), there is a reference to a great, gold necklace of amber. Perhaps this means a golden cord necklace strung with amber as in *Od.* 15. 460.

used is ambiguous. But where the context points clearly to a substance which, upon being rubbed, acquires large amounts of static electricity amber is almost surely meant. Plato (*Timaeus* 80. b-c), for instance, refers to *elektron* together with "Heraclean stones" as possessing attractive qualities; this can be none other than amber. In passages where the context is uncertain, an historical-archaeological and an etymological-philological approach must be used. Information supplied by archaeologists, historians, and linguists show that ancient words for amber are deeply rooted in folklore. Sometimes the name amber derives from its peculiar qualities, or is a transferred name from people who traded in amber.

J. M. De Navarro's study of amber trade routes provides an excellent basis for an historical-archaeological approach. Beginning sometime in the early Aunzetitz civilization of northern Europe and continuing to its zenith about the middle of the seventh century B.C., amber was exported from northern Europe to the Mediterranean peoples.[4] Randall-MacIver reports that at Bologna there are amber finds in graves from the Second Benacci period (*ca.* 9th century B.C.).[5] Schliemann reported a quantity of amber beads in graves at Mycenae (*ca.* 1600-1100 B.C.).[6] Under a temple gate at Assur and in a grave in the inner city of Babylon amber beads have been found.[7] Such evidence tends to corroborate the quotations from Homer as to the probable existence of amber in early Greece.

The Hebrew text of Ezekiel mentions *ghashmal* in three verses (1:4,27; 8:2). The Septuagint translated this as *elektron* (in its Greek form), whereas the Vulgate of Jerome uses the Latinized *electrum*. It is possible but not likely that this is a Hebrew term for amber itself. Wallis, in his *Egyptian Hieroglyphic Dictionary,* suggests a relation between the Hebrew *ghashmal* and the Egyptian term *hesmen,* meaning merely "amber-coloured plated bronze."[8] Writing on the meaning of

[4] De Navarro, "Prehistoric Routes between Northern Europe and Italy Defined by the Amber Trade," *The Geographical Journal,* LXVI (1925), 485, 502. A more recent study (but primarily based on de Navarro's research) is Spekke, *The Ancient Amber Routes and the Geographical Discovery of the Eastern Baltic* (Stockholm, 1957); see also the earlier study, still valid on some points, by Pierson, *Elektron oder Über die Vorfahren, die Verwandtschaft und den Namen der alten Preussen* ... (Berlin, 1869).
[5] Randall-MacIver, *Italy before the Romans* (Oxford, 1928), 59-60.
[6] Schuchhardt, *Schliemann's Excavations...* Translated by Eugénie Sellers (London, 1891), 196.
[7] Ebeling and Meissner, eds., *Reallexikon der Assyriologie...* (Berlin and Leipzig, 1938), II, 1.
[8] Wallis, *An Egyptian Hieroglyphic Dictionary...,* 512. In the Syrian translation of the Hebrew version of Ezekiel there is no word for *ghashmal.* However, Hirth (*China and the Roman Orient...,* 245) and Williamson (*The Book of Amber,* 58) noted that amber is frequently found in the vicinity of Sidon. Jules Oppert (*L'Ambre Jaune chez les Assyriens,* 6) translates an Assyrian cuneiform inscription which, he feels, indicates the presence of amber from the Baltic and

amber in Homer, Giguet takes *ghashmal* in Ezekiel to be nothing other than the metal alloy elektron.⁹

Heracles' shield as described by Hesiod (*Shield of Heracles* 142) has an orb "a-shimmer with enamel and white ivory and amber." A fragment from Democritos (*Frag.* A 165, Diels II, 128. 41) ascribes attractive qualities to amber. According to Diogenes Laertius (1.24), Thales attributed life to inanimate objects "arguing from the stone of the magnet and from amber."¹⁰ Theophrastus (*On stones* 29) noted that amber was a stone found in Liguria that possessed qualities of attraction.¹¹ There can be no doubt that Aristotle in *Meterologica* (4.10.388b) referred to amber, which he said is a compound of the earth that often preserves insects.¹²

Thus, it can be reasonably inferred that Democritos, Diogenes Laertius, Theophrastus, and Aristotle described true amber. In contrast, the Greek term for *elektron* in Sophocles' *Antigone* (1038) is shown by context to refer to a metal: "Gain your gains, drive your trade, if you list, in the silver-gold (*elektros*) of Sardis and the gold of India."¹³ There is no certainty as to the meaning of Aristophanes' description of Cratinus' old age as "Time of which his ambers has reft him" (*Knights* 532). Rogers suggest that ambers here may mean the ornamental studs of a couch, or the pegs of a lyre.¹⁴ Less questionable is the reference to amber by Herodotus (3.115) when he confesses his geographical ignorance of the mythical Eridanus River, whence, he says, amber comes.

Enough references have been cited to permit a preliminary summary of the data before an investigation of later writings. There is great inconsistency in the gender of the Greek word for amber. In the early part of the nineteenth century, Buttmann made a lengthy footnote study

---

consequently very early commercial relations between Assyria and northern Europe.

The word χαλκολίβανον in Rev. 1:15 and Rev. 2:18 has been interpreted as amber but the probable meaning is, as Jerome translated it, *orichalcum,* a yellow copper ore. Finally F. Waldmann (*Der Bernstein im Altertum* ... Landesgymnasium zu Fellin, 7-8) translating *stacte* (Exodus 30:34) suggests a close relationship with the Egyptian *sacal* for amber and the Scythian *scarium* for amber. The only other source for the Egyptian and Scythian forms seems to be Pliny (*H.N.* 37. 11. 36, 40) whose expertness in linguistics is unreliable.

⁹ Giguet, "Sur l'electrum d'Homére," *Révue Archéologique,* XVI (1859-60), 240.

¹⁰ Though as noted by Martin ("Du succin, des ses noms divers et des ses varietés suivant les anciens," *Academie des Inscriptiones et Belles-Lettres,* VI, 299), Diogenes is using Aristotle and Hippias—sources not reliable for the exact word used by Thales. Aristotle (*On animals* 1. 2. 405 a 14) suggests that Thales discovered the attractive qualities of lodestone but does not specifically mention amber.

¹¹ See also Theophrastus *On plants* 9. 18. 2.

¹² Aristophanes, the epitomist of Aelian and Aristotle, in *Epitome of the History of Animals* (57. 15), quotes both Aristotle and Herodotus on amber.

¹³ Cf. Pliny (*H.N.* 37. 11. 40) citing Sophocles who allegedly says that amber is from the tears of a certain bird beyond India.

¹⁴ Rogers, *The Knights of Aristophanes* (1930), 76, n.

of this problem.[15] The gender is indeterminate in Homer and Hesiod, but in Herodotus, Plato, and Theophrastus, all of whose contexts make identification certain, the gender is neuter.[16] The basis of Buttmann's argument comes with Sophocles' masculine gender (ὁ ἤλεκτρος). Using this as the standard for the metal gold-silver alloy, Buttmann notes that Latin *electrum* always meant metal alloy. Even if modern philologists would accept Buttmann's methodology based on genders, this attempt at a rigid rule breaks down upon application to later Latin and Greek writers. Juvenal (14.307), Martial (8.51), Vergil (*Aeneid* 8.402), Silius Italicus (*Punica* 1.229), and Claudian (*Rape of Proserpine* 1.245) use *electrum* for metal alloy; but Vergil (*Ciris* 434; *Eclogue* 8.54), Claudian (*Epist. ad Serenam* 31.11), and Ovid (*Met.* 2.365) use *electrum* for amber in recounting the myth of its formation. The same inconsistency is noted in Greek literature. In Aristophanes' *Knights* (532) and in later prose the feminine form for amber is used.[17] Pausanias (5.1.12.7) describes a statue of the Emperor Augustus made of amber, then warns his reader that this is the amber "found in nature" and not the alloy of gold and silver. The Hippocratic works (4.38, Littré, ed.) use the term as an adjective "amber-like."

Plutarch (*Plat. Quaest.* 7.7; *Quest. Convival.* 2.7.1) uses the term in the neuter gender to describe the phenomenon of attraction in a context which makes it certain that he is referring to amber. Again (*Plat. Quaest.* 7.1), discussing Plato's ideas on motion, Plutarch uses the term in the feminine gender.

Diodorus of Sicily (5.23.1-4) writes of the origin of amber as follows: "Concerning the tin of Britain we shall rest content with what has been said, and we shall now discuss the so-called amber." Diodorus continues concerning the amber cast up by the sea on the coast of Basileia. If Basileia is the island of Heligoland, as some think, Diodorus is geographically correct. In his *Geography* (15.1.38 c 703), Strabo mentions the attraction of chaff to amber. Galen's (13.549, Kühn, ed.) prescription of pills of amber corresponds with similar uses in premodern medicine.

In order to understand the etymological development of the word *elektron* it is well to recall the myth of amber's origin. Phaëthon, the son of Helios, as a youth desired to follow in the same profession as his father. But when he persuaded Helios to allow him to drive the four-horse sun-chariot across the sky, the task proved too difficult. Traversing the heavens in an erratic manner, he set the sky afire producing the Milky Way. Jupiter (Zeus) forthwith smote Phaëthon who fell until he reached the mouth of the river Padus, probably the Po,

---

[15] Buttmann, "Über das Elektron," *Abhandlungen der Königlichen Akademie der Wissenschafter in Berlin* (1818-9), 46, n.
[16] Cf. Aristotle *Meteorologica* 4. 10, 388 b.
[17] Liddell and Scott, "elektron," *A Greek-English Lexicon*. 9th rev. ed.

where his body was committed to the lapping waters.[18] The sisters of Phaëthon, in grief for their brother, stood dripping tears on the bank of the Padus.[19] For one, two, three seasons they continued mourning until they underwent a metamorphosis, becoming poplar trees. In this form, the sisters of Phaëthon at the same time each year drip tears into the waters of the river. When the tears harden in the cold water, they become amber.

According to De Navarro's study on trade routes, it seems certain that an avenue by which amber came to the Greeks was through northern Italy. Müllenhoff, Spekke, Oppert, Waldmann, Williamson[20] and others have tied the import trade with the Ligurians and the Phoenicians, who could be expected to have introduced amber to the Greeks and Hebrews. Jules Oppert has traced the etymology of the Assyrian *kar-ku-ma eri*, which he translates "amber" from a cuneiform inscription, through the Hebrew by which the Assyrian word is able to mean *la pierre attractive,* or "a magnetic stone."[21] Buttmann advanced the theory that *elektron* is a corruption of the more primitive form derived from the verb ἕλκειν, "to attract."[22] The metal alloy, because of its likeness to real amber in luster, assumed the same name as amber.

Buttmann's early explanation of the etymology of the Greek *elektron* was successfully refuted by Martin, even though Martin's case was unaided by modern archaeology. Although Martin did not know that amber existed in earliest times, his assumption was corroborated by later scholars. Taking his cue from the poetic simile of *elektron* and *elektor,* "shining," he assumed that the word for amber was derived from the Greek because of its close alliance with the color of the sun and the Phaëthon legend.[23]

In 1860, Schmidt, a philologist, analyzed the word *aityron* in Hesychius, which he thought might have some connection with amber.

---

[18] The Phaëthon legend is preserved or alluded to in the following works: Pliny *H.N.* 37. 11. 31; Alexander of Aphrodisias *Questiones* 23. 137. 24-5 (see also 13. 139. 141); Diodorus *Library* 5. 23. 4; Eustathius *Com. to Dion. Periegeta* 38, and *Com. to Homer Od.* 366. 30 (1483. 24-5); Claudian *Epistula ad Serenam* 31. 11; (pseudo) Aristotle *On marvellous things heard* 81 (*Minor Works* 836 b 4); Strabo *Geog.* 5. 1. 9. c 215; Stephanus Byzantinus, 299-300, Meinekii, ed.; Apollonius *Argon.* 4. 606; Juvenal 5. 37-9; Lucian *Astrology* 19, and *Amber, or the Swans*; Sidonius *Ad Heronius* 4 (2.355); Herodotus 3. 115; Isidore *Etym.* 16. 8. 6-8; Ovid *Met.* 2. 364-6; Nonnos *Dion.* 23. 93; Pomponius Mela *De situ orbis* 2. 7. 13; Vergil *Ciris* 433-5.

[19] Oldfather, in the Loeb translation of Diodorus of Sicily (5. 23), observes that the word *dakruon* "tears" in the singular, as here, also means "sap."

[20] *Deutsche Altertumskunde* (Berlin, 1890), I, 242. *Amber Routes...*, 17 by implication. *L'Ambre Jaune chez les Assyriens,* 1-2, though not specifically with the Ligurians. *Der Bernstein...*, 9. *The Book of Amber,* 53.

[21] Oppert, *op. cit.* 13-4.

[22] Buttmann, *op. cit.,* 55 ff. A more recent writer, Karl Andrée (*Der Bernstein und seine Bedeutung in Natur- und Geisteswissenschaften...* [Königsberg, 1937], 82) supports this view.

[23] Martin, *op. cit.,* 298 ff.

He rejected the translation "glass" in favor of "sap."[24] Dioscorides (1.83, Wellmann, ed.) identifies *aigeiros* as the sap of the "black poplar" originating as tears from the trees growing by the river Padus. By some, Dioscorides observes, *aigeiros* is called *elektron* and by others *chrysophoron* because it yields upon rubbing a sweet smell and has a golden color. Galen (9.916, Kühn, ed.) has a full entry and description of the medicinal uses of *aigeiros*, but there is no relation or suggestion that this may be amber. Apart from the Phaëthon legend in literary usage, *aigeiros*, or "black poplar," reveals no relation with amber.

Buttmann raised the question: which came first, the gold-silver alloy or the vegetable amber, and, consequently, from which originated the name? Since it is related to the Phaëthon myth, it seems likely that Homer, at least in the *Odyssey* (18.296; 15.460; and, probably, 4.73) referred to amber.[25] Since Homer used the word in the plural when describing beads, it would appear that he was referring to balls of "amber" and not a metal alloy. Liddell and Scott[26] and Waldmann[27] cite the *Odyssey* (15.460), where the gift of the necklace was described as coming from a Phoenician trader. Pierson[28] and Müllenhoff[29] have noted references to tin in the *Iliad* (11.25.34; 18.474.565.574.612; 23.502) and Herodotus' explanation (3.115) that tin and amber come from "the further side of Europe." From this circumstantial evidence that the tin of the *Iliad* came from the Germanic north, Pierson and Müllenhoff ask: why could not the amber of the *Odyssey* also come from that region?[30]

Giguet notes a theory that *elektron* in Homer is neither amber nor the gold-silver alloy, but a kind of enamel used in embossing reliefs. Asserting that the Greek derivation of the word was from the Hebrew and related to the Latin *smaltum*, "enamel," he rejects the identifications of amber in Homer and Hesiod.[31] Murray, translator of the *Odyssey*, believes that it is the metal-alloy that was referred to in the description (4.73) of Menelaus' palace shining with *elektron*. Amber, he holds, is correct for the other two citations.[32] Vergil (*Ciris* 434) makes a

[24] Schmidt, *"Aityron," Zeitschrift für vergleichende sprachforschung*, IX (1860), 399-400. See, Hesychius c. 1621. 3. Pliny (*H.N.* 37. 11. 42) and Tacitus (*Germania* 45) suggest that the Germanic word for amber was *glaesum*, meaning "glass." *Hyalos*, the Greek term for glass, was perhaps loosely applied to designate other transparent substances including amber (Mary Trowbridge, "Philological Studies in Ancient Glass," *University of Illinois Studies in Language and Literature*, XIII, 262).
[25] Müllenhoff, *op. cit.*, 222.
[26] Liddell and Scott, *loc. cit.*
[27] Waldmann, *op. cit.*, 9-10.
[28] Pierson, *op. cit.*, 2.
[29] Müllenhoff, *op. cit.*, I, 242.
[30] See Diodorus (5. 23. 1-4), who discusses amber and tin in juxtaposition.
[31] Giguet, *op. cit.*, 235, 241.
[32] Murray (Loeb ed.).

similar comparison of a palace "rich in frail coral and amber tears (*dives curalio fragili et lacrimoso electro*)." The association of a palace with amber is definite here because of the implication of "amber (*electrum*)" and "tears (*lacrimosa*)" in conjunction with the Phaëthon myth. Since Vergil was thoroughly schooled in Homer, he probably believed that Menelaus' palace (*Od.* 4.73) was decorated with true amber.

The scholiast Eustathius (*Comm. to Homer Od.* 366.30 [1483. 24-32]) warns his readers not to confuse the metal *elektron* with the "mineral" *elektron* "from the hardened sap of tears."[33] The poet Lucian, in his work entitled, "Amber, or the Swans," relates his visit to the Eridanus River where, he said, he expected to supply himself with amber by "holding out a fold of my cloak." When he asked his boatmen where the amber was, Lucian found it necessary to tell him the whole story of Phaëthon. In a brisk manner, the boatmen replied:

Who told you that? said they. The cheat and liar. We never saw any driver fall from a car, and we haven't the poplars you speak of. If we had anything of that sort do you suppose that for two obols we would row or tow our boats upstream, when we could get rich by picking up the tears of the poplars? (Harmon trans., 77)

On the other hand, there is no doubt from the context that Callimachus (*Aetia* 3. R. 75. 31) refers to the gold-silver alloy. Probably the metal *elektron* is meant in Heliodorus (*Aeth.* 22, 80, Bekker, ed.). Aelius Lampridius (*V. Alex.*, 25) records the minting of a coin made of the alloy electrum. There are frequent examples of such coins in Greek numismatics. In the excavations of Troy a small cup was found of one part silver to four parts gold.[34] This fits in generally with the composition of *elektron*.

The comparison of palm dates to amber is made by Xenophon (*Anab.* 2.3.15), and by Athenaeus (*Deip.* 14.651b, citing Xenophon). Even though the simile was probably to a degree a literary standardization, it seems plausible, since a ripe date could have an affinity in resemblance and color to a lump of golden amber.[35]

We turn now from the double meaning of the Greek *elektron* to another word for amber, λιγγούριον. Theophrastus (*On stones* 28) describes it as follows: "*Lyngourion* . . . is remarkable in its powers . . . seals are cut from this too, and it is very hard, like a real stone." It has

---

[33] Eustathius (in *Dion. Periegeta* 38 [5. 294]) warns the reader that, when Dionysius describes tears pressed into golden *elektron*, this is not metal *elektron* but it is a stone which is like gold.

[34] Schuchhardt, *op. cit.*, 62.

[35] However, Gulick, translator of Athenaeus in the Loeb edition (VI, 519), believes that *elektron* means the metal. Philostratus (*Life of Apollonius* 1. 21) employs the adjective "amber-like" to describe palm dates. Cf. the adjective forms also in Hippocrates 4, 38, Littré, ed., and Euripides *Hipp.* 741.

the power of attraction, just as *elektron*.³⁶ Strabo (*Geog.* 4.6.2) explains the situation more definitely: "And they also have in their country excessive quantities of *lyngourion* which by some is called *elektron*."

Theophrastus (*On stones* 28) states that amber is said to be the urine of wild animals, who, jealous of their excretion, bury it, and it subsequently hardens into the stone *lyngourion*. Pliny,³⁷ Dioscorides,³⁸ Ovid (*Met.* 15.412-5), Aelian (*On animals* 4.17), Isidore (*Etymol.* 16.8.6-8), and Claudius (*Epis. ad Ser.* 31.7)³⁹ specify that the animal whose urine is valuable is the lynx.⁴⁰

Exodus (28:19), giving a description of the costume jewels to be worn by the priests, uses the Hebrew word which in the Greek Septuagint was translated into λιγύριον, and in the Latin Vulgate of Jerome into *ligurius*.⁴¹ In a letter, Jerome (64.16), confesses concerning his translation: "Looking over the authors who write on the properties of stones and gems, I am not able to find out about *ligurius*."

The term for *ligurion* is variously spelled in both Greek and Latin. The Greek derivation seems relatively clear: from λύγξ for "lynx"; and οὖρον for "urine."⁴² Theophrastus (*On stones* 16), Strabo (*Geog.*

---

³⁶ See *Theophrastus: On Stones*. translation, Caley and Richards (Columbus, Ohio, 1956), 109-111. Caley and Richards point to various attempts to identify *lyngourion* as beleminite and hyacinth. Because Theophrastus, they suggest (p. 111), in referring to its hardness used the phrase "like-stone," his *lyngourion* is not a stone in the mineral sense. Caley and Richards conclude that *lyngourion* is either amber or "a variety of amber." It seems that the very definite statements by Pliny (*H.N.* 37. 13. 52-3) and Strabo (*Geog.* 4. 6. 2) leave no doubt that Theophrastus was wrong in making any distinction; Theophrastus' *lyngourion* was amber.

³⁷ Pliny *H.N.* 37. 52-3: "De lyncurio proxime dici cogit autorum pertinacia, quippe, etiamsi non electrum id esse contendunt lyncurium, tamen gemmam esse volunt, fieri autem adfirmant ex urina quidem lyncis, sed et genere terrae, protinus eo animali urinam operiente, quoniam invideat homini, ibique lapidescere; esse autem, qualem in sucinis, colorem igneum, scalpique nec folia tantum aut stramenta ad se rapere, sed aeris etiam ac ferri lamnas, quod Diocli cuidam Theophrastus quoque credit. ego falsum id totum arbitror nec visam in aevo nostro gemmam ullam ea appellatione."

³⁸ *Materia Medica* 2. 81, Wellmann, ed. Dioscorides is prescribing *lyngourion* for its pharmaceutical qualities which closely resemble Galen's prescriptions (13. 549, Kühn, ed.) for *elektron*.

³⁹ However, Aelian, Ovid, and Claudius avoid the term itself referring instead to hardened urine.

⁴⁰ Aristotle (*On animals* 3. 2 [Didot 3. 350]) quotes Ctesias who allegedly said that *elektron* was the hardened sperm of the elephant.

⁴¹ Josephus (*Antiquities* 3. 7. 5) is referring to the vestments of the high priest when he used the word *ligurion*. H. St. J. Thackeray, translator of Josephus in the Loeb edition (IV, 395), makes the substance "jacinth" though he allows the possibility of amber. Dio Chrysostom (*Orat.* 13) writes of an "amber costume," which may be amber ornamented similar to that implied in Aristophanes *Knights* (532) but seemingly different from Heliodorus (*Aeth.* 22. 80, Bekker, ed.). In another place Dio (*Orat.* 79) specifies amber in connection with the Celts who he says traffic in it. In both references Dio used the Greek term *elektron*.

⁴² Schmidt, *op. cit.*, 399; Blümmer, "Bernstein," Pauly-Wissowa-Kroll, *Real-Encyclopädie* (Stuttgart, 1894), III, 300-1; and Hesychius' entry.

4.6.2), and Pliny (*H.N.* 37.11.35) connect amber with the Ligurians. The results of De Navarro's study show an amber route ending in the area of the Ligurians which included the ancient port of Massilia (Marseilles).[43] Since the Phoenicians traded with the Ligurians, it can be reasonably conjectured that the Phoenicians, and those to whom they delivered the product, attached to it the ethnic name *ligurion*.[44] From this there later developed the strange etymology of the lynx urine.

It would be useless to argue which name came first, *ligurion,* according to Genthe,[45] or *elektron,* according to Pierson.[46] *Elektron* was more widely used, but this in part can be attributed to Homer, whose works were a part of every Greek's education, thus familiarizing the reading public and later writers with the name. The possibility exists, though evidence is lacking, that there could be a distinction between *ligurion* and *elektron* based on the color of various shades of amber.

Writers of literature can have imprecise meanings with no great consequence, but medical writers must be as accurate as possible. Aetius of Amida (*Libri medicinales* 2.35, Teubner, ed.) warns the reader that *elektron, ligourion,* and *soukinon* are the same thing. The latter word is the Greek form of the Latin word for amber, *sucinum*. Aetius recommends amber for strangury and stomach disorders, but for pains in the stomach he specifies *chryselektron* ("golden amber"). Marcellus (*De medicamentis* 26.114; 29.32) prescribes *sucinum* for the stone and colic, but for goitre and a palpitating heart he says to use "true amber (*sucinum verum*)."[47]

Unlike Greek literature, Roman writings have detailed data on amber. Pliny the Elder admits no uncertainty concerning the Latin *sucinum* for amber. His report on the origin of amber was authoritative until the seventeenth century. He writes:

It is well established that amber is a product of islands in the Northern Ocean, that it is known to the Germans as 'glaesum,' .... To resume, amber is formed of a liquid seeping from the interior of a species of pine, just as the gum in a cherry tree or the resin in a pine bursts forth when the liquid is excessively abundant. The exudation is hardened by frost or perhaps by moderate heat, or else by the sea, after a spring tide has carried off the pieces from the islands. At all events, the amber is washed up on the shores of the mainland, being swept along so easily that it seems to hover in

---

[43] De Navarro, *op. cit.,* 481 ff.

[44] Ridgeway, *The Origin of Metallic Currency and Weight Standards* (Cambridge, 1892), 110; and Blümmer, *loc. cit.*

[45] Genthe, "Über den Antheil der Rheinlande an vorrömischen und römischen Bernsteinhandel," *Monatschrift für rheinischwestfalische Geschichtsforschung und Altertumskunde,* II (1876), 5.

[46] Pierson, *op. cit.,* 47.

[47] For hemoptysis Marcellus (*De medicamentis* 16. 94) prescribes a lozenge of amber (*dielectrum*). Apparently his source is Galen (13. 549, Kühn, ed.), therefore, Marcellus is using Galen's Greek term for amber.

the water without settling on the sea-bed. Even our forebears believed it to be a 'sucus,' or exudation, from a tree, and so named it 'sucinum.' That the tree to which it belongs is a species of pine is shown by the fact that it smells like a pine torch, with the same strongly scented smoke, when it is kindled. (*H.N.* 37. 11. 42-3, Eichholz trans.)

Pliny quotes (*H.N.* 37.11.32) the theories of amber's origin in Greek writings and concludes: "We can forgive them all the more readily for knowing nothing about amber when they betray such monstrous ignorance of geography."

Juvenal (*Sat.* 9.50-3; 6.573) satirizes the custom of Roman ladies carrying balls of amber (*sucina*) probably for the scent and warmth. Discussing odors, Martial (11.8.6) uses the phrase: ". . . of amber warmed by a maiden's hand (. . . *sucina* virginea quod regelata manu)."[48] Ovid (*Met.* 2.365) uses the word *electrum*, which he says was worn by brides. Since Ovid employed the word in conjunction with the Phaëthon legend, he was referring to *sucinum*, or amber, and using poetically the Greek word. As previously noted Martial (8.51), Claudian (*Rape of Proserpine* 1.245), Silius Italicus (*Punica* 1.229), Heliodorus (*Aeth.* 22.80, Bekker, ed.), and Vergil (*Aeneid* 8.402) use *electrum* to mean the metal alloy.

Apuleius (*Met.* 2.19), describing the beautiful glass-ware at a banquet, mentions a vessel carved out of amber (*succinum*). A bowl made of *electrum* is described by the *Scriptores Historiae Augustae* (*trig. tyr. Quietus* 14.5). Martial (8.51) pictures a similar bowl of *electrum* specifically as metal. It seems probable that the bowls in both Martial and the *Scriptores* were of metal alloy, along with the *electrum* mentioned by Juvenal (14.307).

Pliny (*H.N.* 37.11.33) quotes Philemon's statement that amber

is a mineral which is dug up in two different localities in Scythia, in one of which it is of a white, waxen color, and is known as *electrum*; while in the other it is gold-colored, and is called *sualiternicum*.

Pierson has proposed an etymology for *sualiternicum*. The root is from the Lithuanian *swel*, meaning "to burn," to which is attached the suffix *tar* and the frequent ending *nik* giving the meaning of "burning stone."[49] This is close to the modern German *bernstein*, for amber, which probably has the same derivation. The connection of *sualiternicum* and the Scythians probably comes about because of the Baltic-Black Sea trade route and amber traffic.

Pliny also quotes Nicias as reporting an Egyptian word *sacal* for

---

[48] Martial seems to have been impressed by the phenomenon of insects being trapped in the fossilized resin, because he composed three epigrams (4. 32. 59; 6. 15) on a bee, ant, and viper preserved in amber (*sucinum*) for eternity. See also 3. 65. 5; 6. 37. 11.

[49] Pierson, *op. cit.,* 49.

amber; and Pliny refers to Xenocrates' explanation that the Scythian word *sacrium* means amber. The Egyptian word *sacal* seems close to the Hebrew term for "stone."[50] Pierson sees the same base in Egyptian *sacal* and Scythian *sacrium* by reasoning that the introduction of amber into Egypt came from the Black Sea trade routes by way of the Scythians.[51] Thus, the application of this name to the peoples from whom it was obtained and their use of the word falls into the same pattern as the derivation of *ligurion*.

Without drawing dogmatic conclusions, we content ourselves with a few tentative generalizations. The roots of most of the ancient words for amber are shrouded in the shadows which cloud the origins of the languages. Amber's qualities and uses in trade are attested by the words *elektron, sucinum,* and *ligurion*. The background of *sucinum* and *ligurion* seem relatively clear. The confusion of vegetable *elektron* with the metal alloy of the same name may never be resolved, but it seems likely that from Homer on, most writers when using *elektron* were referring to vegetable amber, not metal alloy. Much of the ambiguity of Greek *elektron* and Latin *electrum* is due to the fact that the word attained such wide literary usage that many writers were unaware of its actual meaning.

Wisconsin State College at Eau Claire

[50] This connection was made by John Rostock and H. T. Riley, trans. of *The Natural History of Pliny,* Bohn edition, VI, 399, n.

[51] Pierson, *op. cit.,* 49-50.

TRADITION AGAINST INDEPENDENT INVESTIGATION IN PRE-MODERN CRANIOLOGY

Loren C. MacKinney and Thomas Herndon

The human skull has been a subject of medical interest from earliest times. Archeologists have unearthed skulls from the caves of prehistoric man which show evidences of trepanation and later healing of the bone. Among the ancient Egyptians cranial anatomy received special attention because of their interest in cranial surgery and embalming. The earliest known mention of cranial sutures in medical literature is in the Edwin Smith Surgical Papyrus, which dates from the seventeenth century B.C. but was copied, in part at least, from an original work written a thousand years or more earlier.

The earliest known detailed description of the anatomy of the skull is contained in a treatise by Hippocrates of Cos entitled *On the wounds of the head* (1.1). Therein he wrote as follows: (Withington's translation in the Loeb edition)

Men's heads are not alike nor are the sutures of the head disposed the same way in all. When a man has a prominence in the front of his head—the prominence is a rounded outstanding projection of the bone itself—his sutures are disposed in the head as the letter *tau*, T, is written; for he has the shorter line disposed transversely at the base of the prominence; while he has the other line longitudinally disposed through the middle of the head right to the neck. But when a man has the prominence at the back of his head, the sutures in his case have a disposition the reverse of the former, for while the short line is disposed transversely at the prominence, the longer is disposed through the middle of the head longitudinally right to the forehead. He who has a prominence at each end of his head, both front and back, has the sutures disposed in the way the latter *eta*, H, is written; for the long lines have a transverse disposition at either prominence and the short goes through the middle of the head longitudinally, ending each way at the long lines. He who has no prominence at either end has the sutures of his head as the letter *chi*, X, is written; the lines are disposed one transversely coming down to the temple, the other longitudinally through the middle of the head.

Hippocrates, it should be noted, did not give specific technical names to the cranial bones and sutures, and his descriptions are not completely reliable. For example, he described one normal, and three abnormal, shapes of the cranium, adding unwarranted conclusions to the effect that the pattern of the cranial sutures is determined by the shape of the skull, specifically by the location of bulges or prominences. Modern anatomists reject all such interpretations.

More influential than Hippocrates through the centuries especially in the West, were the voluminous writings of Galen. So far as cranial anatomy is concerned, Galen repeated Hippocrates in substance concerning one normal and three abnormal head shapes and corresponding suture patterns (*On bones for beginners,* 1). In another treatise (*On the use of the parts,* 9.17) he imagined a fourth abnormal type, viz.,

A fourth species of acuminated head might be imagined, but which does not occur, with the head more prominent at the two ears than in front and behind.

This, he continued, is the head of a monster and cannot live because it lacks some of the ventricles of the brain. Also, he maintained that anyone with an abnormal brain cannot be in full possession of his mental powers. It would seem that Galen, on the basis of Hippocratic authority, of personal observation, of keen analysis, and with a modicum of imagination, established what we call the Hippocratic-Galenic tradition concerning the cranium and its sutures. This tradition, as we shall see, dominated the anatomical thinking of many medical men well into the modern era.

In the fourth century, Oribasius, who was called "the ape of Galen," followed the same anatomical precept, quoting Galen as a source (*Medicinalium Collect,* 25.3). Using only Galen's treatise *On bones,* he described over again the one normal and three abnormal skull shapes and suture patterns; he omitted the above-quoted account of the fourth (imagined) skull, to be found only in *On the uses of the parts.*

Reverting chronologically to the pre-Galenic age, we now present two independent-minded writers, one in the Greek East, the other in the Latin West, who disregarded the authorities of classical antiquity. A century before Galen, Celsus, an unusually intelligent Roman encyclopedist, briefly described (in *De medicina,* 8.1) the appearance of the skull and its sutures, as follows:

Generally there are two sutures [i.e., squamosa] above the ears, separating the temples from the upper part of the head; a third [i.e., lambdoidal] stretches to the ears across the vertex, separating the occiput [i.e., the rear portion] from the top of the head; a fourth suture [i.e., sagittal] runs likewise from the vertex over the middle of the head to the forehead itself and ending between the eyebrows. [a sentence concerning the coronal suture may have been in the original version].

Noteworthy in this passage are the absence of data concerning cranial bulges, and the final portion describing the sagittal extension to the nose (which some commentators equate with Hippocrates' and Galen's X, chi pattern). Such extensions are recognized today as an abnormality found in infants and rarely in adults. Celsus deserves credit for having been the earliest known writer to mention (but not by name) the two squamosa (or temporal) sutures.

About a century after Celsus, Rufus of Ephesus, in a Greek treatise *On the names of the parts of the human body* (1.3) manifested complete independence from anatomical tradition. Like Celsus, without reference to varying shapes of the head, he gave a remarkably modern description of a normal skull. He was perhaps the earliest known medical writer to apply the technical terms for coronal and lambdoidal to their respective sutures, and it probably was from him or his Alexandrian colleagues that Galen borrowed these terms. At any rate, Rufus' anatomical knowledge was Alexandrian rather than Hippocratic, and so novel in certain respects that some medical historians have awarded him a "first" in "the realm of anatomical nomenclature."[1]

Whatever Rufus' virtues as an independent thinker, the influence of his famous contemporary, Galen, and his "Ape," Oribasius, dominated the late Roman and early medieval centuries. However, the worshipful "transmitters" of ancient medical lore to this somewhat "dark" age, paid little attention to cranial anatomy. Even a Moslem expert such as Rasis, as late as the tenth century had little to report concerning the human skull. He merely recorded (*Almansor*, 1.2) that normally it is round, with anterior and posterior prominences; he made no reference to sutures. His contemporary, Isaac Judaeus (*Pantegni*, Theory, 2.2), described the normal skull in a confused and uncertain fashion. It seems that Moslem medical authorities followed the classical tradition, but "afar off." However, there were exceptions.

A few years after Rasis, Haly Abbas (*The Royal Book*, 2.3) repeated Galen's description of normal and abnormal skulls but dismissed the abnormal sutures with the remark that "any shape deviating from the normal is unnatural." On the other hand, he probably contributed to cranial nomenclature the term "sagittal" for the longitudinal suture. Haly's work contained the first detailed treatment of human anatomy after that of Galen. It is likely that he would have turned the attention of medieval anatomists away from the abnormalities of the skull, had his treatise not been eclipsed (after the eleventh century) by the brilliant writings of Avicenna. Avicenna, who might (with some justice) be called "The Moslem Ape of Galen," repeated almost verbatim the Galenic description of skulls (*Canon*, 1.1.5. ch.2), thus bringing back to the thinking of Moslems and Christians alike, the classical tradition of human skulls; including three (or more) abnormal types with intricately and fantastically interrelated prominences and sutures. Avicenna's medical works, like Haly's, were soon current in Latin translations in the West, where they tended to eclipse Haly and to rival Galen.

At long last, under such inspiring influence, thirteenth-century Christian writers began to treat of anatomy in some detail in their medical, and even non-medical, compilations. But Vincent of Beauvais,

---

[1] Charles Singer's *Short History of Anatomy*, New York, 1956, 42.

one of the most popular of thirteenth-century encyclopedists described only normal skulls in his section on humans (*Speculum Naturale,* 28.10). Turning to the more scientific compilers, Albertus Magnus, one of the leading spirits of thirteenth century learning, is found in the camp of the classical traditionalists; he followed the Galenic pattern of skulls implicity (*De animalibus,* 1.2.5). At about the turn of the century (ca. 1300) Italian physicians such as Peter of Abano (*Conciliator,* 82; 1472, ed. Mantua) and Lanfranc of Milan (*Practica,* 2. ch.1) followed suit. Without further examples of achievements from this remarkable century, we pause to take stock of the situation with regard to concepts of cranial anatomy.

Thus far (to ca. 1300) our survey would seem to indicate that whereas Celsus and Rufus described the normal human skull, Galen, building on Hippocratic ideas, established a classical tradition comprising (1) a *normal* pattern of skulls (with bulging prominences both fore and aft, intersected by three sutures in an H-eta pattern); and (2) three or more *abnormal* types of skulls in which the lack of prominences in certain sections eliminated the normal sutures of these sections, thus creating intersecting sutures that resembled either a T-tau, or the same figure in reverse, or a X-chi. This general concept (of one normal and three abnormals) seems to have prevailed widely throughout ancient and medieval times in the Greek East, the Latin West, and throughout the far flung Moslem world. Deviations from the Hippocratic-Galenic-Avicennan concept were rare, thanks to the widespread reputations of the three as medical authorities.

From about the year 1300, however, there is a marked break in this continuity. Certain aspects of the traditional concept, already fading in a few times and places, tended to pass out of anatomical thinking in and about 1300; again in the early 1500s there is a rather violent break. To the general trend during these centuries, and to the two periods of sudden change, we now turn our attention. In the first episode, Italians and Frenchmen play the leading role. Well publicized by modern historians of medicine has been the role of Italy and Italians in medieval medical progress. Salernitan, Bolognese and other Italian surgeons; Constantine of Monte Cassino, Roger and Roland, Copho the dissector of pigs, the Bologna autopsists, Roger II and Frederick II, organizers of formal medical and surgical education; and so on, Italy has rightly been hailed as the home of pre-renaissance medical and anatomical science. From the very end of the thirteenth century emerges the name of Mundinus (Mondino de Luzzi) who has been called "the founder of modern anatomy," because of his highly practical handbook on dissection.

Such adulation rests on generally accepted facts and critical judgments. Be that as it may, we propose to turn elsewhere, namely to France, for the start of the late medieval shift of emphasis in cranial anatomy, for the first major break in the classical tradition. Henri de Mondeville, physician-surgeon to French kings during the first two decades of the fourteenth century, is the major figure in the scene. Having been educated in North-Italian medical schools, he may have profited by advanced ideas circulating in Lombardy, where his teacher, Thaddaeus Florentinus was a progressive anatomist. However, the quality and detail of Henri's cranial data surpass, and in some cases antedate those of much-lauded Italians. For example, the famous handbook of Mundinus, which had a brief unimpressive account of skulls, was completed in 1319, twelve years after Mondeville's illustrated *Anatomy,* which contained precise detail on skulls (disregarding the outworn abnormal patterns of the classical tradition), together with accounts of demonstrations using actual or artificial skulls and illustrations, and references to actual skulls for evidence concerning cranial anatomy.[2] After demonstrating (with illustrations at the Universities of Montpellier and Paris in 1304 and 1306, Mondeville revised his *Anatomy* (in 1306), modifying the original set of illustrations. Thirteen illustrations, revised once more, and in color, were incorporated in his French treatise on surgery (1320). Several of these illustrations, because of their full-length, naturalistic artistry are thought (gratuitously, we believe) to have inspired certain of Vesalius' illustrations over two centuries later. Somewhat more credible, perhaps, is the tendency of certain modern historians to credit Mondeville with "breaking the power of tradition" by his objective use of actual skeletons, as well as pictures. In any case, we prefer to present his achievements without benefit of dubious imaginary generalizations such as "the first," "the reviver, restorer, rejuvenator" etc. As a matter of fact, he was NOT "the first" to use anatomical illustrations;[3] however, he seems to have been the first to use illustrations in large-scale anatomical-surgical treatises. Finally, it can be said, we believe without exaggeration, that he, more than any other one person of his age, contributed to the first marked break in traditional cranial anatomy. This he did in the following ways: (1) he carried on first-hand observation, using actual or artificial skulls, and anatomical pictures for study and demonstration; (2) on the basis of observable skulls, he categorically denied, as a popular error, the Aristotelean assertion concerning circular sutures in females; (3) he minimized Galen's "wish" concerning abnormal configurations of skulls;

[2] For details, see Loren MacKinney, "The Beginnings of Western Scientific Anatomy; new evidence and a new interpretation of Henri de Mondeville's role," *Medical History,* 6 (1962).
[3] MacKinney, "A Thirteenth-Century Medical Case History in Miniatures," *Speculum,* 35 (1960), 251-6, esp. 254.

and (4) he eliminated from his revised *Anatomy* illustrations and descriptions of the abnormal sutures of the traditional classical concept.[4]

From the time of Mondeville (ca. 1300) to the galaxy of anatomical "greats" of the sixteenth century, anatomical knowledge and illustrations improved steadily, though slowly and often crudely. This period we characterize as an evolution between two episodes that we designate by the term "breakthrough." Mondeville's successors seemed more inclined to follow his exposition of cranial anatomy than to forge ahead independently. Gui de Chauliac, his famous and highly popular successor in surgery repeated, in substance, the Mondeville description of normal sutures (*Chirurgie,* 1.1.2. ch.1). But, he used no anatomical illustrations, and somewhat grudgingly referred to Mondeville as the one who had "demonstrated anatomy with thirteen pictures." A century later, Nicholas Falcutius manifested a similar lack of enthusiasm for illustrations or novelties in anatomical theory (*Sermones medicinales,* 3.2.1. ch.2). Illustrations were much used, nevertheless, though most of the examples are found in anonymous manuscript treatises. In our own collection of approximately 4000 microfilm reproductions of medical miniatures there are cranial illustrations that parallel Mondeville's models; one dates from the thirteenth century, three from the fourteenth, and six from the fifteenth. Similar types in block prints are to be found in late fifteenth and early sixteenth-century printed works on anatomy. The most noteworthy of these is Berengario da Carpi's *Isagoge brevis* (1522) recently translated by Professor L. R. Lind with photo-reproductions of the illustrations. The importance of this treatise lies in the fact that, like Mondeville's *Anatomy* over two centuries earlier, it marks a break (the second) in traditional craniology.[5] Therein, da Carpi, like Mondeville, disregarded the classical abnormals in skull anatomy, and used illustrations successfully to portray the normal pattern. "Sense experience [he once wrote] is my guiding star," and on such grounds he denied certain Galenic theories.

After da Carpi, events moved swiftly, and controversially, in the field of anatomy. Jacques Dubois, Vesalius' teacher, and Vesalius himself, repeated the entire Hippocratic-Galenic craniology. In fact Vesalius strengthened it immeasurably by adding to the descriptive text in his *Fabrica* (1543) the famous naturalistic illustrations, including five skulls, four of which vividly portrayed the traditional abnormals. He also asserted that he had seen in human remains examined personally at Venice and Bologna actual examples of a fourth abnormal skull which

[4] *Ibid.*
[5] Da Carpi's importance has also been stressed recently by Gernot Rath, in "Pre-Vesalian Anatomy in the Light of Modern Research," *Bulletin Hist. Medicine,* 35 (1961), 142-8. Designated as "first rejuvenator of anatomy" by his successors, he was long eclipsed by Vesalius; now he seems to be enjoying deserved recognition.

Galen had "imagined." With such encouragement many scholars joined the ranks of the classical traditionalists; among them, Francesco Sansovino, Guido Guidi (Vido Vidius), Joannis Argenterius, Bartholomaeus Eustachius, Ambroise Paré, John Banister, and other sixteenth-century notables.

Da Carpi's efforts at objective criticism gained support with Realdo Colombo's tacit denial of the sacrosanct X suture pattern, which by his day might well be designated the "Hippocratic-Galenic-Avicennan-Vesalian" tradition. In his *De re anatomica* (1559) published sixteen years after the *Fabrica* of his former master, and now bitter rival, Colombo wrote as follows:

I have found the sutures of the head existing in various ways.... However, I must confess that I have never seen that shape resembling the Greek letter X which Hippocrates and Galen mention, even though I have often sought it with, as it were, the eyes of a lynx.[6]

Falloppius, Vesalius' successor at the University of Padua, supported Colombo, writing (in *Observationes anatomicae,* 1561) as follows: "I cannot assert that I ever saw that particular decussation in the skull, nor have I met anyone who has." Falloppius expressed further surprise that his predecessors had been so credulous of Hippocrates' ideas concerning cranial sutures. He himself had found no coronal suture in skulls with the frontal prominence, and likewise no lambdoidal suture in skulls with the rear prominence; he also noted suture-less skulls with both frontal and rear prominences. No known anatomist had ever so devastatingly attacked traditional craniology. Shortly thereafter Joannis Riolanis asserted that none of the traditional abnormals existed except in old men. Thus the battle was joined, to continue through the two succeeding centuries.

From the outset a curious aspect was the fact that the leaders of both factions were experienced scientific observers. Da Carpi had a hundred dissections to his credit; Colombo claimed as many as fourteen per year; Vesalius and Falloppius mentioned the many human remains they had examined in Italian towns. Most of these careful observers set high standards of objectivity and reliance on fact rather than tradition. Da Carpi stressed the supremacy of "sense experience" as his "guiding star"; Charles Estienne held that one should trust "his own vision" rather than "anatomical books," even suggesting that the great Galen "withheld certain facts." Giovanni Canano urged the anatomist to "trust your own eyes more than Galen's testimony."[7] A somewhat disappointing counter-influence, however, is the evidence that those who

[6] For details on Colombo, see Robert J. Moes and C. D. O'Malley, "Realdo Colombo: 'On Those Things Rarely Found in Anatomy'," *Bulletin History Medicine,* 34 (1960), 508-28, esp. 520.

[7] Rath, *op. cit.,* passim.

advocated such high standards did not always practice them. Present day critics of Vesalius' inflated reputation have cited occasions on which he stubbornly upheld Galenic theories even in the face of observed anatomical facts.[8] Meanwhile, in the *opposing* camp, Da Carpi and other anti-traditionalists sometimes manifested unusual tenderness toward Galen personally, if not toward his theories. Like Mondeville centuries earlier, da Carpi never flatly denied Galenic craniology, and at times criticized him apologetically in polite terms. All of which is explicable when one recollects the popularity of classical antiquity during this period. Furthermore, Galen was the most eminent and long-standing of medical authorities, not to be attacked with impunity. Hippocrates' craniology also was excused, by Falloppius, as merely intended for the lay populace. None the less, in view of Vesalius' slow evolution to anti-authoritarianism, da Carpi, Colombo and Falloppius merit the leading position in the sixteenth-century break with traditional craniology. Had Vesalius joined them in the anti-Galenic crusade, instead of strengthening the classical concept of cranial anatomy, the sixteenth century might have witnessed a complete triumph for modern scientific craniology. As it was the controversy continued for almost two hundred years.

In the seventeenth century, Thomas Bartholin embellished the Hippocratic-Galenic-Avicennan-Vesalian tradition by adding to Galen's four abnormal skulls seven more, making a total of eleven. Many of these, however were merely variations of the Galenic types. But Bartholin went further, attributing to them abnormal pathological conditions such as hydrocephaly and epilepsy. He also maintained that the third abnormal skull (with the X pattern of sutures) was peculiar to Turks and Greenlanders, who bound the heads of infants. Other traditionalists of the post-Vesalian period need only be mentioned; among them, Caspar Bartholin, father of Thomas, Caspar Bauthin, Joannis Scultetus, and somewhat later Joannis Platnere, William Cheselden and John Bell. It also should be noted that by no means all early modern anatomists took a definite stand on the question of the Hippocratic-Galenic abnormalities. There were those who, like some of their medieval predecessors, quietly ignored the issue contenting themselves with descriptions of the traditionally normal types. Such was Thomas Vicary whose sixteenth-century *Anatomie of the Bodie* of Man merely transcribed a normal account, representative of the Mondeville period, from a fourteenth-century manuscript. The keenly objective Frenchman, Charles Estienne, of the famous Parisian publishing family, in his treatise *On the dissection of the Parts of the Human Body*, took a similarly middle-ground position; as also did Leonhart Fuchs, in his *Compendium medicinae*.

Without further prolonging our survey, we call attention to the fact that the X suture and other abnormal cranial phenomena were not the

[8] *Ibid.*, 147.

only questions with which early modern anatomists were concerned. Through the centuries Aristotle's theories concerning skulls (*History of Animals,* 1.7) were remarkably persistent, considering the opposition they evoked. Mondeville categorically denied the existence of suture-less skulls, and others in pre-modern times attributed them to old age. Vesalius re-stated the "old-age" explanation, which was accepted by many of his contemporaries and successors. Charles Estienne, Paré, Thomas Bartholin and others accepted sature-less skulls as a rarity. Colombo once attributed a young man's death, accompanied by severe headaches, to the absence of sutures. Aristotle's assertion (widely held by medieval encyclopedists) that women had only a single circular suture whereas men had three which intersected, was doubted by Peter of Abano and denied by Mondeville (ca. 1300) and by Vesalius and other sixteenth-century anatomists. Aristotle's craniology seems to have been criticized more severely throughout the centuries than that of any other of the ancients.

In summarizing our survey of the Hippocratic-Galenic-Avicennan-Vesalian tradition of human skulls we note that it was attacked only sporadically and indirectly during ancient and medieval times. Even the doubters of the Mondeville era restricted their out-and-out negations to Aristotle, politely giving to Galen the benefit of doubt. During the sixteenth century frontal attacks were made on the Hippocratic and Galenic positions, but even here anatomists hesitated unreservedly to condemn the authorities of old.

The most dramatic instance is that of Falloppius. Having disproved Hippocrates' statements concerning abnormal suture patterns by the evidence from numerous skulls, he expressed surprise that earlier anatomists had accepted these false theories. Later, however, he excused the error on the ground that Hippocrates' description was merely theory, not meant to be taken seriously since it was popular non-professional opinion that he himself did not believe. This sixteenth-century solution is remarkably similar to a late-nineteenth-century solution of the same problem, expressed as follows by an eminent authority (Francis Adams) in his translation and commentary on the works of Hippocrates (Vol I, p. 357f.) :

..... I have imagined that what Hippocrates meant was to express himself to the following effect: when the forehead is remarkably prominent, and, at the same time, there is a great depression behind, the cranium, if looked upon from above, will show the coronal suture running across the fore part of the head, and the sagittal through its middle, while the lambdoid will be inconspicuous, from being below the level of the coronal. The two together, then, would form some resemblance to the letter T. When, on the other hand, the forehead is low, that is to say, wants a normal development, and the occiput is unusually prominent, the lambdoid suture joins the sagittal, so as to present some appearance of the same letter reversed. But in a square-built head, where the frontal and occipital regions have protuberances equally developed, the coronal and lambdoid sutures run nearly parallel to one another, and are joined in the middle by the sagittal, in which case the three sutures may be imagined to present some resemblance to the Greek letter H. When there is no protuberance either before or behind, and the sagittal suture passes through the middle of the bone down to the nasal process, the coronal suture intersects it, so as to give them something like the shape of the Greek letter X. I offer this explanation, however, merely as a conjecture, and wish the reader to judge of it accordingly.

The "reader," we believe, will "judge" the T and X explanations without hesitation as "conjecture." Furthermore, considering the fact that Hippocrates, Galen, Avicenna, Vesalius and other traditionalists are thought to have been objective scientists who examined skulls in a thorough and critical manner, one is led to wonder (with Falloppius) how so many medical experts have accepted their theories without protest, in fact with politely unconvincing excuses.

University of North Carolina
Chapel Hill

THE *SATOR*-FORMULA: AN EVALUATION
Herbert L. Bodman, Jr.

Wherever Christians have travelled the *sator*-formula has followed. It has fascinated peasants and professors; its tantalizing enigma has drawn many scholars to extremes of fancy and then to impassioned defenses of their imagination. Once the problem was considered solved, but in the light of new evidence a few supporters of the suggested solution have expressed their doubt. An evaluation of the whole question would appear to be in order.

This significant puzzle is composed of twenty-five letters divided into five words of equal length. The form usually assumed is that of a square:

SATOR		ROTAS
AREPO		OPERA
TENET	or	TENET
OPERA		AREPO
ROTAS		SATOR

Occasionally it is found written as a sentence and thus may be defined as a palindrome. But more frequently the squared form is preferred with the added characteristic that it can be read vertically.

Four of the five words are Latin. *Sator* means a "sower" or "planter" and by extension "begetter," "father," "producer," or "causer." *Tenet* is the third person singular of the verb *teneo*, "to hold," "to possess," "to defend," and extensions. *Opera* means "trouble," "pains," "effort," "exertion," "time for work," or "workman." The last-named meaning is generally in the plural. *Rotas* is the accusative plural of *rota* meaning "wheel."

Arepo is the only non-Latin word; furthermore, in this form it exists in no language. Yet, as will be seen, numerous attempts have been made to give this word meaning in order to derive a translation for the formula, it being assumed that the formulator used "palindromic license." Although predominantly Latin the words of the formula have been frequently transliterated into Greek, Coptic and Ethiopic because the formula was used in the cultures associated with these languages.

The history of this formula covers a period of over eighteen hundred years and its uses appear to have varied. It has often been accompanied by phrases or symbols which may have been intended to clarify the purpose of its inscription and which therefore may be considered indications of the meaning attributed to the formula at that time.

The earliest examples yet found are at Pompeii, one a fragment in a private home and the other a complete square scratched on a column in the *palaestra*, both of them beginning with the word *rotas*. They may be dated between 50 and 79 A.D., because the decoration of the house is in a style generally agreed to have been developed after 50 A.D.,[1] and Pompeii was destroyed in 79 A.D.

Four examples of the *sator*-formula were found in the excavation of the temple of Artemis Azzanathcona at Dura-Europos, the Syrian city that for the last years of its existence (ca. 165 to 256 A.D.) was an important *limes* fortress in the Roman military defenses against Parthia and then Sassanian Persia. The camp of the Romans was located in the section of the city in which the formula inscriptions were found and it is apparent that the rooms of the temple were taken over by the military probably at the beginning of the third century when the garrison was considerably increased by local Semitic recruits. A number of the inscriptions are of a cabalistic character: alphabets, magic signs and symbols, pentagrams, evil eyes, a magic animal, and several hermetic texts in mystic alphabets.[2] The room in which the *sator*-formulae were found also contained a large number of graffiti relating to military affairs and indicate that it was a clerical office for the garrison.[3] Many of the inscriptions are Latin written in Greek alphabet. Two of the three *sator*-formulae substitute Greek letters for the Latin, the earliest example of this common practice.

The *terminus ante quem* of the Dura examples is fixed again by the destruction of the city, in 256 A.D. by the second Sassanian attack. They massacred or carried away its inhabitants into slavery. The *terminus post quem* is more difficult to place, but if the *sator*-formulae are to be associated with the military inscriptions, which seems plausible, then a date in the neighborhood of 200 A.D. is probable. Further, one may assume that the inscriber or inscribers of the Dura formulae were members of the Roman military more familiar with Greek than Latin, probably local Semitic recruits.

This assumption attains greater significance when to it is added the facts that the Pompeii *palaestra* was used as a barracks[4] and that the next example chronologically (fourth century A.D.) was found near Cirencester, England and is definitely associated with the Roman mili-

---

[1] Reale Instituto di Archeologia e Storia dell'Arte, "Notizie degli Scavi di Antichità," *Atti della Reale Accademia Nazionale dei Lincei* 5 (1929) 449; 15 (1939) 263; Matteo Della Corte, "Il Crittogramma della Pater Noster," *RendNap* 17 (1937) 93.

[2] M. I. Rostovtzeff, *et al.*, *The Excavations at Dura-Europos: Preliminary Report of the Sixth Season of Work, October 1932-March 1933* (New Haven 1936) 482.

[3] *Ibid.*

[4] Della Corte, "Il Crittogramma," *RendNap* 17 (1937) 93.

tary occupiers of the island.⁵ The other areas where early examples are found are in Egypt and Cappadocia, both tentatively dated in the fourth or fifth century A.D.⁶ It would seem correct, therefore, to assume that the initial vehicle of dissemination for the *sator*-formula, as with so many other cultural items, was the Roman army.

The earliest Egyptian example presents no concrete evidence of a Christian association, it being merely the formula inscribed in Coptic letters on a papyrus.⁷ There is then a gap in the evidence in that area for about two centuries after which several Coptic and Ethiopic examples in striking Christian contexts are found. One in Coptic of the Sa'idic dialect, dated by its orthography in the sixth or seventh centuries, is preceded by three crosses.⁸ In the desert west of Faras in Nubia an inscription in a tomb consists of a prayer dated 739 A.D. for the soul of a certain Theophilus. The *sator*-formula is included in columns of inscriptions among which is a Coptic version of the apocryphal letter from Jesus to Abgar V, king of Edessa, a letter widely employed by the Copts as a prophylactic against illness. Another list records the names of the forty martyrs of Sabaste, also a talisman against disease. The final list consists of the *sator*-formula in linear form preceded by the phrase: "These are the names of the nails of Christ."⁹ The phrase descriptive of the nails in the cross in association with the *sator*-formula occurs again in the Ethiopic work, the *Lefâfa Ṣeḍek* or "Bandlet of Righteousness," where the formula is repeated four times in garbled but identifiable form and preceded once by the sentence: "In the five nails of the Cross of our Lord Jesus Christ, I thy servant Stephen have taken refuge." Another introduction to the formula in the same work is: "I demand this by the five nails which were driven into Thy Body on the Glorious Cross, being . . . [the *sator*-formula is then given]."¹⁰ Other Coptic examples tie the *sator*-formula with that of the *alpha-omega,* a device used in the same manner, and with the cross. One of these clearly indicates that it is part of a prayer for the healing of a foot.¹¹

⁵ *EphEp* IX 519; F. Haverfield, "A Roman Charm from Cirencester," *ArchJ* 56 (1899) 319; Donald Atkinson, "The *Sator*-formula and Christianity," *Bulletin of the John Rylands Library, Manchester* 22 (1938) 420 (hereinafter cited as Atkinson, "The *Sator*-formula.")

⁶ Adolf Erman and Fritz Kreba, *Aus den Papyrus der Königlichen Museen* (Berlin 1899) 262; Oscar Wulff, ed., *Altchristliche und Mittelalterliche Byzantinische und Italienische Bildwerke* (Königliche Museen zu Berlin, "Beschreibung der Bildwerke der Christlichen Epoche," 3; Berlin 1909) I 317, no. 1669.

⁷ Erman and Krebs, *op. cit.,* 262.

⁸ Victor Stegemann, "Die Koptischen Zaubertexte der Sammlung Papyrus Erzherzog Rainer in Wien," *SBHeid,* 1, Philos.-hist. Kl., 1933-1934, 26, 74-75 (hereinafter cited as Stegemann, "Zaubertexte.")

⁹ F. L. Griffith, ed., *EEF: Archaeological Report, 1897-1898,* 63; A. H. Sayce, "Gleanings from the Land of Egypt," *RecTrav* 20 (1898) 176.

¹⁰ Sir E. A. Wallis Budge, ed. and tr., *The Bandlet of Righteousness, an Ethiopian Book of the Dead* (London 1929) 37, 75, 101.

¹¹ Walter Ewing Crum, *Coptic Monuments, Catalogue générale des Antiquités*

The first evidence of the *sator*-formula from Asia Minor, dated in the fourth or fifth century, has definite Christian associations: the fish and the formula IC+XC.[12] But there is some question whether the dating is accurate for this bronze amulet, since the minuscule *pi* in the Greek transliteration of *arepo* and *opera* is rendered as an *omega* with a line above it and the *tau* in two of the four times it occurs in the formula is written as a 7. According to a leading authority on the alphabet, these forms of the letters were not used until the ninth century and the twelfth to fourteenth centuries, respectively.[13] If these objections are sustained, then the earliest Christian use of the formula, indicated by associated formulae, must be the Coptic examples of the sixth to the eighth centuries.

In Cappadocia the words of the *sator*-formula became the names of the shepherds of the Nativity. In the rupestral churches of the Ürgüp region there are several Nativity scenes, classifiable roughly into two categories: an early group, ninth to eleventh centuries, of frescoes with strong eastern influence, and a later group, dating from the eleventh century, in which the paintings reveal a decided Byzantine influence. The words of the formula occur primarily in the first group. In the church of Saint Eustathius the shepherds are named CATOP for the young man; APEΠO for the old man; and TENETO for the musician. The words are placed next to the head in the oriental fashion so the intention of the artist cannot be misunderstood.[14] At Toqale Kilissé the young man is named APEΠON and TENETON seems to designate the musician while the old man is unidentified.[15] In another case the musician is entitled ΠEPAPOTAC, a composite of *opera* and *rotas*.[16] Among the second group of frescoes the shepherds are usually unnamed. In one case, however, only the musician is named and he CATOP.[17] It is notable, then, that there is a definite link between the words of the *sator*-formula and the shepherds of the Nativity but that no tradition appears to exist connecting a specific shepherd with a particular word of the formula.

During the Middle Ages the *sator*-formula was introduced into Europe. It received wide cognizance in Germany, ample favor in Italy

---

égyptiennes du Musée de Caire (Cairo 1902) 42; Stegemann, "Zaubertexte," 18, 38, 52, 78.
[12] Oscar Wulff, ed., *op. cit.*, I 317, no. 1669.
[13] David Diringer, *The Alphabet, a Key to the History of Mankind* (New York 1948) 457, columns 8 and 10 of table.
[14] Guillaume de Jerphanion, *Une Nouvelle Province de l'Art Byzantine: Les Eglises Rupestres de Cappadoce* (Paris 1925) I, pt. 1 78 and pl. 38 fig. 1; Guillaume de Jerphanion, "La Formule Magique Sator Arepo ou Rotas Opera," *RecSciRel* 25 (1935) 202, n. 35.
[15] Jerphanion, *Les Eglises Rupestres de Cappadoce*, I, pt. 1 273 and pl. 68 fig. 1.
[16] *Ibid.*, II, pt. 1 155 and pl. 152 fig. 2.
[17] *Ibid.*, I, pt. 2 411 and pl. 104 fig. 3.

and France, but slight recognition in England. A sampling may indicate the close association of the formula with Christian superstition.

The majority of the German examples of the *sator*-formula are to be found on medals and plaques generally accompanied by epithets of God. These are in Latin, Hebrew and pseudo-Hebrew. One in the numismatic collection of Gotha is a silver medallion on which the formula is encircled with the words Saraot (Sabaot), Emanuel, Soter, Helian, Usion, Tetragrammaton, Onagia and Ealuaet. On the reverse is a heart in which is engraved Jahveh and Schadai in Hebrew and INRI (Iesus Nazarenus Rex Iudaeorum). Emerging from the heart are the hands and feet of Christ, marked with wounds, arranged in a manner suggestive of a cross. Encompassing these are Adonai, Eloy, Eloah, Elohim, Ehohrah, Seday and Zebaot.[18] An elaborate periapt in the Nürnberg National Museum contains, in addition, the phrases *Verbum caro factum est, Agla, consummatum est* and two arrows pointing heavenwards.[19] These phrases indicate that the formula, among others, was used to call upon supernatural power to extinguish fires. This is confirmed by an edict published in 1743 by Duke Ernst Auguste of Saxe-Weimar ordering that all towns and villages should manufacture such fire disks to serve as means of quenching conflagrations which endangered the community.[20] The practice was to throw the fire disk into the fire to extinguish it.

In Bosnia the formula was used as a remedy for headache and for hydrophobia and in Iceland it was scratched on the fingernails of the patient as a cure for jaundice.[21]

In France and Italy use as a prophylactic appears to have accompanied the employment of the formula in churches and chapels as a protective device. For several centuries a sachet had been handed down, unopened, in a family from Aurillac in southern France. As the potency of the contents had become suspect, the sachet was opened revealing a wealth of medieval curative incantations and charms. One of the finds was a parchment divided into squares on both sides and containing recipes to combat various illnesses. The lower rows of squares are filled with occult devices, each labelled in Latin. The *sator*-formula is described by the following sentence in garbled Latin: *"Hanc figuram mostra mulierem in partu et peperit"* for *"Hanc figuram monstra mulieri in partu et*

[18] S. Seligmann, "Die Satorformel," *Hessische Blätter für Volkskunde* 13 (1914) 162 (hereinafter cited as Seligmann, "Satorformel").
[19] Correspondence from A. Treichel, *Verhandlungen der Berliner Gesellschaft für Anthropologie, Ethnologie und Urgeschichte* 15 (1883) 354.
[20] Seligmann, "Satorformel," 174.
[21] Auguste Allmer, *Revue Épigraphique du Midi de la France* III, no. 74 (1894) 302; Jon Arnason, *Islenzkar bjodsögur og Aefintýri* as quoted in Seligmann, "Satorformel," 170.

pariet (Show this figure to a woman in childbirth and she will produce)."
The script would indicate a date *circa* the fourteenth century.[22]

Michaelo Savonarola, an Italian doctor and father of the famous monk and religious reformer Girolamo Savonarola, directed in a manuscript of 1466 that the formula should be affixed as a plaster on the afflicted part of the patient's body without his knowledge.[23]

The *sator*-formula embellishes a Latin Bible unearthed from the ancient foundations of the Abbey St. Germain-des-Prés. The elaborate and ingenious design adorns the final page for the manuscript which is dated "anno requante domno Hludovicus VIII" which was 822 A.D.[24] but there is a distinct possibility that the formula is a gloss.

The device has been found in a walled-up section of the chapel of Saint-Laurent in Rochemaure, Ardèche, the ruined convent of Santa Maria di Campomarzo in Verona, the church of Santa Lucia of Magliano in Aquila, the cathedral at Sienna, and the church of San Pietro ad Oratorium in Capestrano.[25] It has even crossed the Atlantic, having been found in Brazil in the 1840's and in 1894 among the enclaves of Germans in the Allegheny Mountains of the United States where it was used to prevent fire, stop fits, and prevent miscarriage.[26]

Efforts to derive a solution to the *sator*-formula date as far back as the fourteenth or fifteenth century. The Bibliothèque Nationale in Paris possesses a manuscript of Byzantine origin with an attempt at a translation.[27] It would be hardly surprising that attempts at solution are not confined to modern scholarship because the appearance of the figure invites closer inspection and implies delitescence. Its employment as an amulet served to reinforce suspicions of obscure import beyond the obvious meanings of the words themselves. The words, moreover, hardly express a coherent thought even allowing for palindromic license.

But all attempts at translation have foundered on the meaning to be given the word *arepo*. As the word stands there is no evidence of its use in any language conceivably known to the Romans of the first century A.D. The Byzantine manuscript translates it as "plough" but this necessitates wide variation between $αρεπο$ and $αροτρου$.

The most common explanation is that *arepo* is a form of the Gallic

[22] Alphonse Aymar, "Contribution à l'Etude du Folklore de la Haute-Auvergne: Le Sachet Accoucheur et ses Mystères," *Les Annales du Midi* 38 (1926) 306.
[23] Seligmann, "Satorformel," 171.
[24] R. Mowat, "Le Plus Ancien Carré de Mots *Sator Arepo Tenet Opera Rotas*," *MAntFr* 64 (1905) 61.
[25] Jerphanion, "La Formule Magique," 208, 210-211.
[26] J. Hampden Porter, "Folklore of the Mountain Whites of the Alleghenies," *Journal of American Folklore* 7 (1894) 113.
[27] Seligmann, "Satorformel," 174.

arepennis, aripennis, arap, or *arapennis,* meaning a half-acre of land.²⁸ A modern French derivative is *arpent*. The etymology of the word is unknown; the stem may be similar to *arepo* and it is true that it is in keeping with the agricultural flavor of the other words in the palindrome. But the gap between *arepennis* and *arepo* can hardly be bridged grammatically or under the rules of etymology. More likely this interpretation is the product of wishful thinking.

Other explications have included *arrepor,* "I creep along," and *adrepo,* "I walk along side."²⁹ While they are Latin words, they assume that a letter has been omitted. If this is assumed, any number of words in Latin or other language could be conceived that might make sense, allowing for palindromic license. C. W. King, who favors *adrepo,* translates the formula as: "The worker (*opera*) holds (*tenet*) the wheels (*rotas*) [of the plough]; I the sower (*sator*) walk along side (*arepo*)."³⁰ C. Wescher, using the Byzantine manuscript's hypothetical Greek equivalents of the words, renders the following: "The sower is at the plough; the work (of plowing) occupies the wheels."³¹ J. Palma took *arepo* to be a proper name, that of the "sower," and produced: "An indefatigable sower, the worker Arepo, holds the works, the wheels." He then interpreted this translation to mean, "God, the creator, holds in his hand both his vases of clay known by the name of man and all the force of the round machine."³² Other types of solutions suggested have been that the formula should be read in a line, separated into words at other points than every fifth letter, or that it should be read boustrephedon, that is, the first line from left to right, the second from right to left, etc.³³ Neither of these is acceptable: the first required the interpolation of additional letters to derive a meaning, and the second presupposed a transitional phase in writing between cultures with writings in opposite directions. Although this condition existed between Semitic languages and Latin, it would imply that the formula was evolved in a Semitic culture. There is no evidence at this point to suggest that this was the case.

In 1926 Felix Grosser published in *Archiv für Religionswissenschaft*³⁴ a solution which departed radically from those which sought to

---

²⁸ E. A. Andrews, *A Copious and Critical Latin-English Lexicon* (New York 1854) "Arepennis."

²⁹ Seligmann, "Satorformel," 173; C. W. King as quoted in observation of E. Egger, *BAntFr* 1875, 96.

³⁰ *Ibid.*

³¹ C. Wescher, "Note sur l'Interpretation d'une Inscription Provenant de Rochemaure (Ardèche)," *BAntFr* 1874, 153.

³² Anonymous note, *L'Intermédiaire des Chercheurs et Curieux* 3 (1866) 476-477.

³³ W. Deonna, "Talismans Magiques trouvés dans l'Ile de Thasos," *REG* 20 (1907) 371-372; anonymous note, *L'Intermédiaire des Chercheurs et Curieux* 3 (1866) 522-524.

³⁴ Felix Grosser, "Ein Neuer Vorschlag sur Deutung der *Sator*-Formel," *ArchRW* 24 (1926) 165-169.

find meaning in the words themselves. He treated the formula as an anagram, disregarding the words themselves and rearranging the twenty-five letters in such a way that they twice formed the initial words of the Latin Lord's Prayer, Pater Noster, placed in the pattern of a cross with the letter N as the nexus. Four letters remained, two A's and two O's. These were placed at the extremities of the cross. The completed figure took this form:

```
                A
                P
                A
                T
                E
                R
A  P A T E R N O S T E R  O
                O
                S
                T
                E
                R
                O
```

Thus from behind the framework of the word-square are revealed three common Christian formulae: the cross, the *pater noster,* and the *alpha* and *omega,* the first signifying Christ, the second the foremost supplicatory prayer of the church, and the third the eternity of God. Grosser believed that the square originated at a time in the early history of Christianity when its adherents were persecuted and desired a profession of faith which would be sufficiently obscure to protect them from Roman prejudice. This the *sator*-formula, as his solution interpreted it, admirably fulfilled.

Guillaume de Jerphanion, one of the more prolific writers on the *sator*-formula, noticed in his favorable critique of Grosser's solution that the word-square supplied guarded hints of its true nature, if Grosser's solution were accepted. The cross is represented five times, four of them the Greek *tau* cross (the word *tenet* used twice to form a cross and the four T's in the two words).[85]

All of the early examples of the palindrome began with the word *rotas*. The first instance of the inverted form is the Coptic papyrus amulet of the fourth or fifth century. There has been some speculation as to the cause of this change. In the light of Grosser's proposed solution, Jerphanion observed and Atkinson also noted that the *sator* pattern provided a more satisfactory placement of the A's and O's: the *alpha*

[85] Jerphanion, "La Formule Magique," 223.

preceded the *omega* in the first two words.³⁶ It may also be suggested that if the cryptogram originated at the time of persecution, its secret had to be well concealed. But by the time of the Coptic papyrus anti-Christian prejudice had ceased, Constantine had been converted, and there was little need of complete subterfuge. It may then, or even previously, have been realized that the word *sator* alone of all the words in the formula embodied the three elements of the solution: the cross represented by the *tau*, the *alpha* and *omega* flanking it, and God by the meaning of the word itself.

Grosser suggested his solution of the *sator*-formula before the earliest examples of the formula had been discovered, namely, those at Pompeii and those at Dura-Europos. The Dura examples posed no particular problem but in Jerphanion's opinion the discovery of the Pompeii examples and the conclusion they forced that the formula had been devised prior to 79 A.D. presented major obstacles. Jerphanion based his objections on the following points:

1. The existence of Christians at Pompeii has not been conclusively proven.

2. Since Greek was the language of the Christian catechism and liturgy, the word-square should have been born in a center of the Greek language. Had early Christians wished to evolve a cryptogram containing the first words of the Lord's Prayer, they would have employed the Greek πάτερ ἡῶν, not the Latin *Pater Noster*.

3. The letters A and O must refer to the infinity of God or Christ. Yet the first definite instances of Christian reference to the ancient Greek expression AΩ for "the beginning and the end" occurs in the Apocalypse dated post 79 A.D. Jerphanion rejects the argument that the expression was in common usage and borrowed by the Christians for their own purposes.

4. Considering the delay in the utilization of the cross in Christian iconography and symbolism, Jerphanion doubts its existence at the nascence of the palindrome. He predicates such a statement on the assumption that the *sator*-formula was a prophylactic device from its inception, while admitting that the cross was endowed with salvatory virtue in the New Testament.

5. The law of the *cruces dissimulates* did not really exist before the beginning of the third century. Although it was developed from previous experience, Jerphanion is skeptical that the spiritual state and Christian custom existing prior to 79 A.D. was of a character such as to produce such an arcane device as the *sator*-formula.³⁷

---

³⁶ *Ibid.*, 210; Atkinson, "The *Sator*-formula," 424, n. 18.
³⁷ Guillaume de Jerphanion, "A Propos des Nouveaux Exemplaires trouvés à Pompei du Carré Magique 'Sator'," *CRAI* 1937, *passim*.

Matteo Della Corte and Atkinson have published articles seeking to refute these criticisms of Grosser's proposed solution. Basing his conclusions on a thorough study of the Pompeii graffiti, Della Corte is certain that Christians were present in Pompeii, although probably not in great numbers. Among his proofs he offers the epigraph [C]*ristiani* found in the *atrium* of the *Hospitium* and a cross in bas relief over a corner shrine in the house of Pansa.[38] Both Della Corte and Atkinson hold that the Lord's Prayer was recited immediately by all Christians and was translated into Latin at an early date. A Greek book, *The Doctrine of the Twelve Apostles* (Διδαχὴ τῶν δώδεκα αποστολων), written definitely in the first century, adjures all Christians to repeat the prayer thrice daily.[39] Atkinson states that the catechetical use of the Lord's Prayer in the private devotions of converts was common and that there was a minority of Latin-speaking converts at Rome numerous enough to have given rise to a Latin name for the Lord's Prayer.[40] The latter author adds, "It may be regarded as the strongest confirmation of Grosser's explanation that the letters additional to the double *Paternoster* are A and O twice repeated." He asserts that the author of the Apocalypse is

quoting in its Greek form a well-known "saying of the Lord." And this, as far as our evidence reaches, in the Aramaic form in which Christ must have uttered it, was original with him, though perhaps suggested by passages in Isaiah.[41]

The so-called "sayings of the Lord" are thought to be a written collection not preserved but believed to have been used by at least Matthew and Luke.[42]

Clearly no solution embodying a translation of the formula's words can be accepted without a reasonable interpretation of *arepo*. At this juncture it would appear impossible for one to be found. Of the proposals based on other criteria, none but that of Grosser is acceptable. Grosser's suggestion is ingenious but if he had the ingenuity to develop it, can one deny that an unknown Latin of the first century A.D. had the requisite genius to devise such a means of communicating the essentials of the Christian message among a persecuted minority? What is perhaps more difficult to reconcile is that precise knowledge of the message underlying the formula could have been retained over more than a century to dictate an inversion from the previously common *rotas* form to the subsequently more usual *sator* form. Yet perhaps an unnecessary degree of knowledge is assumed. Perhaps the simple fact

---

[38] Matteo Della Corte, "I Christiani a Pompei," *RendNap* 19 (1939) 6.
[39] *Ibid.*, 13.
[40] Atkinson, "The *Sator*-formula," 426-427.
[41] *Ibid.*, 433.
[42] Vincent Taylor, *The Gospels, a Short Introduction* (London 1945) 20.

that the word *sator* means "sower," a concept long associated with God, would be sufficient to cause the inversion.

No example of the formula has yet been found outside an environment in which at least a good claim for Christian presence can be made. Since the sixth, and possibly the fourth, century the context has definitely been Christian. It would seem that not only on the grounds of elimination of other solutions proposed but also on the grounds of inherent plausibility, the Grosser suggestion should be accorded the term "solution" without any qualifying adjective, at least until some nefarious archaeologist may unearth a *sator* square definitely datable before Christ.

University of North Carolina
Chapel Hill

PUBLICATIONS BY WALLACE E. CALDWELL

BOOKS

Hellenic Conceptions of Peace. Studies in History, Economics and Public Law, LXXXIV, no. 2. New York: Columbia University Press, 1919.

The Ancient World. New York: Farrar and Rinehart, 1937. Second revised edition. New York: Rinehart, 1949.

——— and E. H. Merrill. *World History.* Chicago: Sanborn, 1949.

——— and E. H. Merrill. *Popular Illustrated History of the World.* New York: Graystone Press, 1950. Second Edition. New York: Graystone Press, 1954.

——— and W. C. McDermott. *Readings in the History of the Ancient World.* New York: Rinehart, 1951.

TRANSLATIONS

from the French: *Thebes: The Glory of a Great Past* by Jean Capart, New York: Dial Press, 1926.

ARTICLES

"The Place of Ancient History in the Social Studies," *Journal of Social Forces* I (1923), 237-240.

"The Content and Teaching of Ancient History," *Journal of Social Forces* I (1923), 550-555.

"The Age of Pericles: An Interpretation," *South Atlantic Quarterly* XXVIII (1929), 354-369.

"A Foreword," *Bulletin of the Archaeological Society of North Carolina* I (1934), no. 1, 2-3; no. 2, 1-2.

"Education in the Social Sciences and the New Deal," *High School Journal* XVIII (1935), 87-92.

"The Humanities at the University of North Carolina, 1795-1945, A Historical Survey," *A State University Surveys the Humanities.* Chapel Hill: University of North Carolina Press, 1945.

"The Writing of a World History," *High School Journal* XXIX (1946), 40-42.

"Why a Liberal Education?", *Carolina Quarterly* (Spring, 1949). 5.

"The Rise and Fall of the Individual in Classical Antiquity," *University of North Carolina Extension Bulletin* XXIII, no. 3 (1953).

"An Estimate of Pompey," *Studies Presented to David Moore Robinson* II. St. Louis: Washington University Press, 1953, 954-961.
"Fraternal Orders in Orange County," *Orange County, 1752-1952*. Edited by Hugh T. Lefler and Paul Wager. Chapel Hill: Orange Print Shop, 1953, 318-321.
"Names," *Studies in Honor of B. L. Ullman*. St. Louis: Washington University Press, 1957, 29-34.

REVIEWS

of G. P. Baker, *Twelve Centuries of Rome*. The Classical Journal XXX (1935), 558-559.
— Kurt Pastenaci, *Die Beiden Weltmächte der 500-jährige Kampf der Germanen mit Rom*. Classical Weekly XXXII (1938), 82.
— Werner Jaeger, *Paideia: The Ideals of Greek Culture*. American Historical Review XLV (1940), 689-690.
— C. H. V. Sutherland, *The Romans in Spain*. American Historical Review XLVI (1941), 700.
— A. N. Sherwin-White, *The Roman Citizenship*. Classical Weekly XXIV (1941), 134-135.
— Norman J. DeWitt, *Urbanization and Franchise in Roman Gaul*. Classical Weekly XXIV (1941), 176.
— Cyril E. Robinson, *Zito Hellas: A Popular History of Ancient Greece*. Classical Weekly XLII (1945), 14.
— Louis Gottschalk, Clyde Kluckhohn and Robert Angell, *The Use of Personal Documents in History, Anthropology and Sociology*. Social Forces XXIV (1946), 354-357.
— Social Science Research Council, *Bulletin 54, Theory and Practice in Historical Study*. Social Forces XXV (1947), 358-359.
— Douglas L. Rights, *The American Indian in North Carolina*. Archaeology I (1948), 60.
— C. E. Robinson, Hellas, *A Short History of Ancient Greece*. Classical Weekly XLII (1948), 14. Second review of same book in Classical Weekly XLIII (1950), 158.
— Truesdell S. Brown, *Onesicritus: A Study of Hellenistic Historiography*. Classical Weekly XLIV (1951), 156.
— J. Enoch Powell, *Translation of Herodotus*. Classical Journal XLVII (1951), 56-57.
— Grahame Clark, *Prehistoric Europe*. Social Forces XXXI (1953), 294.
— Jack Finegan, *The Archaeology of World Religions*, and John Murphy, *The Origins and History of Religions*. Social Forces XXXI (1953), 285-286.
— Committee on Historiography, *The Social Sciences in Historical Study*. Social Forces XXXIV (1956), 386.

*MISCELLANEOUS**

"Seeing Greece Through a Tar Heel Tourist's Eyes," *The Charlotte Observer,* May 29, 1932.

Masonry and Democracy. Privately printed, 1941.

"The Rebuilding of the Temple," *Grand Lodge Bulletin.* Grand Lodge of Iowa, A. F. and A. M. XLIV (1943), 213-218.

"The Word," *Annals of the Grand Council of the Allied Masonic Degrees of the United States* III, part 1 (1944-1946).

"Patriotism in a Republic," *Daughters of the American Revolution Magazine* (June-July 1961), 472.

UNPUBLISHED

"The Impact on History of Discoveries in the Near East." Read at the American Historical Association Meeting in Chicago, December 1959.

* Complete bibliography of Masonic papers to be published by Robert W. Caldwell.

INDEX

A, Alpha, 138; 139.
Aelian, 112; 117.
Aeneas, 78; 81.
Aeneid, See Vergil.
Africa, 86; 100.
Agesilaus, 35; 36.
Alexander the Great, 34-44; 83.
Allies, Italian, 53f; Latin, 53f.
Alloy, 110; 112; 113; 114-116; 119; 120. *See also* electrum, elektron.
Alphabets, 132-134.
Amber, 110-120, *passim*; forests, 110; trade routes, 111.
Amicitia Caesaris, 96.
Amicitiam renuntiare, 92; 94.
Amphora, Panathenaic, 27.
Amulet, 134; 136; 138.
Anchises, 75; 78; 83.
Antony (M. Antonius), 45; 46; 75; 86.
Apocalypse, 139; 140.
Apollo, on Chalcidian coins, 28; 29; 31; 32; 33.
Arepo, word in *Sator*-formula, 131; 134; 136; 140; etymology of, 137.
Aristophanes, 11; 12; 21; 112; 113.
Aristotle, 112; 113; 114; 117; 125; 129.
Arrian, 34-44.
Arsites, Satrap of Phrygia, 34; 35.
Artabazos, 29.
Asia, 100; Asia Minor, 134.
Assur (Assyria), 111-112.
Athena, 30; 96.
Athens, 3-14; 26-33; agora of, 16, 23; tribute lists of, 28-33.
Attic standard of coinage, 30.
Atticus, 45-30.
Augustus, 75; 78; 88; 89; 90; 91; 92; 113.
Avicenna, 123; 130.

Belgae, 102.
Bellum Civile, 84; 85; 86; 87-89; 90. *See also* Caesar, Lucan.
Bernstein (amber), 119
Bottiaioi, coins of, 29; 32.
Boudicca, 101; revolt of, 104.
Britain, 84; 99-109; 113; agriculture in, 107f; coinage in, 102; 104; underdeveloped economy of, 103; mining in, 106f; resources of, 101; 102; 106; Roman roads in, 103; 104; tribes of, 101-105.
British island, 84.
Britons, 101; 103; 104.

Brutus, 86; 96.
Byzantine, influence, 134; manuscripts, 136; 137; origin, 136.

Caesar, Julius, 45-50; 51; 73-90; 94; 102; 103.
Cairns, 16-19.
Capital, forced savings as, 104; private investment of, 104; 105-107; "social overhead", 100; 105; 109.
Cappadocia, 133; 134.
Car-dykes, Cambridgeshire, 105; Lincolnshire, 105.
Cavalry, Persian, 35-42; Thessalian, 41.
Cassius, 84; 85.
Catiline, 74.
Cato, M. Porcius, 53; 84; 85; 86; 89; 95; 96.
Catullus, 12; 63; 76.
Celsus, 122; 123; 124.
Celti (Celts), 102; 117.
Chalcidice, Chalcidians, 28-33.
Chalkis of Euboea, 30.
Chichester, 106.
Chi pattern of skull suture, 122; 124; 127; 128.
Christ, 135; 138; 140; 141.
Christian, association, 133; 134; catechism, 139; churches, 135-138; context, 133; converts, 140; custom, 139; formulae, 138; iconography, 139; living in Pompeii, 139; message, 140; presence of, 141; reference, 139; superstition, 135; use, 134.
Christians, 123; 131; 133-135; 138-141.
Christianity, 138.
Cicero, 8; *concordia ordinum* of, 51-62; 73-77; 81; 84; 87-88; hoped-for triumph, 45-50.
Civil War. *See Bellum Civile*.
Classicianus, Julius, 105; 108.
Claudian, 113; 119.
Claudius, Emperor, 99; 102; 104; 117.
Clementia, 88; 92.
Cleopatra, 88.
Cogidumnus, 106.
Coinage, Attic, 30; Bottiaioi, 29; 32; British, 102; Chalcidic, 27-33; Ichnei, 30; Orreskioi, 30; Phoenician, 30; Roman, 104; Sermilia, 31; Tyntenoi, 30.
Colchester (Camulodunum), 102; 104; 105.
Concord, Temple to, 53; 56.

146 INDEX

Concordia ordinum, 48; 51-62. See also Cicero.
Coptic, script, 131; 133; Sator formulae in, 133-134; papyri, 138; 139.
Coronal suture of skull, 127; 130.
Cranial anatomy, 121; 122; 125; 126; surgery, 121.
Crassus, 76; 86; 87.
Cryptogram, 139.
Cunobelinus, 102.
Cups, Little-Master, 19.
Curio, 47; 49; 84.
Cybele, 78; 79; 80; 81.
Cynthia, 64-69.
Cyrus, 14.

Darius III, 35; 36; 39; 43.
Decianus, Catus, 104.
Delphi, 94.
Demetrius the Grammarian in Britain, 108.
Democracy, 5-9.
Dictator, 86; 89.
Dio Cassius, 76; 93; 104.
Diodorus of Sicily, 34-44; 41; 103; 113; 114; 115.
Diocles of Halae, 24-25.
Dioscorides, 115; 117.
Dipolia, 7; 10.
Dolabella, 50; 85.
Dominus, 87; 89.
Domitian, 108.
Dux, 85; 87; 89.

Economy, "developed", 99; "underdeveloped", 99-103.
Egypt, 86; 88; 120; 133.
Egyptian, 111-112; court, 88; sacal, 112; Sator formulae from, 133.
Electrum, 110; 111; 113; 116; 119-120.
Elektron, 110-120.
Emperor's Displeasure. See Amicitiam renuntiare.
Emperors, 91-92.
Empire, 81; 88; 91.
England, 134.
Ennius, 75; 77.
Epicurus, 3; 4.
Epistedeuma, 5; 6.
Equestrian class, 53-55.
Eta pattern of skull suture, 124.
Europe, 115; 134; northern, 111-112.
Ezekiel, text of, 111-112.

Falloppius, 127-130.
Fens, 105; 107-109.
Flaccus, 84; 85.
Flavian era, 105; 107-108.
Formula. See Sator formula.
Fortune, 83; 87.

Fragments, 95; 112; 132.
France, 125; 135.
Freedom, 3-14.
Freedom of speech in the Roman Empire, 92.

Galen, 115; 117; 118; 122-130.
Gallic, arepennis (half-acre), 136; campaigns, 90; Samian ware, 105.
Gashmal, or ghashmall, 111; 112.
Gaugamela, 34; 36; 43.
Gaul, 86; 102; 108.
Germany, 86; 99; 110; 134; northern, 115; wars of, 96.
Glaesum, 115; 118.
God, as Creator, 137; as Sator, 139.
Gracchi, 53-54.
Gracchus, C. Sempronius, tribune, 55; 75.
Gracchus, T. Sempronius the Elder, 54; T. Sempronius, tribune, 54-55.
Granicus, Battle of, 34-44.

Heracles, 20; 21; 25-27; shield of, 112.
Hermes, tiles dedicated to, 16-19.
Herodotus, 5; 6; 13; 14; 29; 30; 32; 112; 113; 114; 115.
Hesiod, 12; 112; 113; 115.
Hesychius, 114; 115; 117.
Hippocrates of Cos, 116; 121; 122; 127-130.
Hippocratic tradition, 122; 124; 126-129.
Homer, 12; 110; 112; 113; 115; 116; 118; 120; Iliad, 115; Odyssey, 110; 115.
Homeric, 80; 110.
Horace, v; 76.

Illiad. See Homer.
Imperator, 84; 85; 86; 89.
Inscriptions, from Miletus, 17; on pottery, 15-27.
Instar, 77-78.
Ionia, 36; 42.
Iove, 76; Iovi, 80.
Issus, 34.
Italy, 80; 124; 134; 135; northern, 114.

Jerome, 112; 117.
Josephus, 117.
Julia, 85; 86; 87.
Julii, 83.
Jupiter, 76; 78; 80; 87; 88; 113; Capitolinus, 73; 77; Latiaris, 73.
Juvenal, 94; 99; 108; 113-114; 119.
Juvenalia of 59, 93.

INDEX 147

Kalos-name, 20; 23.
Kings of Macedon, 28; 29; 31; 33.
Korinthos, 21-23.

Lambdoidal suture of the skull, 127; 129; 130.
Lapiths, 25-27; battle with Centaurs, 25-27.
Latin West, 122.
Latium, 88.
Law of Treason, or *Lèse Majesté*, 92; 95; 97.
Lictors, Cicero and, 47-50.
Liguria, 112; 118.
Ligourion, 117; various spellings of, 117-120.
"Liquidity Preference", 104.
Livius Drusus, M. (the Elder), 55-57.
Livy (Titus Livius), historian, 52; 82.
London, 104-105.
Lord's Prayer (Pater noster), 138; 139-140.
Lucan, 73; 74; 76; 77-82; 85; 87-90; 96-98.
Lucian, 114; 116.
Lucilius, 94-95.
Lucretius, 75; 79.
Lynceus, addressee of Propertius, 63-65.

Macedon, 28; 29; 31; 33; Macedonia, 99.
Magna Mater, 78; 80.
Mansiones, 104.
Martial, 81; 113; 119.
Materia medica, 117
Megabyzus, 5.
Mekyberna, 29; 30.
Memnon, mercenary commander, 34; 35; 36; 42.
Menelaus, 110; 115; 116.
Mondeville, Henri de, 125-129.
Moslem, 122-123.
Mutationes, 104.

Nero, 77; 90; 92-100; 104; 105; 106; as Canace, 94; as Capaneus, 95; as Nauplius, 94; as Niobe, 95.
Neronia, 96.
Nicias, Peace of, 31-32; treaty of, 29; quoted by Pliny, 119.

O, Omega, 134; 138.
Octavian, 45-46.
Odysseus, 110.
Odyssey. See Homer.
Olynthus, Olynthians, 28-33.
Opera, word in *Sator* formula, 131; 134; "worker", 137.
Opimius, 53; 56; 75.
Orestes, 94.

Oribasius, 122; 123.
Otanes, 5.
Ovid (P. Ovidius Naso), 78; 80; 113; 114; 117; 119.

Padua, 93; University of, 127.
Padus (Po) river, 113-114; 115.
Paré, Ambroise, 127; 129.
Parmenio, 37; 41; 43.
Parthia, 76; 132.
Pater noster. See Lord's Prayer.
Patria, 73-75; 77; 81; communis, 74; 75.
Patricians, 52-55.
Pausanius, 110; 113.
Pax Augusta, 75.
Pericles, 5; funeral oration of, 5-8.
Persians, at the Granicus, 34-44; Sassanians, 132.
Petrarch, 45; 47.
Petronius, 81; 95; 99.
Phaethon, tears of, 113-116; 119.
Pharsalia, battle of, 77; 83; 85-86; 90.
Philostratus, Apollonius, 94; 116.
Phoenician, 114; 115; 118; coinage of, 30-32.
Piso, L. Calpurnius, 97; conspiracy of, 90; 92; 95; 97; 98.
Plato, 3; 4; 11; 23; 110; 111; 113.
Pleasure, 3-14.
Plebeians, 52-55.
Pliny the Elder, 96; 106; 107; 110; 112; 114; 115; 117; 118; 119; 120.
Plutarch, 34-36; 76; 80; 83; 113.
Poetry, erotic. *See* Propertius.
Politeia, 5-6.
Polybius, 4; 46.
Pompeii, 139; 140; palaestra of, 132.
Pompey the Great, 45-50; 51; 73; 75; 76; 77; 80; 84; 85; 86; 87; 88; 89; 96.
Pottery, Attic, 15-27; inscribed, 15-27; painters of, 15; 20; 21; 23; 25-28.
Pre-conditions, economic, 99-100.
Princeps, 83; 89; 92; *furens*, 86.
Principate, 82; 97.
Principatus, 84.
Proletariat, Roman, 53-55.
Propertius, elegies, 2.34, 63-68; 3.20, 68-72.
Pseudo-Xenophon, or the "Old Oligarch", 3; 8-11; 13.

Quaestorship of Lucan, 96.
Quintilian, 73.
Quirinus, 73.

Republic, Roman, 74; 75; 81; 82; 86; 88; 90; Republican, 83.
Res Romanae, 83.

INDEX

Roma, 73-79; 81; dea Roma, 81; Romaglauben, 75; martia Roma, 79; Roma patria, 74.
Roman (Romano), army, 133; Britain, 99; 100; 108; -British sculpture, 106; Empire, 91; 97; 98-99; 100; field systems, 107; historiae, 83; legions, 103-104; 108; prejudice, 138; roads to Britain, 104; trade, 103.
Romans (Romani), 74; 101; 103; 104; 107; 132; 136.
Rome, 77; 78; 82; 86; 87; 93; 94; 99; 106; 109; 140.
Rotas, word in *Sator* formula, 131; 134; "wheels", 137. *See also Sator* formula.
Rubicon, 73; 76; 80; 81; 89.

Sacal, 119; 120.
Sages, Seven, 4.
Saint Albans, 104; 105.
Sator, meaning of, 131; 133; 134; 135; 136-141.
Sator formula, 131-141; Anagram of, 138; early appearance of, 131; examples of, 131-137; 139-140; evidence of, 133-134; 137; 141; history of, 131-138; interpretations of, 131; 136-137; 138-141; inversion of to *Rotas* form, 131; 132; 134; 138; 140-141; languages of, 131-141; pattern of, 132; 138; uses of, 131-133; 135-136; 139; words of, 135, 140.
Scipio Africanus, P. Cornelius (Minor), 54; 55; 77.
Scythia, Scythians, 112; 119; 120.
Semitic cultures, 137; Semitic recruits, 132.
Senate, Roman, 92; 93; 97; house, 94.
Seneca the Elder, 82; 83; 85; 86; 87; 90; 92; 104.
Seneca the Younger, 82; 85; 87; 90.
"Setting", economic, 99; 100; 105; 109.
Sidonius, 114.
Silius Italicus, 80; 113; 119.
Skable, 29; 30.
Socrates, 11; 86.
Sophocles, 94; 112; 113.
Spain, 80; 85; 86; 106.
Stoic, doctrines, 85; saint, 85.
Stolos, 29; 30.
Strabo, 4; 101; 102; 103; 110; 113; 114; 117.
Sucinam (Succinan), 118; 119; 120.

Suetonius, C. Tranquillus, 77; 81; 83; 84; 86; 88; 91; 92; 93; 95-97.
Suetonius, Paulinus, 105.
Sustained growth, economic, 100; 105.

Tacitus, P. Cornelius, 91; 93; 94; 95; 97; 98; 101; 104; 107; 108; 115; *Ann.*, 75; 91; 93-98.
Tactics, Persian, 34-44.
"Take-off", economic, 99; 100; 101; 105; 109.
Tau form, 134; 138; 139.
Tau pattern of skull sutures, 124.
Tenet, Teneto, or *Teneton,* word in *Sator* formula, 131; 134; 138.
Theophrastus, 112; 113; 116; 117.
Theseus, 21; 25.
Thrasea Paetus, P. Clodius, 93; 94; 96.
Thucydides, 3; 5; 9; 11; 13; 28; 29; 30; 32.
Tiberius, Emperor, 90; 92.
Triumvir, 83; 87.
Triumvirate, 84.
Turpilianus, P. Petronius, 105; 108.

Underdeveloped area, or underdeveloped economy, 99; 100; 103.
University, of Montpelier, 125; of Padua, 127; of Paris, 125.

Valerius Maximus, 82; 84; 85.
Vases, Attic, 19; Meidian, 23; painters of, 15-25. *See also* Pottery.
Velleius Paterculis, 82; 83; 84; 87.
Venus, 81; 83; 86; Genetrix, 86.
Vergil, 63; 67; 75; 77; 79; 80; 81; 113; 114; 115; 116; 119; *Aeneid*, 75; 77; 78; 80; 81; 113; 119; *Eclogues*, 78; 113; *Georgics*, 78; 117.
Vergilian, 78.
Vesalius, Andeas, 125-130.
Vespasian, Emperor, 106; 109.
Vesta, 73; 76.
Vestae, 74; 76.

Wales, 103; 107; 108.
Weald, 106, 107.
Word-square, 138; 139. *See Sator* formula.

Xenocrates, 120.
Xenophon, 116.

Zeus, 21; 80; 113.

THE JAMES SPRUNT STUDIES IN HISTORY AND POLITICAL SCIENCE

No. 1. PERSONNEL OF THE CONVENTION OF 1861. By John Gilchrist McCormick }
LEGISLATION OF THE CONVENTION OF 1861. By Kemp P. Battle. } (Out of print.)

No. 2. THE CONGRESSIONAL CAREER OF NATHANIEL MACON. By Edwin Mood Wilson. (Out of print.)

No. 3. THE LETTERS OF NATHANIEL MACON, JOHN STEELE, AND WILLIAM BARRY GROVE, WITH NOTES By Kemp P. Battle. (Out of print.)

No. 4. LETTERS AND DOCUMENTS RELATING TO THE EARLY HISTORY OF THE LOWER CAPE FEAR, WITH INTRODUCTION AND NOTES. By Kemp P. Battle. (Out of print.)

No. 5. MINUTES OF THE KEHUKEY ASSOCIATION, WITH INTRODUCTION AND NOTES. By Kemp P. Battle. (Out of print.)

No. 6. DIARY OF A GEOLOGICAL TOUR BY ELISHA MITCHELL IN 1827 AND 1828, WITH INTRODUCTION AND NOTES. By Kemp P. Battle. (Out of print.)

No. 7. WILLIAM RICHARDSON DAVIE: A MEMOIR. By J. G. de Roulhac Hamilton.
LETTERS OF WILLIAM RICHARDSON DAVIE, WITH NOTES. By Kemp P. Battle.

No. 8. THE PROVINCIAL COUNCIL AND COMMITTEES OF SAFETY IN NORTH CAROLINA. By Bessie Lewis Whitaker.

VOL. 9, No. 1. THE SOCIETY FOR THE PROPAGATION OF THE GOSPEL IN THE PROVINCE OF NORTH CAROLINA. By D. D. Oliver.
CORRESPONDENCE OF JOHN RUST EATON. Edited by J. G. de Roulhac Hamilton.

VOL. 9, No. 2. FEDERALISM IN NORTH CAROLINA. By Henry M. Wagstaff.
LETTERS OF WILLIAM BARRY GROVE. Edited by Henry M. Wagstaff

VOL. 10, No. 1. BENJAMIN SHERWOOD HEDRICK. By J. G. de Roulhac Hamilton.

VOL. 10, No. 2. BARTLETT YANCEY. By George A. Anderson.
THE POLITICAL AND PROFESSIONAL CAREER OF BARTLETT YANCEY. By J. G. de Roulhac Hamilton.
LETTERS TO BARTLETT YANCEY.

VOL. 11, No. 1. COUNTY GOVERNMENT IN COLONIAL NORTH CAROLINA. By W. C. Guess.

VOL. 11, No. 2. THE NORTH CAROLINA CONSTITUTION OF 1776, AND ITS MAKERS. By Frank Nash.
THE GERMAN SETTLERS OF LINCOLN COUNTY AND WESTERN NORTH CAROLINA. By Joseph R. Nixon.

VOL. 12, No. 1. THE GOVERNOR, COUNCIL, AND ASSEMBLY IN ROYAL NORTH CAROLINA. By C. S. Cooke
LAND TENURE IN PROPRIETARY NORTH CAROLINA. By L. N. Morgan.

VOL. 12, No. 2. THE NORTH CAROLINA INDIANS. By James Hall Rand.

VOL. 13, No. 1. THE GRANVILLE DISTRICT. By E. Merton Coulter.
THE NORTH CAROLINA COLONIAL BAR. By E. H. Alderman.

VOL. 13, No. 2. THE HARRINGTON LETTERS. Edited by Henry M. Wagstaff.

VOL. 14, No. 1. THE HARRIS LETTERS. Edited by Henry M. Wagstaff.

VOL. 14, No. 2. SOME COLONIAL HISTORY OF BEAUFORT COUNTY. By Francis H. Cooper.

VOL. 15, Nos. 1 and 2. PARTY POLITICS IN NORTH CAROLINA, 1835-1860. By J. G. de Roulhac Hamilton.

VOL. 16, No. 1. A COLONIAL HISTORY OF ROWAN COUNTY, NORTH CAROLINA. By S. J. Ervin. (Out of print.)

VOL. 16, No. 2. THE DIARY OF BARTLETT YANCEY MALONE. Edited by Wm. Whatley Pierson, Jr.
THE PROVINCIAL AGENTS OF NORTH CAROLINA. By Samuel James Ervin, Jr. (Out of print.)

VOL. 17, No. 1. THE FREE NEGRO IN NORTH CAROLINA. By Rosser Howard Taylor.
SOME COLONIAL HISTORY OF CRAVEN COUNTY, NORTH CAROLINA. By Francis H. Cooper.

VOL. 17, No. 2. JOURNAL OF A TOUR OF NORTH CAROLINA BY WILLIAM ATTMORE, 1787. Edited by Lida Tunstall Rodman. (Out of print.)

VOL. 18, Nos. 1 and 2. SLAVEHOLDING IN NORTH CAROLINA: AN ECONOMIC VIEW. By Rosser Howard Taylor. (Out of print.)

VOL. 19, No. 1. PRESENT STATUS OF MODERN EUROPEAN HISTORY IN THE UNITED STATES. By Chester Penn Higby.

THE JAMES SPRUNT STUDIES IN HISTORY AND POLITICAL SCIENCE

Vol. 19, No. 2. STUDIES IN HISPANIC-AMERICAN HISTORY. Edited by William Whatley Pierson, Jr.

Vol. 20, No. 1. NORTH CAROLINA NEWSPAPERS BEFORE 1790. By Charles Christopher Crittenden.

Vol. 20, No. 2. THE JAMES A. GRAHAM PAPERS, 1861-1884. Edited by Henry M. Wagstaff.

Vol. 21, Nos. 1 and 2. THE DEMOCRATIC PARTY IN ANTE-BELLUM NORTH CAROLINA, 1835-1861. By Clarence Clifford Norton.

Vol. 22, Nos. 1 and 2. MINUTES OF THE NORTH CAROLINA MANUMISSION SOCIETY, 1816-1834. Edited by Henry M. Wagstaff.

Vol. 23, No. 1. THE PRESIDENTIAL ELECTION OF 1824 IN NORTH CAROLINA. By Albert Ray Newsome

Vol. 23, No. 2. THE SECESSION MOVEMENT IN NORTH CAROLINA. By Joseph Carlyle Sitterson.

Vol. 24, No. 1. JEFFERSONIAN DEMOCRACY IN SOUTH CAROLINA. By John Harold Wolfe.

Vol. 24, No. 2. GUIDE TO THE MANUSCRIPTS IN THE SOUTHERN HISTORICAL COLLECTION OF THE UNIVERSITY OF NORTH CAROLINA.

Vol. 25, No. 1. NORTH CAROLINA BOUNDARY DISPUTES INVOLVING HER SOUTHERN LINE. By Marvin L Skaggs.

Vol. 25, No. 2. ANTE-BELLUM SOUTH CAROLINA: A SOCIAL AND CULTURAL HISTORY. By Rosser H. Taylor

Vol. 26, No. 1. THE PROHIBITION MOVEMENT IN ALABAMA, 1702 TO 1943. By James Benson Sellers.

VOLUME 27. PROHIBITION IN NORTH CAROLINA, 1715-1945. By Daniel Jay Whitener.

VOLUME 28. THE NEGRO IN MISSISSIPPI, 1865-1890. By Vernon Lane Wharton. (Out of print.)

VOLUME 29. THE WHIG PARTY IN GEORGIA, 1825-1853. By Paul Murray.

VOLUME 30. THE SOUTH IN ACTION: A SECTIONAL CRUSADE AGAINST FREIGHT RATE DISCRIMINATION. By Robert A. Lively.

VOLUME 31. ESSAYS IN SOUTHERN HISTORY. Edited by Fletcher Melvin Green.

VOLUME 32. SOUTH CAROLINA GOES TO WAR. By Charles Edward Cauthen. (Out of print.)

VOLUME 33. REVOLUTIONARY JUSTICE: A STUDY OF THE ORGANIZATION, PERSONNEL, AND PROCEDURE OF THE PARIS TRIBUNAL, 1793-1795. By James Logan Godfrey.

VOLUME 34. THE POLITICAL LIBERALISM OF THE NEW YORK *Nation*, 1865-1932. By Alan Pendleton Grimes.

VOLUME 35. WAR LABOR BOARDS IN THE FIELD. By Allan R. Richards.

VOLUME 36. THE RALEIGH REGISTER, 1799-1863. By Robert Neal Elliott, Jr.

VOLUME 37. CONSTITUTIONAL DEVELOPMENT IN ALABAMA, 1798-1901: A STUDY IN POLITICS, THE NEGRO AND SECTIONALISM. By Malcolm Cook McMillan. (Out of print.)

VOLUME 38. AGRICULTURAL DEVELOPMENTS IN NORTH CAROLINA, 1783-1860. By Cornelius Oliver Cathey.

VOLUME 39. STUDIES IN SOUTHERN HISTORY. Edited by J. Carlyle Sitterson.

VOLUME 40. ANDREW JACKSON AND NORTH CAROLINA POLITICS. By William S. Hoffmann.

VOLUME 41. PHARAONIC POLICIES AND ADMINISTRATION. By Mary Francis Gyles.

VOLUME 42. JACKSONIAN DEMOCRACY IN MISSISSIPPI. By Edwin Arthur Miles.

VOLUME 43. FERRY HILL PLANTATION JOURNAL, JANUARY 4, 1838-JANUARY 15, 1839. Edited by Fletcher Melvin Green.

VOLUME 44. DEMOCRATIC PARTY DISSENSION IN NORTH CAROLINA, 1928-1936. By Elmer L. Puryear.

VOLUME 45. POLITICAL FACTIONS IN ALEPPO, 1760-1826. By Herbert L. Bodman, Jr.

Vol. 46. LAUDATORES TEMPORIS ACTI: Studies in Memory of Wallace Everett Caldwell, Professor of History at the University of North Carolina, by His Friends and Students. Edited by Mary Francis Gyles and Eugene Wood Davis.

www.ingramcontent.com/pod-product-compliance
Lightning Source LLC
Chambersburg PA
CBHW030114010526
44116CB00005B/242